Chivalry and the Perfect Prince

Habent sua fata libelli

CHIVALRY *the* & PERFECT PRINCE

Tournaments,
Art, and Armor
at the Spanish
Habsburg Court

BRADEN FRIEDER

Sixteenth Century Essays & Studies 81
Truman State University Press

Cover art: *Titian*, Portrait of Philip II, 1549. Oil on canvas. Madrid, Museo del Prado (411). Used by permission.

Cover design: Teresa Wheeler
Type: Goudy Old Style, © URW
Printed by: Thomson-Shore, Dexter, Michigan USA

Library of Congress Cataloging-in-Publication Data

Frieder, Braden K.
Chivalry and the perfect prince : tournaments, art, and armor at the Spanish Habsburg court, 1504–1605 / Braden K. Frieder.
    p. cm. — (Sixteenth century essays & studies ; v. 81)
Includes bibliographical references and index.
ISBN 978-1-931112-69-7 (hardback : alk. paper)
1. Armor, Renaissance—Spain. 2. Tournaments, Medieval—Spain. 3. Charles V, Holy Roman Emperor, 1500–1558. 4. Philip II, King of Spain, 1527–1598. 5. Knights and knighthood in art. 6. Kings and rulers in art. I. Title.
NK6662.A1F75 2008
394'.70946—dc22

2008000748

To My Wife

Contents

Figures

Preface

The origin of this book was a visit to the Royal Armory in Madrid. As a young history student, I was attracted to the suits of decorated armor made for Emperor Charles V and his son, Philip II of Spain. Renaissance princes wore decorated armors not only for protection, but also as status symbols. I was intrigued by the idea that these suits of armor were really costumes for a kind of royal theater in which the ruler appeared to his people as the descendant of ancient gods and Christian heroes. The stages on which the prince acted out this role were the tournaments, state entries, and military campaigns of the Renaissance. The actors in these events commissioned armor and other artworks specifically for these occasions, their collective iconography expressing Renaissance ideas of the perfect prince. This common vocabulary of chivalric imagery was linked to historical events and to the unique problems faced by the Habsburg regime. By the middle of the sixteenth century, European monarchs rarely led their own troops into battle, though the worth of a ruler was still conceptualized in military terms. The ruling dynasty used the visual language of the tournament and martial display to symbolically affirm the legitimacy of their rule and the identity of the prince as a divinely appointed deliverer.

When I began my study, I found that, although there is a fair amount of literature on the connoisseurship of Renaissance armor, relatively little had been published on the context and meaning of these splendid artifacts. Shifting my research to courtly spectacle and festival art in the sixteenth century, I found that books and articles in recent years have tended to sideline the tournaments that accompanied the ceremonial entries of visiting princes. A closer examination of Renaissance spectacle shows that the tournament in the sixteenth century was not peripheral to the royal entry, but central to it. A search through the available literature on tournaments provided better hunting, but the main object of the chase still proved elusive. Compared to the large volume of material published on military history, only a handful of books were devoted to the tournament itself. For the most part, these studies focused on medieval tournaments, with the Renaissance tournament treated as a kind of denouement. This seems strange indeed, considering that the tournament as an art form reached its apogee in the Renaissance. The tournaments held at the courts of sixteenth-century European monarchs were unsurpassed in size and splendor, and were remembered in these terms by contemporary writers on the subject. Their descriptions proved to be the most fruitful primary sources for my study, and form the basis for this book.

As Malcolm Vale points out in *War and Chivalry*, the comparative lack of interest in later chivalry can probably be traced to the writings of the cultural historian Johan Huizinga (1872–1945). Echoing the German philosopher Hegel, Huizinga believed every age in history was pervaded by its own fundamental spirit that determined all forms of cultural life. In the late Middle Ages, when the tournament-as-spectacle took shape at the courts of Burgundy and Flanders, the spirit of the age, according to Huizinga, was one of decadence and decline. This view continues to inform much of the current scholarship on chivalry and tournaments. Modern historians have also emphasized the widening gap between chivalry and real life at the end of the Middle Ages. People living in the Renaissance, however, were unaware that chivalry was in decline. The *Jouvencel*, based on a fourteenth-century manual of knighthood, went through five printed editions between 1493 and 1529. The tournament was still alive and well at the courts of Queen Elizabeth and King James of Scotland at the beginning of the seventeenth century. Apart from religion, chivalry remained the strongest of all ethical considerations, particularly among the ruling classes. Contemporary views on the subject are suggested by a curious incident alleged to have taken place following the Battle of Pavia in 1525. Emperor Charles V, exasperated with Francis I for breaking an oath taken as a condition of his release from captivity after the battle, challenged the king to personal combat as a way of settling their differences. Knightly warfare may have been out of date, but chivalric values were not.

The visual arts provide another invaluable source of information on the aristocratic ideals of warfare and the tournament in the sixteenth century. Renaissance artists were closely attuned to the needs of their patrons, and provided portraits and other artworks designed to appeal to their self-image. As the imperial family, the Habsburgs patronized some of the finest painters, sculptors, and armorers of the Renaissance. The imagery used to decorate Habsburg armor and artworks depicting important people wearing it was not simply arbitrary, but filled with constructed meanings pointing to the larger Habsburg agenda. In many cases, these artworks can be tied to sixteenth-century current events. Studied together in their original context, art and armor began to make more sense. Recent studies by Alan Young and others suggest a change in the air, and have returned to the tournament as an integral part of a wider spectrum of chivalric life and culture, which lost none of its vitality in the Renaissance. Tournaments at the Spanish Habsburg court, however, are still understudied. It is to address these areas that this book was undertaken.

Acknowledgments

A great number of people have assisted me in developing this project over the years, far too many to acknowledge here. First, I thank Andy Mancuso and Howard Rodee for encouraging an early interest. Funding for my preliminary research at the University of Wisconsin–Madison and travel to Europe was provided in part by grants from the Shorger Fund for Studies in Italian Art. In Spain, I would like to thank the staff at the Archivo General de Simancas, especially Dra. Isabel Aguirre Landa, for her help in navigating the labyrinth. I am forever indebted to Dr. Alvaro Soler del Campo, director of the Royal Armory in Madrid, who patiently stood by and answered all my questions while I photographed the armors under his care. In Italy, my thanks go to the staff of the Biblioteca Nazionale and the reading room at the Palazzo Medici-Riccardi in Florence. The staff at the Archivio di Stato and the Biblioteca Braidense, Milan, were also enormously helpful, and fielded both scholarly and nonscholarly questions about getting around in Milan. The work of historians Geoffrey Parker and Henry Kamen was of inestimable value in reconstructing the childhood interests of Philip II. My thanks also to Professors Narciso Menocal, Gail Geiger, and Jane Campbell Hutchison at the University of Wisconsin–Madison, who as members of my dissertation committee read and critiqued my initial research for this book. Silvia Giorgini checked my Italian translations. I would also like to express my appreciation to Professor Steven Orso for his advice and interest in my project. My wife lent constant support and also provided invaluable editorial assistance. And I will always remember Juan Antonio, Rubén, and Víctor for their friendship and encouragement. *Sí, vale la pena.*

A Note on Sources

The primary sources for Renaissance tournaments are festival books, which are eyewitness accounts published to commemorate the visits of rulers and other important people to major cities in the sixteenth century. Translating this material into something resembling modern English proved an enormous task, though an extremely rewarding one. These accounts often include detailed descriptions of the tournaments and other pageantry that followed the ceremonial entries of Habsburg princes. Festival books themselves were modeled on contemporary chivalric literature, especially the prose cycle of *Amadís of Gaul*, a medieval romance that was eventually published and proved enormously popular in the Renaissance.

Inventories of the possessions of Emperor Charles V and his successor, King Philip II, have also survived, having been placed for safekeeping in the royal archives at Simancas near Valladolid, Spain. These documents were helpful in tracking down tournament armors and related artworks belonging to the emperor and his son. Original account books of the royal household are also preserved in the archives at Simancas. The records of payment are occasionally detailed enough to allow us to link armors and other artworks to specific events, or at least narrow the gap a bit.

The translations in this book are my own. Translation sometimes involves making a compromise between strict grammatical accuracy and conveying the sense of a word or phrase into the target language. Where this was the case, I ask the reader's indulgence for rendering the source into what seemed the appropriate English style.

Chivalry and the Perfect Prince

The European Empire of Charles V, ca. 1548–51.

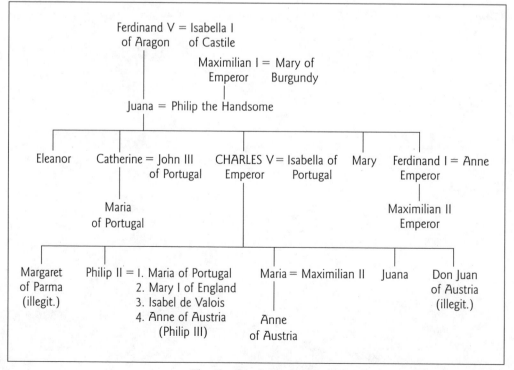

The Family of Charles V.

Chapter I

A Sport For Princes

The Art of the Tournament in the Renaissance

IN 1547, LUCAS CRANACH THE ELDER met with Emperor Charles V to paint his portrait, and the two recalled their first meeting when His Majesty was a boy of eight. Charles, bored with the tedium of sitting for a portrait, had been unable to hold still for the artist to complete a preliminary sketch. Charles's tutor hung a polished weapon on the wall and this finally held the boy's attention long enough for Cranach to complete his portrait.[1] For Charles, this was the beginning of a lifelong fascination with the tools and craft of war. An inventory of the emperor's possessions made just before his death in 1558 lists what was then probably the single largest collection of arms and armor owned by a European monarch. Charles's son Philip II was an equally enthusiastic patron of the armorer's art and added substantially to his father's collection before his own death in 1598.

Charles V of the house of Habsburg stood on the brink of resurrecting the European empire of Charlemagne. The Low Countries, Austria, Spain, and most of Italy were already his, and in 1521 and 1533 Spanish conquistadors added the American empires of Mexico and the Inca to the Habsburg territories. In 1547 Charles defeated the German princes arrayed against him at Mühlberg. France stood perilously close to encirclement and there was talk of a renewed Habsburg alliance with the house of Tudor,

---

[1]Campbell, *Renaissance Portraits,* 180.

3

the hereditary enemies of the Valois kings. The emperor's son, Philip of Spain, came of age in 1545 and it was time to introduce him to his future subjects. The political situation in the north was extremely delicate, however, and the Protestant princes had already expressed their unwillingness to accept a distant Catholic monarch as overlord. On the eve of his confirmation as successor to Charles V, Philip made a ceremonial progress through Italy, Austria, Germany, and Flanders, culminating in a reunion with his father in Brussels and their attendance at the Imperial Diet at Augsburg in 1550, where the emperor's heir would be presented as the ideal Christian prince, the scion of an illustrious line of rulers whose lineage could be traced back to the gods and heroes of antiquity.

An essential part of the prince's tour was the ritual combat of the tournament. In addition to their entertainment value, tournaments served an important social and political function. To gain the respect of the nobility, the prince had to display his skill at arms, still regarded as the primary measure of a ruler's worth in the sixteenth century. It was also important that the prince be seen interacting smoothly with the local gentry, assuring them not only of his potential as a military leader, but also of his respect for their own hereditary rights and privileges. The value of the tournament as a tool of statecraft should not be underestimated. Renaissance princes spent vast sums on the organization and equipment for tournaments, and fully understood their political worth.

In the later Middle Ages, the tournament began its transformation from training for warfare into a form of martial spectacle. Tournaments in the earlier Middle Ages had been rough-and-ready affairs, where armies of combatants attacked each other all at once and with real weapons. Serious injuries and death were common in early tournaments and the church periodically tried to ban them. As time went on, steps were gradually taken to increase the safety of tournament competition and decrease the loss of life and limb. Blunt or rebated weapons had appeared in European tournaments as early as the thirteenth century. The various types of tournament combat were regulated and formalized in the fifteenth century, especially at the court of Burgundy, which eventually became part of the Habsburg patrimony. By the Renaissance, skill and grace were replacing brute strength to overcome an opponent, though the tournament remained a rough sport with an element of real danger. Tempers sometimes flared and accidents occurred. The most notorious incident involved King Henry II of France, who was fatally injured in a tournament in 1559. The king's opponent failed to drop his shattered lance in time and a huge splinter penetrated the occularium of the king's helmet, piercing his brain through the eye. The kings of France refrained from jousting after this famous mishap and stories of the horrific event circulated throughout Europe. The comparative safety of later medieval and Renaissance tournaments has probably been exaggerated by modern historians, and it is important to note that tournaments were still considered training for war in some parts of Europe until well into the seventeenth century.

The dangers of the tournament, however, did not excuse the rest of the nobility from participating in them. Fifteenth-century writer Christine de Pisan believed that those holding the rank of knight should be obliged to fight in tournaments to develop the strength and endurance necessary for war (exceptions were made for elderly or overweight men).[2] Historians are quick to point out that Renaissance tournaments bore little or no relation to the harsh realities of war, but Renaissance writers on the subject certainly believed they did. Aristocratic warriors in particular regarded war as simply an extension of the tournament into a different arena, and often behaved this way when they commanded armies on the battlefield.[3] The real relationship between tournaments and warfare in the Renaissance, however, was more complex, with the development of the tournament sometimes (though not always) paralleling contemporary developments on the battlefield.

The ceremonial entry of the prince and his entourage into a city or town preceded the tournament. In the Renaissance, the entry of a visiting prince was cast in the form of a Roman triumph, complete with temporary arches and other *apparati* made of wood and plaster. The prince would then attend Mass in the local church or cathedral before retiring to his host's palace. The tournament itself was initiated with a formal challenge issued by an individual knight or a group of knights, and delivered on their behalf in court by a herald. Knights issuing the challenge—called the *tenans*, or "challengers"—declared the rules for that particular tournament. Those who accepted the challenge were called the *venans*, or "comers." Tournaments might take place anywhere that provided sufficient space, though by the late Middle Ages, they were usually held in the town square or in the courtyard of the main palace or public building of a city or town. A wooden stockade was erected around the perimeter of the tournament area, which was now called the tiltyard or "lists." The size of the enclosure varied, though the space required for jousting averaged around a hundred yards in length.[4] It is difficult to determine the actual attendance at medieval and Renaissance tournaments, though something like twelve thousand people may have witnessed a tournament at Greenwich in 1517.[5] Major continental tournaments were probably considerably larger. Spectators were charged

[2]Vale, *Chivalry*, 63.
[3]Vale, *Chivalry*, esp. 79.
[4]Young, *Tudor and Jacobean Tournaments*, 74, 76.
[5]Young, *Tudor and Jacobean Tournaments*, 74.

admission and had to stand at the stockade from dawn to dusk to see all the competitions.[6] Grandstands were built alongside the enclosure to accommodate the more important spectators. The ruler and his immediate entourage sat, comfortably screened from the sun, in a separate set of seats overlooking the center of the lists. A separate box was also reserved for the judges of the tournament.

The competitors entered the lists one by one to a fanfare of trumpets, wearing jackets or skirts over their armor in the colors of their coats of arms and with figurative crests on their helms. Each contestant was accompanied by his servants and retainers, who wore liveries in their master's colors. The horses were clad in colorful trappers, again repeating the colors of the knight's coat of arms. The heraldic trappings worn by the knight and his retainers were often embellished with a motto and a personal device or emblem called an *impresa*. Mottoes and *imprese* could be changed to suit the occasion and were repeated on the knight's ceremonial shield, which was borne before him into the arena. A page preceded his master into the lists, shouting his master's war cry as he entered. After entering the lists, the contestants took a turn about the stockade and presented themselves to the judges, who entered their names on a roster. The contestants promised to abide by the rules of the competition, which varied from event to event and were publicized beforehand.

The martial display of the tournament typically began with the joust, a formalized combat in which a pair of armored horsemen rode at each other with leveled lances. Each horseman couched his lance under his right arm and held it at an angle across his body. The object of the joust was to unseat one's opponent or shatter one's lance with a well-placed blow to the opponent's shield (fig. 1.1). Medieval and Renaissance knights rode standing in the stirrups with their legs held straight. High, armored saddles protected their hips and kept them firmly in their seats. In addition to good aim, jousting required coordination and a well-developed sense of timing. At a prearranged signal, the knights charged at each other down the course, leaning slightly forward in the saddle and lowering their lances as they charged. At the moment of impact, the jouster tensed his legs and straightened slightly at the waist, setting his body into the blow and pulling his torso up and back. This last move was especially important for avoiding the splinters of an opponent's lance, which otherwise might enter the occularium or vision slit on the jousting helm. Judges closely observed each blow, or "attaint," made by the contestants, keeping track of the scores on special sheets called jousting checks. Original examples of Renaissance jousting checks occasionally survive, with the scoring boxes filled in with the names of the contes-

[6]Young, *Tudor and Jacobean Tournaments*, 74.

Figure 1.1 Joust of Emperor Maximilian I of Habsburg, from a German tournament book, early sixteenth century. Reproduced from R. Coltan Clephan, *The Tournament* (London: Methuen, 1919), plate 3.

tants and their scores. Interestingly, it has been noted that the language and ritual structure of the joust closely resembled the old medieval judicial duel, or trial by combat. In addition to proving their martial skills, knights sometimes used jousting matches to settle personal differences.[7]

Sometime in the fourteenth century, a cloth barrier was introduced to separate the combatants. A wooden fence or palisade, called a tilt barrier, gradually replaced the cloth barrier in the fifteenth and sixteenth centuries. The tilt barrier prevented collisions and kept the contestants at an optimum angle for shattering the lance (between about twenty and thirty degrees). In the sixteenth century, the ends of the tilt barrier were sometimes turned out in opposite directions. The precise reason for this

[7]Vale, *Chivalry*, 76.

feature is unknown, though it may have kept the knights' horses from swerving into the wrong end of the lists at the beginning of the charge, and ensured that contestants (who may have been stunned from the impact) were headed in the proper direction after the encounter.[8] Jousts without a tilt barrier, however, remained popular in some parts of Europe until well into the sixteenth century. Jousting over a tilt barrier may have been a southern idea, since in Germany and other northern countries, jousts of this type were called foreign or Italian jousts.

By about 1400, European armor had evolved into a complete suit of steel plates protecting all parts of the wearer. Armorers continued to improve on this basic arrangement for the remainder of the century. By 1500, the craft of shaping and assembling contoured steel plates closely tailored to the human figure reached its apogee in Europe (fig. 1.2). Armor at the beginning of the sixteenth century featured smooth and functional-looking surfaces, with the edges of the principal plates angled to deflect the blows of lances and other weapons. The principal centers for armor-making were Milan and southern Germany, though smaller local centers existed in other major cities of the Low Countries and England. In Spain, a small armor industry specializing in helmets and brigandines (a type of light body armor) existed at Zaragoza, but for the most part the Spanish nobility bought their armor from northern Italian workshops. Regular armor for war was worn in tournaments until well into the sixteenth century, though new kinds of armor were also developed for specialized types of tournament combat.

Reinforcing pieces of armor made especially for the tournament were added to the basic armor for war as early as the fourteenth century. By about 1480, suits of armor were being made specifically for the joust with rebated lances (fig. 1.3). Jousting armor sacrificed mobility for the maximum amount of protection, and was made from the thickest plates of steel. An armor for the German joust, or *gestech*, consisted of a heavy breastplate with tassets, a massive great helm, or *heaume*, bolted directly to the breastplate, special armor for the bridle arm, and a small curved shield, which was tied to the breastplate under the left shoulder. Blows below the waist were forbidden and armor for the legs was usually dispensed with, especially in Germany. To strike an opponent's horse was expressly forbidden and horse armor was generally not used in jousting. A small plate protection for the horse's head called a *chamfron* was often retained, however, along with a thick padded collar, the *stechsack*, to protect the horse's chest from collisions in jousts run without a tilt barrier. Occasionally, the animal's eyes were completely covered, probably to prevent shying at the moment of impact. Armor like this was worn for

[8]Young, *Tudor and Jacobean Tournaments*, 76.

Figure 1.2 Italian or Flemish, armor of Henry VIII, ca. 1515. London, HM Tower of London. Used by permission.

Figure 1.3 South German, armor for the *Gestech*, ca. 1490. Vienna, Kunsthistorisches Museum (HJRK S VIII). Used by permission.

jousting across Europe until about the middle of the sixteenth century. In Spain, this type of joust was known as the *justa real*, or "royal joust."

Weapons for tournament combat were outfitted with extra equipment for accuracy and safety. By the thirteenth century, jousting lances were normally fitted with triple-pronged heads called coronels to reduce their penetrating power (fig. 1.4). Knights still ran courses with sharp points (called jousts of war), however, in Spain and the German Empire until the middle of the sixteenth century. A lance rest on the breastplate supported the leveled lance and jousting armors were sometimes fitted with an additional brace, called a *queue*, extending behind the jouster's right arm, which ensured that the lance was aimed at the proper angle. A ring near the butt of the lance, a *graper*, was fitted with rows of teeth that bit into a piece of wood wedged in a socket under the lance rest and kept the lance from sliding backwards. A metal guard on the lance, called a vamplate, protected the knight's hand and, by the end of the fifteenth century, had expanded to protect the entire lower arm. After 1500, lances for jousting were often made hollow and fluted, which almost guaranteed a dramatic explosion of splinters in the air as the jousters collided. The fluted lance, called a *bordonasse*, reached up to twelve feet in length[9] and weighed close to forty pounds (fig. 1.5). A squire or page was usually required to assist the knight into his armor and hand him his lance.

Following the joust, tournament competitors went on to other types of combat on horseback and on foot. A day of jousting typically ended with the *mêlée* or *Freiturnier*, in which the contestants divided into two teams and charged each other all at once with their lances. Confusingly, this type of combat was also sometimes called the *tournois* or tourney. The *mêlée* was a holdover from earlier medieval tournaments and was run in regular armor for war, though with reinforcing pieces added to the left side of the body (a variant on the *mêlée* called the club tourney required a special helmet and armor for the upper arms). Once the lances were shivered, the contestants drew their swords and fought on until the final trumpet at sunset signaled the end of the day's combats. Like the tournament lance, special swords were also designed for the *mêlée*. Sixteenth-century tournament swords were made with actual steel blades, but with dull edges and rounded points for safety. A German *Freiturnier* of the early sixteenth century is illustrated in a 1509 print by Lucas Cranach the Elder (fig. 1.6), showing knights wearing full armor for war, fighting on horseback with tournament swords in a palatial courtyard. Pages scramble to retrieve the knight's lances, which have been cast to the ground following the initial charge. At center left, one knight's horse has collapsed from the impact. Ladies

[9]Gravett, *Knights at Tournament*, 50.

Figure 1.4 English, rebated lance point (coronel), early sixteenth century. London, HM Tower of London. Used by permission.

Figure 1.5 English, bordonasse, first half of sixteenth century. London, HM Tower of London. Used by permission.

watch from the balcony on the left, and draped over the windowsill of the judges' box is a tapestry depicting the deeds of the biblical strongman Samson. The *mêlée* might last anywhere from two to four hours and required a great deal of stamina.[10] The image of the hero, whose strength was given to him by God, was intended to inspire the exhausted knights to further effort.

Tournament combats between armored knights fighting on foot also existed from at least as early as the fifteenth century. A separate enclosure, the *champ clos*, was set aside for dismounted combats. Knights sparred with pollaxes and other staff weapons, two-handed swords, or even their daggers. By the late fifteenth century, a special type of armor for tournament combat on foot had appeared, consisting of a massive helmet with a moveable visor, full plate protection for the body, and a wide skirt of steel hoops from the waist to the knees. The entire tournament—jousts, the *mêlée*, and combats on foot—was often collectively referred to as a *pas d'armes*, or "passage of arms."

Around 1500, Habsburg emperor Maximilian I added a bewildering variety of combats. The chivalrous emperor personally developed new forms of jousting and tournament armor, including courses with fancy special effects such as disappearing and exploding shields. The principal object of the joust continued to be unhorsing one's opponent, or at least striking shields with a spectacular shattering of lances. For those so inclined, imperial tournaments retained a course with sharpened lances and special armor, called the *Scharfrennen*. A new type of decoration for armor in which rows of elegant vertical flutes were added to the brightly polished steel plates also appeared near the end of the emperor's reign. This armor, which combined German-style decoration with the burlier outline of Italian armor, quickly spread across Europe and was dubbed the Maximilian style (fig. 1.7).

[10]Vale, *Chivalry*, 80.

Figure 1.6 Lucas Cranach the Elder, *A Tournament*, 1509. Woodcut, London, British Museum (1895-1-22-277). Used by permission.

Figure 1.7 Colman Helmschmied, armor for man and horse of Ferdinand I with reinforcing pieces, ca. 1526. Vienna, Kunsthistorisches Museum (HJRK A 349). Used by permission.

By about 1540, however, European tournaments had returned to something like their former simplicity. Four principal types of tournament combat emerged. The *Plankengestech*, or joust, was run over a barrier with either smooth or barred shields, called *manteaux*. The *tilt* was another type of joust, presumably over a barrier, though with a special set of massive reinforcements for the left side of the body called a *grand guard*. The *Freiturnier* or *mêlée* was run at large (with no tilt barrier), again with special reinforcements for the helmet and the left side of the armor. The *Fusskampf* was essentially the old combat on foot in the

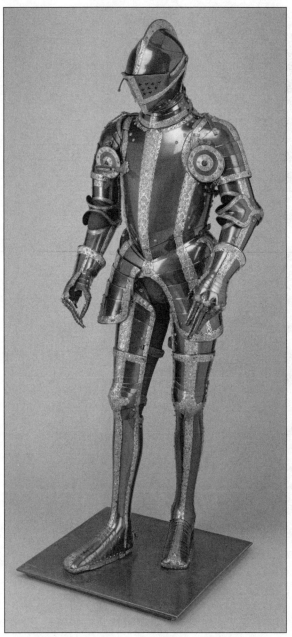

Figure 1.8 German (Augsburg), blued and gilded armor of Maximilian II, 1557. Vienna, Kunsthistorischen Museum (HJRK A 578). Used by permission.

champ clos, with a variety of weapons including javelins, pole arms, and two-handed swords.

Armor around the middle of the sixteenth century lost the fancy fluting of the Maximilian style, recalling something of the elegance of earlier plate armor (fig. 1.8). The breastplate developed a sharp keel, which dipped downwards towards the center of the waist. The surfaces of the armor were now left smooth, with the decoration confined to broad vertical bands of scrolling ornament, following the fashion in civilian clothes. The smooth parts of the plates were tinted a dark blue color, using a process similar to the blueing on modern gun barrels, making a striking contrast to the ornamental bands, which were usually covered in gold. The decoration on later armor was typically achieved by acid etching, though embossing and applied ornament were also used.

Beginning around 1540, suits of armor were being made with matching pieces of exchange for war and the tournament (fig. 1.9). The same suit of armor could now be worn for a variety of different combats, both on horseback and on foot. The complete set was called a garniture and might include over a hundred pieces of armor, all decorated en suite with the same ornamental pattern. The old great helm for the joust had been largely abandoned by the end of Maximilian's reign and was replaced by a kind of close helmet with a standing crest like the regular helmet for war. The lower half of the helmet was protected by a reinforcing piece called a *buff*, which prevented the visor from being knocked open by an opponent's lance. Breastplates were drilled with holes for the *manteau* and grand guard, which were screwed directly to the body armor. The barred shield or *manteau d'armes* was

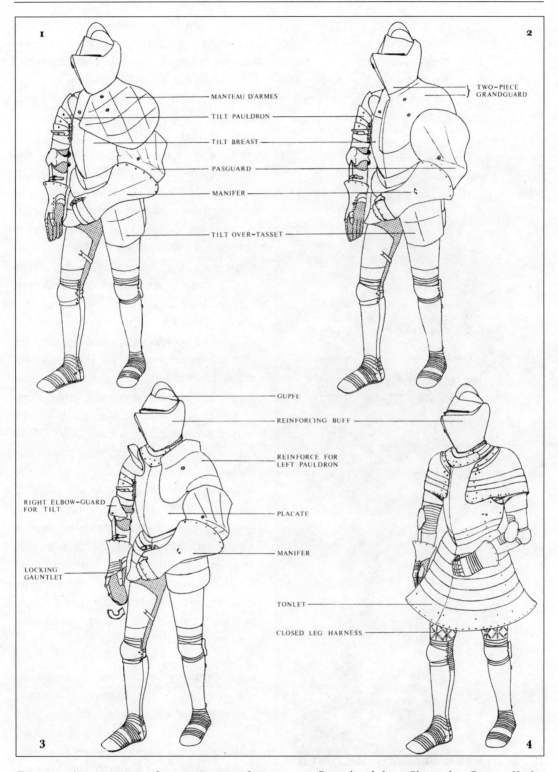

Figure 1.9 Armor garniture for various types of tournament. Reproduced from Christopher Gravett, *Knights at Tournament* (London: Osprey Publishing, © 1988), 58, by permission of the publisher. (1) Armor for the joust with barred shields, (2) armor for the tilt, (3) armor for the *Freiturnier*, (4) Tonlet armor for combat on foot.

embossed with a trellis-shaped pattern, virtually ensuring that an opponent's lance would grab hold and shatter on impact. Other reinforcements were added to the left side of the body, including an oversized gauntlet called a *manifer* and a flaring extension over the elbow called a *pasguard*. The leg harness made something of a comeback in the tiltyard, mostly to avoid injuries from collisions with the barrier. Part of the reason for the revival of leg armor, however, may have been to evoke the chivalric traditions of the past, which were being driven from the battlefield by continuing improvements in firearms. A skull-piece called a *gupfe*, typically decorated with pierced designs, was worn over the helmet as extra protection in the *Freiturnier*. In the sixteenth century, a special suit of armor for combat on foot was also a standard part of a complete garniture for war and the tournament. The armor for dismounted combat was called a tonlet suit, and featured a broad flaring skirt, or *tonlet*, for the waist (fig. 1.10). Unlike armor for mounted combat, the thigh-pieces of a tonlet suit were completely enclosed at front and back, since the wearer did not have to grip the sides of his horse with his legs when fighting on foot. Contestants sometimes wore a special type of gauntlet called a locking gauntlet with the tonlet suit and also for the *Freiturnier*, which prevented contestants from dropping weapons (locking gauntlets were prohibited in some tournaments).

Around the middle of the sixteenth century, a new type of combat on foot called the barriers was introduced to the tournament. In the barriers, contestants struck at each other with slender wooden pikestaffs and swords over a waist-high barrier, usually just a long pole with the ends set on a pair of uprights. A modified half-armor for infantry combat was used when

Figure 1.10 Jôrg Seusenhofer and Hans Perckhammer, tonlet armor of Archduke Ferdinand II of the Tyrol, 1547. Vienna, Kunsthistorischen Museum (HJRK A 638). Used by permission.

Figure 1.11 Northern Italian (Milan), half-armor of the Duke of Dos Aguas for combat on foot, 1575–80. The Art Institute of Chicago, George G. Harding Collection (1982.2172a–o). Used by permission.

fighting at the barriers. Regular half-armor for war usually consisted of a cuirass and arm-harness worn with an open-faced helmet and light armor for the shoulders (fig. 1.11). For the barriers, a fully enclosed helmet and special protection for the left shoulder were substituted immediately before combat. A large round shield was also sometimes added to an armor for the barriers. As in the joust, blows below the waist were forbidden and leg armor was typically not used. The barriers proved extremely popular and by 1600 had completely replaced the previous varieties of dismounted combat. Unlike jousting on horseback, the barriers trained the skills necessary for infantry warfare, which was rapidly replacing the cavalry charge of heavily armored knights on the battlefield (the barrier for foot combat may also have been intended to duplicate conditions when fighting at a wall or palisade during a siege). Entire tournaments, in fact, were sometimes held on foot, and dismounted combats were no longer considered simply an adjunct to the joust. Contestants might fight alone or in groups, though a type of *mêlée* on foot is also mentioned in some accounts.

A combat at the barriers is clearly illustrated in panel 7 of *The Valois Tapestries*. These tapestries were woven around 1580 in Brussels to commemorate two important events in the history of sixteenth-century

France: the meeting of Queen Catherine de Médicis and her daughter Isabella, the queen of Spain, at Bayonne in 1565, followed by the reception of the Polish ambassadors at the French court in 1573.[11] The tapestries illustrate a number of identifiable festivals held at Bayonne and the Tuileries. While *The Valois Tapestries* were not produced specifically for the Habsburg court, they are the single best visual source for European tournaments of the later Renaissance. In the scene illustrating the barriers, the contestants wear half-armor and appear to be thrusting across the barrier at each other with the ends of their staves (fig. 1.12). Fragments of staves and broken sword-hilts litter the ground beneath their feet. The two contestants in the center wear close-helmets to protect their faces, while gentlemen waiting their turn to fight wear light open-faced helmets. In the foreground, a page hands his master his helmet. Another small page, his back turned to us, holds a round shield for the Duke of Anjou, with his master's helmet (which is much too large for him) perched on his head. The tapestry illustration suggests fighting at the barriers was a vigorous physical activity, though contemporary writers on the subject complained the exercises bore little resemblance to actual combat.[12]

Costumes and disguises were worn at tournaments from as early as the thirteenth century. Contestants might enter the lists dressed as characters from the Arthurian legends and other medieval romances. Others masqueraded as Turks, wild men, monks, or even women. In the Renaissance, tournaments and their attendant pageantry were increasingly centered on princely courts, completing the transformation of the tournament into a kind of royal theater. The ruler or prince played the starring role in the costume tournament, or *tournois à thème*, attended by a court nobility with closely prescribed parts in the drama. Tournament competitors and their ladies arrived in gilt pageant cars, dressed as characters from Greek mythology or medieval romance, their real identities disguised by masks. Unlike medieval tournaments, chivalric role-playing in the sixteenth century took place inside a fashionable décor derived from classical antiquity. Processional avenues were punctuated by temporary triumphal arches and heroic statues in the antique style and tournament spaces were embellished with classical statues, pilasters, and festoons. The architectural setting might also feature an entire mock castle or fortress, which was besieged by squads of knights and foot soldiers. Assaults on wooden ships made especially for the occasion imitated naval combats. All the tricks of Renaissance stagecraft were employed to heighten the realism of these spectacles, which were sometimes held at night or even indoors to enhance the effect. These techniques were

---

[11]Yates, *Valois Tapestries*, xxiv.
[12]Anglo, *Martial Arts of Renaissance Europe*, 168–71.

Figure 1.12 After Antoine Caron, *The Valois Tapestries*, panel 7: A Fight at the Barriers, ca. 1580. Tapestry, Florence, Galleria degli Uffizi. Used by permission.

surprisingly sophisticated and included sounds, artificial illumination, and atmospheric effects. Hidden machinery operated by pulleys opened doors and lowered stairways or moved painted clouds from side to side. These contraptions resembled the type of stage machinery devised for Renaissance and baroque theaters, of which drawings occasionally survive. Spectacular displays of fireworks enlivened combats held at night. In addition to mock fortresses and ships, *apparati* in the form of colossal animals and fantastic beasts might be wheeled into the lists, sometimes fitted with moving parts or filled with gunpowder that exploded when put to the torch. Panel 8 of *The Valois Tapestries* shows an attack on an *apparatus* shaped like an elephant, defended by soldiers wearing Roman costume (fig. 1.13). The attackers are dressed as Moors, Turks, Celts, Romans, and Hungarians, supported by squads of cavalry and arquebusiers. The artillery consists of firepots or smokebombs, hurled by attackers and defenders alike, to the great delight of a pair of yapping dogs at the bottom of the scene.

During the Renaissance, it was understood that the Greeks and Romans had engaged in triumphal entries and martial contests, though the precise nature and appearance of these spectacles was unknown. In medieval art, figures from the distant past were usually dressed in contemporary garb. Military saints and ancient heroes, for example, were given the triangular shields and chain mail armor of medieval knights. A type of pseudo-antique costume for ancient characters reappeared in the Renaissance, including muscled breastplates like those worn by generals and other high-ranking officers in Greek and Roman art. Around the early 1530s, actual metal armor in the heroic style was revived in Italy. The Negroli family of Milan specialized in the craft of embossing steel armor and the earliest surviving examples of Renaissance armor in the antique manner are from their workshop. Other Italian armorers were soon imitating their style. Metal armor *all'antica* or *alla romana* was usually limited to a panoply of helmet and shield, worn with a costume of leather or cloth tailored to resemble Roman armor.[13] Occasionally, however, entire suits of metal armor were made in the ancient style (fig. 1.14). The mania for historical authenticity extended to the detailing on the breastplate, which in this example includes the head of the Gorgon Medusa, a talisman worn on ancient armor as a protection against evil. Armor garnitures for war also sometimes included pieces of exchange embossed like ancient armor for pageant use. Pageant armor *alla romana* was based on the study of Roman monuments that were known in the Renaissance, including portraits of famous emperors in armor (fig. 1.15) and reliefs on triumphal arches, sarcophagi, and coins. It is also entirely

---

[13]Hayward, "Revival of Roman Armour in the Renaissance," 158.

Figure 1.13 After Antoine Caron, *The Valois Tapestries*, panel 8: Attack on an Elephant, ca. 1580. Tapestry, Florence, Galleria degli Uffizi. Used by permission.

Figure 1.14 Bartolommeo Campi, armor *all'antica* of Guidobaldo II della Rovere, Duke of Urbino, 1546 (later given to Charles V or Philip II). Madrid, Real Armería, A188. Used by permission.

Figure 1.15 Roman, Tiberius, first century AD. Rome, Museo di Villa Torlonia Albani. Reproduced by permission of Alinari/Art Resource, NY.

possible that actual pieces of ancient armor were preserved for study in princely collections.[14] Armor in antique style, of course, was not intended for real sixteenth-century warfare. The raised or embossed decoration on these armors defeated the principle of the glancing surface used on armor made for the battlefield and was reserved for tournament and pageant use. Art historians believe armor like this was worn in processions and parades, and there is some pictorial evidence from the period to support this idea.[15] The Roman triumph, in which a victorious general made a ceremonial entry into the city followed by a train of captives and their spoils, was revived in part in the Renaissance. Paintings and prints illustrating the ceremonial entries of Emperor Charles V and Henry II of France sometimes show participants wearing muscled breastplates in classical style. Historicism and the interest in period costume, however, could be a double-edged sword. Medieval artists had dressed ancient characters in modern armor, but Renaissance nobles could be equally guilty of anachronism and sometimes projected their own chivalric values onto the distant past. Ghillebert de Lannoy, for example, solemnly instructed his son that the Roman Empire was won by chivalry and the pursuit of honor.[16] Heroes from Celtic Britain and the medieval legends of Charlemagne were shown indiscriminately wearing Roman armor in illustrations for chivalric romances such as *Orlando Furioso* and *Amadís of Gaul*, which were avidly consumed by Renaissance readers. With the revival of armor in antique style, Renaissance princes could at least play the roles of ancient heroes while wearing more believable costumes (in spite of humanist wags who pointed out that Cicero never jousted).

The *Valois Tapestries* suggest that armor in antique style was also worn for the *tournois à thème*. Panel 2 of the tapestries documents a carrousel and *mêlée* in antique costume held at Bayonne in 1565 (fig. 1.16). In the dappled sunlight of a midsummer's day, knights dressed as the legendary heroes of Britain and Ireland battle for their ladies, who watch from a stand in the background. Pageant cars decked out like ancient chariots bring ladies costumed as Virtues to the stands, while boys dressed as Cupids present rings to the ladies. In the center of the scene, contestants engage in a *mêlée* with swords while others wait on the sidelines with jousting lances. The combatants wear gilded helmets and carry shields embossed like ancient armor, with body armor of metal scales or muscled corselets in an anachronistic Roman style. Their leg and arm harnesses, however, are mostly made of plain steel in contemporary fashion. For added excitement, exploding firepots have been rolled between the feet of the horses, probably as a signaling device for

[14]Pyhrr and Godoy, *Heroic Armor*, 11–12.
[15]Hayward, "Revival of Roman Armor in the Renaissance," 145.
[16]Vale, *Chivalry*, 16.

Figure 1.16 After Antoine Caron, *The Valois Tapestries*, panel 2, Carrousel and *Mêlée* at Bayonne, ca. 1580. Tapestry, Florence, Galleria degli Uffizi. Used by permission.

all the horses to turn at once.[17] Contemporary festival books also occasionally mention contestants at tournaments wearing embossed armor,
presumably decorated in antique style. The *mêlée* in fancy-dress costume
proved very popular in the later Renaissance, and eventually evolved into
the grand carrousel of the seventeenth century, which was primarily an
exercise in horsemanship.

Other types of tournament combat that were sometimes held in
antique costume included the *naumachia* or mock sea battle and jousting
at the *quintain*, a wooden figure carved and painted to resemble fantasti-
cal characters like dragons or Turks (the quintain turned on a pivot and
struck unwary jousters who failed to duck in time). Contemporary
accounts describe another jousting exercise called running at the ring, in
which contestants aimed their lances at rings of various sizes hanging
from a post. Except for running at the ring, all of these exercises in
fancy-dress costume are shown in the Valois Tapestries, including naval
assaults on an island and a sea monster. An English manuscript of
unknown provenance from around 1550 shows a competitor in an
antique-style cuirass fighting in a tournament on foot against an opponent wearing more up-to-date armor, suggesting that embossed armor was
used in this context as well.[18]

In addition to these types of combats, which were fairly standard
throughout most of Europe, games and festivals with a local flavor were
also held. In England, for example, archery contests, wrestling, casting
the bar, and other tests of physical strength enlivened tournaments.[19] In
Spain, knights practiced bullfighting on horseback and another type of
mounted combat, the *juego de cañas* or "cane game." The cane game was
run in Moorish costume with high stirrups and heart-shaped leather
shields known as *adargas* (fig. 1.17). At the signal to begin, opposing
teams dashed at breakneck speed across the arena, casting blunted spears
at each other and then wheeling around to return, protecting their backs
with their shields as they retreated. The movements were repeated until
men and horses were completely exhausted.[20] The cane game probably
originated in the ancient Near East, though late Roman cavalry manuals
describe a type of combat resembling the Spanish cane game. In the
early Middle Ages, barbarian horsemen in southern Europe used similar
tactics, and Byzantine and Carolingian cavalrymen also practiced exercises
resembling the cane game.[21] The light cavalry tactics of the north African Moors, based in turn on an Arabian military tactic known as *karr
wa farr*, or "fight and flight," were the direct ancestors of the Spanish

[17]Yates, *Valois Tapestries*, 55–56.
[18]Young, *Tudor and Jacobean Tournaments*, 99.
[19]Gravett, *Knights at Tournament*, 50.
[20]Marsden, "Fêtes espagnoles," 394.
[21]Nicolle, *Age of Charlemagne*, 13.

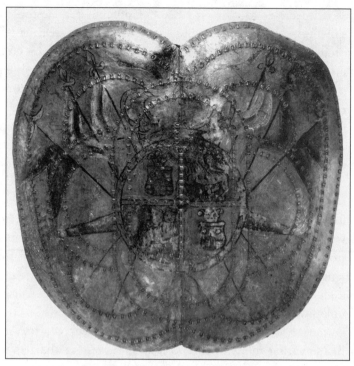

cane game. In this type of combat, lightly armed horsemen tried to exhaust more heavily armored opponents by repeated attacks and retreats. The cane game was also played in the Spanish kingdom of Naples, where it was known as the *gioco de canne*. Italians and northerners alike tended to be critical of these exercises, however, believing that the true merit of a knight was shown in face-to-face combat. Antonio de Ferrara, writing about a Spanish tournament he witnessed in the middle of the sixteenth century, scorned the cane game as a confusion of loud shouting "in Arab fashion," remarking that games of attack and retreat were unworthy of a man of valor.[22] In spite of Ferrara's opinion, the cane game was enormously popular. Arms and armor in pseudo-Islamic or Hungarian style, presumably intended for the cane game, were manufactured in western European workshops, though surviving examples of these are rare. Other more lighthearted games were also played at tournaments, including a Spanish game called *alcancías*, in which contestants hurled balls of earth filled with flowers or perfume at each other (ladies and children might participate in these games).

The main object in later medieval and early Renaissance tournaments was to win the favor of ladies, who bestowed prizes like a ring, a scarf, a feather, or a kiss on the victors. More valuable prizes such as fine weapons or jewels were awarded at later Renaissance tournaments, and the competitors sometimes placed wagers on the outcomes of the

[22]Marsden, "Fêtes espagnoles," 394.

contests. Special stands were sometimes erected for the ladies attending a tournament, especially for lady judges in tourneys of love. A special set of sideboards was sometimes necessary to hold all the prizes, which might include gold and silver plate, medals, chains, jewels, and rings set with precious stones. After the various prizes were awarded, the tournament competitors and their ladies met for rounds of feasting and dancing in the palace. These festivities continued all night and read like manifestoes for the sin of gluttony. Ingenious devices were invented to dispense food and drink. Music, dancing, and masquerades followed the feasting. Like other forms of Renaissance spectacle, the courtly masquerade featured fantastic *apparati* and lavish costumes. Costumes and equipment for the masquerade repeated the motifs of the tournament, sometimes incorporating actual weapons and armor.

In the days following the tournament, a visiting prince would attend to more serious business, holding court from his host's palace. This was standard practice in an age when the idea of a fixed royal residence did not yet exist. Ambassadors from foreign powers had to follow the itinerant courts of European monarchs, bearing gifts from their own rulers prior to receiving an audience from the prince. City councils, foreign nobles, and important potentates like the emperor or pope traditionally sent gifts of fine armor or a ceremonial sword to a visiting prince-elect. Ceremonial weapons and swords of state were not intended for actual battle and were sometimes oversized, their blades etched and gilt with scrolling designs, usually including the name and titles of the giver. Before the prince departed, his host usually invited him to take part in that most aristocratic of pastimes, the hunt. These too were grandiose affairs, requiring specialized weapons and hundreds of huntsmen, retainers, and dogs, all identified by their lord's livery. In addition to the thrill of the chase, the hunt, like the tournament, was believed to develop the skills necessary for war.

Following the prince's visit, an official court chronicler would write a detailed itinerary of the prince's travels, highlighting the major events of his tour. These accounts, known as festival books, were subsequently published at court expense (fig. 1.18). Festival books are fascinating cultural documents in their own right, opening a window into the vanished world of Renaissance courtly spectacle. They were also the primary vehicle by which royal propaganda was disseminated to the reading public in the territories governed by the prince. The tournament combats that punctuated the prince's journey were elevated in the festival books to a level of allegorical significance. The books were typically written in a style intended to imitate popular chivalric romances. They include such stock motifs as the quest, the unknown knight, trial by combat, wizards and fairy enchantments, distressed maidens, lovesick Saracen warriors, and the Sword in the Stone. Local scholars, anxious to secure a position

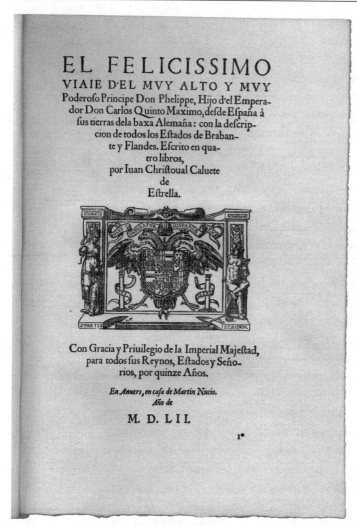

EL FELICISSIMO
VIAIE D'EL MVY ALTO Y MVY
Poderofo Principe Don Phelippe, Hijo d'el Emperador Don Carlos Quinto Maximo, defde Efpaña à
fus tierras dela baxa Alemaña : con la defcrip-
cion de todos los Eftados de Braban-
te y Flandes. Efcrito en qua-
tro libros,
por Iuan Chriftoual Caluete
de
Eftrella.

Con Gracia y Priuilegio de la Imperial Majeftad,
para todos fus Reynos, Eftados y Seño-
rios, por quinze Años.

En Anuers, en cafa de Martin Nucio.
Año de
M. D. LII.

1°

Figure 1.18 Pieter Coecke van Aelst,
title page of Juan Cristobal Calvete
de Estrella, *El Felicíssimo viaje del Príncipe don Phelippe* (Antwerp, 1552).
Reproduced by permission of Wayne
State University Library, Detroit.

at court, scrambled to publish their own accounts of the prince's visit.
Interestingly, these accounts sometimes differ substantially from the official chronicles, or rely on a different type of literary imagery. Italian
chroniclers, for example, often compared visiting princes to figures from
Greek and Roman history and mythology. Festival books were sometimes
illustrated with woodcuts or intaglio prints showing highlights of the
tournaments and other festivities on the prince's tour. Court humanists
were also consulted on the construction of appropriate emblems for the
occasion, which were reproduced on coins and medals and also on
armor and tournament shields. The development of the Renaissance
emblem, in fact, was closely tied to the chivalric ambience of the tournament, in which personal emblems and mottoes first appeared. By the
Renaissance, emblems were replacing heraldry as a means of identifying
noble warriors, both on and off the battlefield.[23] Artists worked from

[23]Vale, *Chivalry*, 97.

emblem books first published in the sixteenth century, most notably by Alciati and Piero Valeriano. They also borrowed emblems from a book of hieroglyphs allegedly written by a mysterious ancient philosopher known as Horapollo, whose writings were known in the Renaissance.[24]

Alongside the production of a distinctive type of tournament literature, artists employed by princely courts gave visual form to Renaissance ideas of the ideal ruler. Paintings and sculptures of Renaissance princes often show the sitter dressed in contemporary armor, which was illustrated from life and can sometimes be matched to actual pieces of armor in royal and princely collections. Aristocrats wore armor in portraits as a badge of social rank and military authority, accompanied by a symbolic visual language designed to remind the viewer of the virtues of the prince. Habsburg emperor Maximilian I and his successor, Charles V, made every effort to attract talented artists to their courts. Habsburg patronage included such famous painters as Albrecht Dürer (1471-1528), Parmigianino (1503-40), and Titian (1488/90-1576). Titian was official court painter to Charles V, and also painted portraits of his son, Philip II. As an indication of the esteem in which the emperor held Titian, he ennobled the artist and gave him a skullcap and gold chain of office in 1533.[25] Important sculptural portraits of Charles V and Philip II were entrusted to the Milanese sculptor and goldsmith Leone Leoni (1509-90), whose son Pompeo Leoni (1533-1608) later became court sculptor to Philip II. Other major artists who worked for Philip II were the Dutch painter Anthonis Mor (1517-77), Sofonisba Anguissola (1532-1625), and the Spanish painter Alonso Sánchez-Coello (1531-88). Among their other duties, court artists were also called upon to design triumphal arches and *apparati* for the prince's festivals, along with costumes, banners, horse trappings, and other luxury objects. Few of these perishable artworks have survived, though prints and drawings of them occasionally survive. In addition to formal portraits and festival art, tapestries and frescoes were required to decorate the living areas of castles and urban palaces. These buildings were the staging areas for tournaments and other spectacles, and artworks chosen to decorate them typically illustrate subjects related to the chivalric milieu of warfare and the tournament, the hunt, and other courtly pastimes. Emperor Charles V preferred the tapestry designs of Jan Vermeyen (1500-1559), a Dutch painter and printmaker, and relied on this artist to produce detailed visual accounts of his battles and tournaments.

The only surviving direct connection to the world of the Renaissance tournament is in the decorated suits of armor worn by the nobility. For the decorative enhancement of armor, Renaissance artists copied

[24]Pizarro Gómez, *Arte y espectáculo*, 93-96.
[25]Panofsky, *Problems in Titian*, 7-8.

illustrations of armor from ancient monuments and produced books with decorative designs from which armorers and other craftsmen could work. Famous artists like Leonardo da Vinci, Dürer, and Caravaggio occasionally decorated armor themselves or designed pieces of armor and other military hardware. For the most part, however, the actual production of armor was left to professional armorers and weaponsmiths employed directly by the princely court. Armorers provided illustrated catalogs of their products to aristocratic patrons, and some of these have survived to the present day. Armor could always be bought off the peg, but for important clients, armorers used wax models of the customer's limbs to tailor a custom armor to the correct size. Charles V continued his grandfather Maximilian's patronage of the German imperial armorers, most notably Colman Helmschmied (1471–1532) and his son Desiderius Colman (1513–79) of Augsburg. Following the establishment of Spanish control over the duchy of Milan, the famous armorers of northern Italy were also at the emperor's disposal. Major Italian armorers who worked for Charles V included Filippo Negroli and his brother Francesco (active 1531–61), and Caremolo Modrone (1489–1543) of Milan. Charles patronized both German and Italian armorers equally, though his son Philip showed a definite preference for the Germans. Prince Philip owned fine pieces of armor by Francesco Negroli, Matteus Frauenpreis of Augsburg (active ca. 1525–63), Desiderius Colman, and Wolfgang and Franz Grosschedel of Landshut (active 1545–54). Unlike many court artists, the imperial armorers grew quite rich, and owned fine townhouses in the cities where they worked.[26]

In addition to larger-scale artworks, coins and medals were struck to commemorate important state occasions in the Renaissance. Since ancient times, coins had carried both visual and textual messages glorifying the rulers who produced them and cities where they were produced. Renaissance coins and portrait medals were loosely modeled on Roman coins, which were an important public venue for enhancing the majesty of the state. Coins bearing images of the prince were tossed to the crowd during the entries that preceded Renaissance tournaments, and portrait medals (which imitated the fabric of coins) were often given as tournament prizes. In giving medals to their supporters, the Habsburgs and other Renaissance princes may have been self-consciously imitating the Julio-Claudian emperors of Rome, who granted donatives in coin specially minted for the occasion to the imperial guard upon their accession.[27] Renaissance medals featured a profile portrait of the ruler on the obverse, with a personal emblem or *impresa* on the reverse referring to the special virtues or qualities of the sitter. Italian portrait medals

---

[26]Pfaffenbichler, *Medieval Craftsmen*, esp. 14.
[27]Grant, *Army of the Caesars*, 151–52.

typically show male sitters wearing armor in an imaginative antique style, deliberately recalling the heroic portrait in antiquity and intended to remind the viewer of the continuities between the new and ancient empires (though medals showing the sitter wearing an identifiable suit of real armor have also survived). Emblems and accompanying inscriptions were sometimes composed for specific occasions, though a prince's personal badge or heraldic device was more commonly used. These emblems recycled the imagery used in tournaments and other festival art, including allegorical figures and scenes from classical mythology. In the sixteenth century, Giovanni del Cavino and Leone Leoni, who was employed as a sculptor by the Habsburg court (Leoni was also master of the imperial mint at Milan), revived coins and medals directly imitating Roman imperial types. Other Italian artists who specialized in portrait medals, most notably Jacopo Nizolla da Trezzo (1515/19–1589) of Milan, subsequently imitated Leoni's style. Jacopo made medals for both Philip II and the Gonzagas of Mantua, who were important allies of the imperial house.

Tournaments and courtly spectacles marked the major turning points in the life of a Renaissance prince. His birth, his coming of age, his marriage, and his eventual assumption of power were all attended by formal displays of martial prowess. The climax of the Renaissance tournament coincided with the reign of Charles V and the coming of age of his firstborn son, Prince Philip of Spain. Tournaments and other martial spectacles highlighted Philip's grand tour of the European empire of Charles V on the eve of his succession. A visual rhetoric culled from history and literature, which was carefully chosen to match the occasion, accompanied these events. The type of imagery selected for the tournaments and other artworks associated with Philip's tour was a concrete expression of Renaissance ideas of the ideal ruler and merits a closer look. Out of the mélange of related imagery and ideas, three main themes emerge: the prince as knight-errant and consort, the prince as crusader and defender of the church, and the prince as divine deliverer and heir apparent of the Holy Roman Empire. The following chapters will present case studies of Habsburg tournaments and related artworks in which these themes were most clearly expressed. Together, these ideas painted a picture of the perfect prince, whose lineage was traced to ancient heroes and whose reign was sanctified by heaven.

Chapter 2

BEAUTY, LOVE, AND PLEASURE
The Prince as Knight-Errant and Consort

T HE HABSBURG EMPIRE WAS BUILT by marriage as much as by military conquest. Emperor Maximilian I of Austria combined love and politics by marrying a succession of brides from three of the most important families in Europe. Only the first of these marriages, however, to Mary of Burgundy, was to have any lasting historical significance. Mary died in 1482, leaving her son, Philip the Handsome, to inherit the duchy of Burgundy and the Low Countries. Maximilian then arranged Philip's marriage to Princess Juana of Castile, daughter of Ferdinand and Isabella, the Catholic monarchs of Spain. Juana arrived in Flanders in 1496, promptly fell in love with Philip, and the two journeyed south together to introduce the duke to his future Spanish subjects. In 1500, they celebrated the birth of their firstborn son, Charles of Ghent. By inheritance alone, the heir of Philip and Juana stood to accomplish the old dream of a pan-European empire. Philip, however, failed to gain the allegiance of the Aragonese nobility (who remained loyal to King Ferdinand) and he died in mysterious circumstances in 1506. Several interesting artworks made around the time of Philip's journey refer to the union of Burgundy and Castile and were commissioned in an effort to remind Juana's subjects of Philip's right to rule.

Philip's sojourn in Spain began optimistically enough. Suits of fine armor were commissioned for the young prince, including a pair of Spanish jousting armors probably made for Philip in honor of his marriage. In addition to these, Philip owned a suit of Flemish armor and several light helmets, or *sallets*, decorated in Spanish style.[1] Portions of Philip's Flemish armor are preserved in Madrid, and their decoration alludes to his union with Juana and subsequent status as king of Castile (fig. 2.1). The lightweight helmet for this armor is shaped like a civilian beret, embossed with raised ribs on top suggesting a royal crown. On the upper part of the backplate of the armor, almost hidden from view, is a small etching showing a pair of *putti* bearing a crown. The crown is an obvious reference to kingship and the little *putti*, or *amorini*, who raise it towards Philip's head are ancient symbols of love and matrimony.

Figure 2.1 Flanders, armor of Philip I, ca. 1490–1500. Madrid, Real Armería, A11. Used by permission.

Back in Flanders, the marriage of Philip and Juana was commemorated in a large oil painting of the Last Judgment, completed by a Netherlandish master in the late fifteenth or early sixteenth century (fig. 2.2). In the wings of the triptych stand portraits of Philip and Juana. Philip is shown wearing a full suit of armor and a crowned helmet, recalling the armor made for him around the time of his journey to Spain. Philip raises a decorated ceremonial sword and with a sweep of his hands opens his coronation robe, revealing a surcoat or tabard bearing heraldic emblems, including the arms of Burgundy and Castile. Juana rests her hand on her belly, probably a reference to the birth of their firstborn son and heir, Charles of Ghent. On the threshold of the High Renaissance, the visual language of northern art is still emblematic and hieratic. The marriage of Philip and Juana is shown as an adjunct to

[1] Godoy, "The Royal Armory."

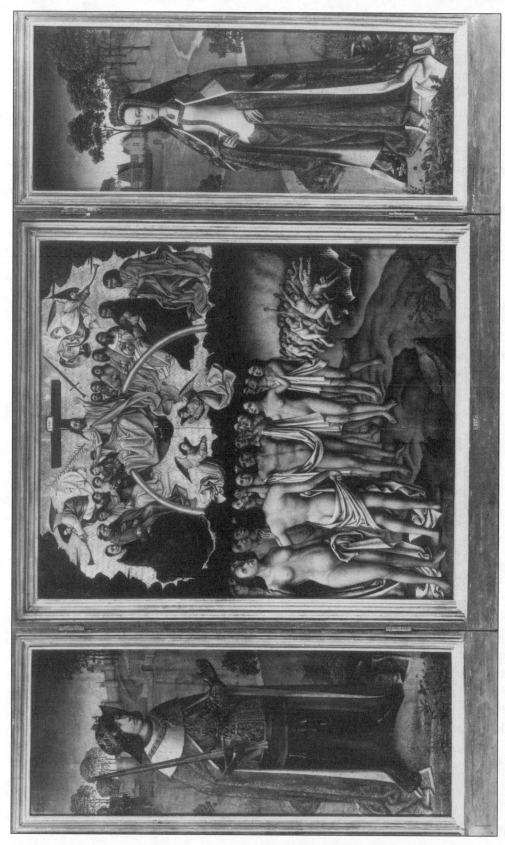

Figure 2.2 Master of Affligem, *Zierikzee Triptych with Portraits of Philip of Burgundy and Juana of Castile*, late fifteenth to early sixteenth century. Oil on panel, Brussels, Musée des Beaux-Arts. Used by permission.

the progress of sacred history, and they are identified primarily by the symbols of rank they carry.

Philip's trip to Spain, though abortive, propped open the European gateway to the Iberian peninsula. In 1517, when his son, Charles of Ghent, Duke of Burgundy and now king of Spain, arrived at the port of Villaviciosa to take up his inheritance, he was seasick and overburdened with possessions and a vast entourage of Flemish nobles. News of his arrival was greeted with less than enthusiasm by Cardinal Cisneros, regent of Spain after the death of Ferdinand the Catholic. The cardinal, however, died not long after Charles landed, removing the last legal obstacle to Charles's assumption of full authority in Spain. The young king and his ponderous train slowly made their way to Valladolid, the capital of old Castile, where a series of tournaments was planned to officially welcome him to Spain. The king entered the city on horseback, wearing a shining corselet of steel.[2]

The tournaments began in December of 1517 and lasted until the end of the following summer. The combats were held in the marketplace of Valladolid and were attended by the king's knights and knights-errant from as far away as France and England. There were masked jousts, jousts of war, royal jousts, and cane games. Laurent Vital, a Flemish nobleman and official chronicler of the king's journey to Spain, witnessed and described the combats. The forms of the combats, Vital claims, were inspired by a vision in a dream shared by two knights-errant of the royal court. According to the dream, a fir tree was to be planted in the middle of the stockade, hung with two shields, one red and charged with gold bezants, another gold and strewn with flowers. Knights who touched the red shield with their lance were to joust in regular armor for war, while those who touched the gold shield were to run at the tilt in jousting armor. Defeated knights were obliged to surrender themselves to the lady of the winner. The rules of the joust were enforced by Murgalante the Large, a fierce Saracen giant some sixteen feet tall who dozed at the foot of the tree (he was represented by a statue in the actual tournament). This spectacle was called the Quest of the Marigold.

The young king himself participated on one occasion. At the height of the combats, Charles left the stands in secret and rode into the lists incognito, where he broke many lances. Charles, who was still unwed, bore on his jacket the motto "Nondum" ("Not Yet"). The combats, the chronicler records, were held in honor of the king's sisters and Germaine de Foix, widow of King Ferdinand of Aragon, and were especially pleasing to the ladies gathered to watch the tournament. The Quest of the Marigold was followed by the Quest of Love, held in honor of the emperor's sister Catalina, who arrived in Valladolid in

[2]Vital, *Primer viaje a España de Carlos I,* 249.

March. This time the jousting lasted three days and featured a course with sharpened lances. The tournaments were not without their mishaps. Vital reports that during the jousting, five horses fell dead to the ground with broken backs, which he blames on the narrow confines of the marketplace. One knight was severely injured, his shoulders dislocated and the stump of his opponent's lance left in his body, causing great loss of blood.[3]

The underlying message of the tournaments at Valladolid, of course, was that Charles and the other younger members of the Habsburg family were suitable and available for marriage. To get their message across, the organizers of the tournaments plumbed the repertoire of courtly love and chivalric romance. Vital compares the dream of the two knights-errant to the stories of Sir Launcelot, Tristram of Lyonesse, and King Perceforest, all knights of the Round Table who engaged in dangerous quests on behalf of love. Vital describes the knights who jousted at Valladolid as unusually brave and provides detailed descriptions of the accidents to underscore his point. Chivalric ideals assumed that noblemen instinctively had the urge to fight, bleed, and even die before their beloved, and the physical dangers of the combats were partly intended to heighten the attractiveness of the jousters to female spectators. Love imagery and references to the sexual desirability of the young king abound in the chronicler's description of the tournament and its attendant festivities; at one point, Vital exclaims that if he had a gold doubloon for each of the pretty girls who wanted to kiss King Charles, his purse would be full. The Unknown Knight, usually a fair and untried youth who entered the lists incognito or in disguise, was another standard literary motif borrowed from the Arthurian legends, and was used to increase the excitement and anticipation of female spectators. The social occasion of the tournament also provided opportunities for a kind of limited political dialogue between the ruler and his new subjects. During Charles's stop in Valladolid, defamatory *cartellinos* were posted on the door of the church of San Pablo, claiming that the king cared little for Spain and that he would soon leave the country.[4]

King Charles's stay in Spain, in fact, was brief. In June 1519, after news of the death of Emperor Maximilian, Charles was elected Holy Roman Emperor. France, however, also claimed the imperial crown, and Charles embarked from La Coruña in 1520 to secure his election in Germany. During his absence, Charles was faced with the revolts of the Comuneros and the Germanías in Spain, which were put down with great difficulty and involved some compromises on Charles's part. The king had to learn Castilian and show proper respect for Spanish customs.

[3]Vital, *Primer viaje a España de Carlos I*, 278–327, passim.
[4]Vital, *Primer viaje a España de Carlos I*, 255–354, passim.

Charles returned to Spain as Holy Roman Emperor and married Isabella of Portugal in 1526. Their wedding took place in Seville and was celebrated with tournaments and cane games in Spanish style. In May 1527, Charles V and Isabella celebrated the birth of their firstborn son, Prince Philip of Spain. The birth of a male heir was welcomed in Valladolid in the usual fashion, with rounds of feasting, dancing, and tournaments. According to Spanish tradition, the emperor himself began the festivities by killing a bull in the arena.[5] The entertainment continued for almost a month, the imperial ambassador remarking that the tournaments surpassed the mythical adventures of Amadís of Gaul.[6]

The outdated image of Philip II as a compulsive bureaucrat who tried to rule the world from his desk was based mostly on descriptions of the king in old age mixed with a heavy dose of Protestant propaganda. As far as we can tell, the prince grew up with all the usual preoccupations of sixteenth-century aristocratic boys. Young Philip showed a keen interest in chivalry and the martial arts. An early inventory of the prince's possessions describes a toy knight that he kept in his room; it was made of silver with a complete suit of armor and a miniature horse and lance.[7] Toy knights made for Renaissance boys occasionally survive. Fitted with wheels and attachment points for strings, the model could be pulled across a tabletop in a miniature joust (fig. 2.3). The same document also records a real armor "with all its pieces," noting that His Highness gave it to one of his companions when he outgrew it. Philip also owned a number of swords and crossbows, a golden shield (which he gave to one of his pages), and seven model cannons of gold and bronze.[8]

In 1535, Charles appointed Don Juan de Zúñiga, *comendador mayor* of Castile, to teach the prince how to ride a horse and handle a spear and a sword. As Philip's governor, Zúñiga also acted as a kind of guardian of the prince's morals, reporting Philip's conduct and development directly to the emperor.[9] When he was ten years old, the prince arranged a little joust with his companions, after which he danced with his younger sister María.[10] Philip also greatly enjoyed hunting in the mesas around Valladolid. Eventually, even the old warrior Zúñiga could not keep up with him. An expedition that seemed like two hours to the prince, Zúñiga growled in one of his letters, seemed more like twelve to him.[11]

[5]Grierson, *King of Two Worlds*, 19. The event was later immortalized in a sketch by Goya.
[6]Kamen, *Philip of Spain*, 2.
[7]AGS, *Casa y Sitios Reales*, legajo 36, fol. 7/5r. Illustrations of aristocratic boys playing with toy knights are sometimes found in contemporary German prints.
[8]AGS, *Casa y Sitios Reales*, legajo 36, fols. 21r–21v, 24r–24v.
[9]Parker, *Philip II*, 7–9, 21.
[10]Kamen, *Philip of Spain*, 6.
[11]Parker, *Philip II*, 9.

Figure 2.3 Nuremberg, model of a knight, ca. 1540. Munich, Bayerisches National Museum (W940). Used by permission.

Relatively few artworks that actually illustrate tournaments held at the western Habsburg court have survived and information about Philip's tournaments is mostly documentary. A painting and a preliminary drawing illustrating a Spanish cane game, however, were completed by Jan Vermeyen sometime around 1539, when Charles V was visiting Toledo (fig. 2.4). The games were held in honor of Empress Isabella, who was pregnant again and is shown seated next to Charles in the imperial box. A young boy, presumably Philip, is shown in an adjoining box along with two pretty girls (one of whom is probably his little sister María), who are intent on the action taking place in the arena. The spectators are paired as couples and arranged by social rank, the ladies sharing the

Figure 2.4 Jan Cornelisz Vermeyen, *The Game of Canes*, 1539. Oil on panel, private collection. Image reproduced from Hendrick J. Horn, *Jan Cornelisz Vermeyen, Painter of Charles V and His Conquest of Tunis* (Meppel: Davaco, 1989), by permission of the publisher.

excitement of the spectacle along with the men and boys. Philip delicately holds a flower in his right hand, an allusion, perhaps, to his upcoming betrothal to the Princess of Portugal.[12]

Empress Isabella died of a miscarriage in 1539, when Philip was eleven years old. According to custom, the nearest available relatives were required to identify the body of the deceased and accompany the funeral procession to the place of burial. The story goes that the emperor admonished his son not to cry in front of the dour Spanish nobles, but when the coffin was opened Philip lost his composure and burst into tears. The empress's death was a double blow to Charles, who not only loved his wife but had depended on her to govern as regent during his long absences from the country. The emperor was now forced to rely on Philip instead,[13] charging him with real responsibilities at the age of sixteen.

Philip's education in language and the humanities also began in earnest around this time. In spite of flattering reports concerning the prince's academic progress, one gets the impression that Philip was actually a rather mediocre student. The emperor dismissed Philip's first tutor as too lenient and appointed sterner teachers to instruct him. Juan Cristóbal Calvete de Estrella managed to teach the prince at least some Latin and Greek. Honorato Juan and Juan Ginés de Sepulveda were employed to teach him mathematics and architecture, geography, and history. Books were purchased for Philip in Salamanca and Medina del Campo: the Bible, of course, along with works by Virgil, Ovid, Vitruvius, Boccaccio, Petrarch, Serlio, and the collected writings of Erasmus, including *The Education of a Christian Prince*. Philip also learned to dance and play the *vihuela*, an early form of Spanish guitar.[14] Philip had trouble with mathematics and perhaps some difficulty with foreign languages (he was afraid of making the inevitable mistakes), but he did develop genuine interests in nature, military history, and art. The prince's favorite books, however, were chivalric romances. He was especially fond of *Amadis of Gaul*,[15] a Spanish tale of knights and derring-do set in Britain around the time of Christ.

Philip's passion for tournaments continued alongside his academic pursuits. In 1540, his tutor Siliceo diplomatically reported that, after study, the prince's main interests were hunting and jousting.[16] Philip's allowance was increased to thirty ducats a month, with which he bought, among other things, practice swords and light lances for running

[12]The painting was probably completed sometime after the event, and varies slightly in detail from the preliminary drawing.

[13]Kamen, *Philip of Spain*, 7–8.

[14]Parker, *Philip II*, 6–7, 8; and Kamen, *Philip of Spain*, 4–6.

[15]Parker, *Philip II*, 15.

[16]Kamen, *Philip of Spain*, 4.

at the ring.[17] When Philip was sixteen, Zúñiga wrote proudly that the prince was the best man-at-arms at court,[18] though Zúñiga's opinion of his protégé's abilities sounds a bit optimistic.

The emperor returned to Spain in November 1541. At the age of fifteen, Philip was taken on a tour of Old Castile, Catalonia, and Valencia, where the prince had to swear to uphold the ancient privileges of the realms.[19] The ceremonies at Valencia were punctuated by tournaments and other martial games, though Philip may not have taken part in the more dangerous types of combat yet. Fiestas were held on the day of the Immaculate Conception to celebrate his arrival. On 11 December, the emperor and Philip attended jousts and a *juego de alcancías*, a lighthearted game in which male and female contestants hurled balls of earth stuffed with flowers at each other. The next day, the emperor assisted in a combat on foot at the barriers at the house of the Duchess of Calabria. The festivities at Valencia concluded on 13 December with a cane game attended by the emperor and Philip.[20] The cane game was more vigorous and dangerous than the other activities, but was probably safer than running a course with leveled lances in heavy armor.

Philip's participation in the games at Valencia was an integral part of his acceptance as Charles's heir in the Spanish kingdoms. As the eldest son of Charles V, Philip was also the most eligible bachelor in Europe and the emperor was already searching for a suitable bride for his son. With the exception of the cane games, the games at Valencia also had erotic connotations. The game of *alcancías* is better documented, and definitely had sexual undertones. Unlike the joust and other forms of armored combat, the *alcancías* was a unisex game. The weapons—earthen bombs designed to splatter on contact—were utterly harmless, filled only with sweet-smelling blossoms or other scents. In addition to their immediate sensual impact, flowers and perfume were love tokens in the sixteenth century, as they are today. The image of flowers emerging from the earth also suggested springtime, the season for lovers in the Renaissance.

As soon as Philip was confirmed as *principe heredero* by the various estates, the emperor set sail from Pálamos, beginning his last and longest absence from Spain. Philip was designated regent until his return. Before his departure, Charles left the first of a set of special instructions for the prince with Zúñiga. These documents, written in the emperor's own hand, contain detailed advice on the prince's political and personal

---

[17]Parker, *Philip II*, 9.
[18]Kamen, *Philip of Spain*, 6.
[19]Kamen, *Philip of Spain*, 10.
[20]Foronda y Aguilera, *Estancias y viajes de Carlos V*, 532–33.

affairs, including sexual matters.[21] "I would have you perfect," the emperor is said to have once lectured his son.[22]

The next major event in Philip's life was his marriage to Princess María Manuela of Portugal. The two had been betrothed in 1542, when Philip was fifteen, and the marriage took place in November the following year in Salamanca. The prince was entertained with a mock battle when he arrived at the gates of the city. After the wedding ceremony there were bullfights, tournaments, banquets, and masques.[23] Philip returned with his bride to Valladolid, stopping briefly at Medina del Campo, where they were greeted with a triumphal entry and a tournament featuring sham battles between Christians, Gypsies, and Moors.[24]

An especially grand series of tournaments was planned in Valladolid after the young couple arrived in late November 1543. The spectacles continued for months, ending the following summer of 1544. Lists of the prince's expenses that year suggest the hectic preparations involved. The accounts bristle with orders for swords, plumes, jewels, sculptures, tapestries and painted cloth, silver (for decorating armor), gold, lances, sword hilts, and blades. Philip and his companions planned a different livery for each adventure, and hundreds of yards of luxury cloth also had to be purchased. For the first round of combats, green velvet and satin from Cuenca and Granada were required to make skirts and hose for the prince and the Duke of Alba. Suits of green satin from Valencia and Segovia were tailored for a minstrel and the black jester Perico de Santervas, accompanied by six footmen in the same livery. A war-saddle for Philip's horse Haro was needed, and more green cloth for the hangings for some trumpets; even the scabbards for the tournament swords were to be green. A length of orange-colored satin was ordered from Toledo for Don Alvaro de Córdoba, who was to wear costumes in Hungarian and Turkish style. Philip also paid for the liveries of the princess and her party, which were black and yellow lined with white fustian and cloth of silver, with trimmings of crimson murrey and Florentine gold. In March, more cloth was purchased for an all-white livery for the prince, then red velvet and crimson satin in May, along with a pair of armored saddles and seven trappings of twisted cloth, for the horses of the knights who accompanied His Highness.[25]

The colors chosen for the tournaments are interesting and worth a closer look. In the chivalric culture of the later Middle Ages, colors had acquired symbolic meanings beyond their ordinary heraldic use. These meanings were still current in the sixteenth century, especially in

[21]Parker, *Philip II*, 17–19.
[22]Grierson, *Two Worlds*, 19.
[23]Grierson, *Two Worlds*, 21.
[24]Marsden, "Fêtes espagnoles," 397, 399.
[25]AGS, *Casa y Sitios Reales*, legajo 36, fol. 1, esp. 3r–10v.

Flanders and areas where Flemish influence was strong, including Spain. Certain colors, for example, were associated with sexual union and fertility and thus would have been appropriate choices for ceremonies honoring a marriage. Green symbolized passion and was the premier color for lovers. Reds and vermilions were other colors denoting passion, as they still do today. Virginal white was also associated with love, in token of the purity of its higher forms. Black, usually considered a mourning color, also signified the sorrow suffered by true lovers.[26] The choice of these colors should not surprise us in Habsburg Spain: Charles V had been born in Flanders and, although Prince Philip was born in Spain, he certainly understood his dual Iberian and Burgundian heritage.

The first of the wedding tournaments at Valladolid took place in early March of 1544, having been delayed for two months by the poor health of the prince. The combats took place in the racing grounds outside the city. The tournament was arranged by Don Luis Enríquez, admiral of Castile, who stipulated the rules for the competition: the combats were to be on horseback, beginning with a running of lances in regular armor for war, followed by separate combats with axe and sword. Classical mythology and medieval chivalry were freely combined in setting the stage for the tournament. Actors impersonating Jupiter and the court of Olympus stood guard at the gates, the goddesses forbidding the entry of the knights until each had declared the beauty of his lady. The goddesses also reminded the competitors to present themselves at least one hour before the combats, so that their names could be recorded for posterity. Some of the highest nobles of the realm took part, each accompanied by a triumphal car decked out with allegorical figures related to love and marriage.

The procession into the arena began with the admiral's invention, a giant apparatus in the shape of a seven-headed serpent, jetting smoke and fire from all its mouths. The admiral's pageant was trailed by a band of fearsome savages, all wearing helmets and collars of ivy. The field marshalls of the tourney were accompanied by an immense three-tiered float inhabited by fantastic creatures: nymphs in white taffeta seated on cushions of silver brocade, with satyrs seated on the corners blowing rustic horns (the real music was supplied by professional musicians hidden inside the car). The nymphs bore lances painted red and white, from which dangled the helmets and shields of the competitors with their coats of arms. At the back of the car rode a dwarf, clad in

---

[26]Huizinga, *Waning of the Middle Ages*, 270–72, esp. nn1–2: "You will have to dress in green, It is the livery of lovers…. Some dress themselves for her in green, Another in Blue, another in white, Another dresses himself in vermilion like blood, And he who desires her most Because of his great sorrow, dresses in black." Medieval color symbolism is complex and changed depending on its context. The erotic connotations of green have pre-Christian roots and are found in the *livre vert* of May Day celebrations in northern Europe.

red and white velvet and armed with a little whip. The car was pulled by four white horses decked out to resemble unicorns, ridden by pages dressed in red and white silk. Around the car walked eighteen men-at-arms, all wearing antique-style armor. The cars of the other combatants followed this pageant, which the chronicler assures us were equally splendid, each more outlandish than the last. The car of Don Alonso Pimentel and his companions carried figures dressed as Venus and Cupid with nymphs playing fiddles. The car of Fadrique and Luis Enríquez was enlivened by the antics of two madmen dressed in green; another pageant featured a ship under sail, complete with a revolving globe and the goddess Fortune accompanied by sirens and swans. The prince's own pageant was led by a real camel bearing a mock castle set on a two-tiered rock, with the jester Perico on the first level and a terrified-looking bugle player swaying back and forth on the upper level. Other unusual pageants followed this, including a Samson covered entirely in hair and an African, naked except for a black loincloth.

At last the prince himself arrived. As Philip passed before the palace, he and his companions put their horses through a practiced set of jumps and turns to impress his bride, who was watching from a window. Philip and his knights jousted first, the prince breaking a lance against his adversary. After this he fought with an axe until it shattered, then on to the combat with swords. Meanwhile, a second round of pageants was presented to the judges: an exploding shield was lowered into the arena and fantastic dragons appeared, along with figures representing Fame and Time, Venus and Mars caught in the act by Vulcan, cyclopes, real Peruvian llamas, and a pair of enchantresses (good and bad). An adventurer called the Knight of the Serpent challenged anyone to defy him and a ship filled with fireworks was wheeled into the lists. Another pageant showed a starry sky and a virtual eclipse of the sun and moon. Eventually the tournament drew to a close and the competitors returned to their lodgings to disarm. A fiesta was held afterwards and the various prizes were given to the winners of the combats. A gold medal was presented to the admiral of Castile for the most inventive pageant seen that day.[27]

Like the tournaments held earlier for Charles as the new king of Spain, the tournament of the race ground at Valladolid was filled with visual allusions to love and matrimony. Classical, biblical, and medieval sources were mined to produce allegorical tableaux suitable for the occasion. The seven-headed serpent, associated with the Whore of Babylon

---

[27]Philip's first tournament at Valladolid is described at length by an anonymous chronicler whose account is reproduced in Sociedad de Bibliófilos Españoles, *Relaciones de los Reinados de Carlos V y Felipe II*, 1:71-94. The iconography of the pageants is analyzed in detail by Marsden, "Fêtes espagnoles," 393-94.

in Renaissance art, was an apropos symbol of earthly desire. White unicorns were likewise associated with love, but since they could be tamed
by a virgin, they were also symbols of the chastity necessary to maintain
the matrimonial state. Satyrs and their earthy music were long-standing
symbols of sexual desire, necessary in order to consummate a marriage.
Venus and Cupid, of course, were the prime movers of love, and Samson lost his hair (along with his virility) as a result of falling in love.
Cars like the ones described at Philip's tournaments are occasionally
illustrated in Renaissance art. Pageant cars carrying allegorical figures are
shown on the backs of the famous marriage portraits of Battista Sforza
and Guidobaldo da Montefeltro of Urbino, and in prints depicting the
pageants of Queen Elizabeth of England.

More tournaments were held in the summer of 1544. The precise
location of these tournaments is unknown, though the documents suggest a number of different sites in and around Valladolid. Philip's secretary Gonzalo Pérez noted that the prince organized a pair of
tournaments in March and May that year. The May tourney, he adds,
took place in the countryside and was a great success, with nearly a
hundred competitors taking part.[28] Another tournament, held in early
June, took place in the gardens of a certain Galván. In addition to the
jousting, Philip and ten knights took part in a combat on foot in the
garden of Luis Tristán on St. Peter's Day, 27 June.[29] The climax of the
wedding festivals in 1544 was a splendid tournament, supposed to take
place on an island in the Rio Pisuerga at the end of June. The expedition ended in disaster, however. A boat carrying the competitors, who
were all in glittering armor, sank under the extra weight, nearly drown-
ing the prince and several of his companions. Eventually the boat was
refloated and the adventurers set out again, but after a second dunking
the tournament was called off.[30] The list of Philip's expenses that summer includes the following interesting entries:

> Mas treinta y çinco varas de tafetan naranjado y blanco doble
> para vn toldo al barco de corsino para el dicho dia del tor-
> neo que lleua çinco personas....[31]

> [Item, thirty-five yards of double taffeta, of orange and white,
> for an awning for the boat for the said day of the tourna-
> ment, which carries five persons....]

And:

---

[28]Kamen, *Philip of Spain*, 20.

[29]AGS, *Casa y Sitios Reales*, legajo 36, fols. 1/19r, 15r.

[30]Parker, *Philip II*, 15. The alleged site of the mishap is still pointed out to visitors, a narrow
strip of land in the river as it passes on the southwest side of Valladolid near Calle Puente Colgante.

[31]AGS, *Casa y Sitios Reales*, legajo 36, fol. 1/15r.

> Mas treinta y çinco varas de Tafetan naranjado que dio en Valladolid postrero de junio del dicho año...de Treinta y vna uanderas que han de Yr en el varco de corsino, y en otro pequeño en que uan su alteza y todos los otros torneadores....[32]

> [Item, thirty-five yards of orange-colored taffeta, purchased in Valladolid at the end of June of said year...(for) thirty-one banners that have to go on the boat, and on another little one in which His Highness and all the other tourneyers are going....]

Two years later, another island combat was staged on a small lake near Guadalajara. This time Philip was injured in both legs and had to walk with a cane for several weeks.[33] Expenses for other tournaments held by the prince were recorded in 1545 and 1547–48, including payments for coverings painted with coats of arms and a wooden building worth some 150 escudos.[34]

The motif of the island combat is common in medieval epic and romance, occurring in the Arthurian legend of Sir Tristram of Lyonesse and even in the Viking sagas. Island combats are also found in chivalric literature popular in the Renaissance, including the cycle of Amadís of Gaul, which Philip had loved from childhood. In book 2 of *Amadís*, the hero sails in a fairy galley to the Firm Island, an abode of giants laid under a strange enchantment by its first ruler, Prince Apolidón of Greece. An arch was erected at the entry to the island, surmounted by a figure of brass bearing a magic trumpet. Knights unworthy of their ladies were laid low by a blast from the horn if they tried to pass beneath the arch. The knight who was steadfast in love, however, was allowed to pass unharmed and his name was inscribed in magic letters on a tablet of jasper, raised on crystal pillars. Guided by the father of his beloved Oriana, Amadís gains entrance to the island. There he sees the shields of those knights who had successfully passed the arch but failed the final test, the Adventure of the Forbidden Chamber, which was guarded by demons and jinni. Eventually the hero overcomes the guardians and enters the ivory chamber, where he gazes upon the ancient statues of Apolidón and his bride.[35] The similarities between Amadís' journey by boat to the Firm Island and Philip's island tourneys of 1544 and 1546 (or what little is known about them) are intriguing.

[32]AGS, *Casa y Sitios Reales*, legajo 36, fol. 15v.
[33]Parker, *Philip II*, 15.
[34]AGS, *Casa y Sitios Reales*, legajo 36, fol. 1, 285r.
[35]Anonymous, *Amadís de Gaula, Tomo II*, ed. Place, esp. 357–59. Later on in the story, the same arch is referred to as the Arch of the True Lovers. The Firm Island appears again in the story of Esplandián, the sequel to the Amadís stories.

The prince was certainly familiar with the stories and it is tempting to suggest a connection.[36]

Armor made for the young prince around the time of the wedding tournaments at Valladolid is preserved today in the Royal Armory in Madrid. In 1544, the first pieces of a grand garniture ordered by the emperor for Philip were delivered to Spain by Desiderius Colman, son of Colman Helmschmied of Augsburg, the emperor's chief armorer.[37] This garniture was the first complete suit of armor owned by the prince.[38] A substantial part of this armor survives today, including portions of a light armor for the joust (fig. 2.5). The proportions of the armor are short and slender, reflecting Philip's small build as a teenager. The right pauldron and vambrace of the jousting armor are decorated like the puffed and slashed costume of the period, but they do not match the rest of the armor, suggesting that these pieces may have been won in a tournament.[39] The decoration on this armor is extremely fine, consisting of interlacing bands enclosing tiny blossoms or pine cones, the emblem of the armorers of Augsburg. These delicate patterns gave the armor its name, the *lacerías* or "strapwork" garniture. The actual etching is in the German style, though Philip insisted that the drawings for the designs be provided by his own Spanish artist, Diego del Arroyo.[40] The armor was apparently completed over a period

[36]Parker also notes that some of Philip's early tournaments were modeled on the Amadís stories; Parker, *Philip II*, 15.

[37]Unlike most armorers from this period, the Helmschmied family is relatively well known to scholars today. In 1439, a certain Jörg Helmschmied (George the Helmet-maker) was paying taxes in Augsburg, and in 1496 was paid a hundred florins for a helmet and chamfron. The principal armoring dynasty of the north was founded by Lorenz Helmschmied (active 1467–1515), who made fine armors for Frederick III and Maximilian I. His son Colman Helmschmied (1471–1532), regarded as the greatest of the Augsburg armorers, was court armorer to Charles V. The use of the Star of David on their punch mark and the prevalence of the name Colman (Koloman) suggest that the family may have been Jewish, perhaps of Hungarian or eastern European origin. Several portraits and medals depicting Colman Helmschmied have survived. Desiderius Colman (1513–79) was the son of Colman Helmschmied. Desiderius was apprenticed to an armorer named Lutzenberger, who married Desiderius's stepmother in 1545. In 1532, Desiderius took over his father's workshop in the Mauerburg district in Augsburg, which the Helmschmieds had shared with the Burgkmair family. Desiderius formed a partnership with the Augsburg goldsmith Jörg Sigman, who married into the family. By 1550, Desiderius Colman was a member of the city council, and in 1556 he was appointed court armorer to Charles V. Desiderius's title was renewed by Maximilian II. Desiderius used the same mark as his father (a jousting helm, surmounted by a Star of David), which has led to some confusion between their works. Works ascribed to Desiderius Colman are found in Madrid/Royal Armory, A 157–58, A 189–216, A 217–30, A 239–40, and A 242. See AGS, *Secretaría de Estado*, libro 71, fols. 44v, 74r–74v, 93r, 108v, 110v; and Crooke y Navarrot, *Catálogo historico-descriptivo de la Real Armería*, 57, 74, 77–78nn1, 2, 80.

[38]Crooke y Navarrot, *Catálogo historico-descriptivo de la Real Armería*, 68.

[39]Crooke y Navarrot, *Catálogo historico-descriptivo de la Real Armería*, 71.

[40]Diego del Arroyo is mentioned in the prince's account books in February 1544, when he was paid three ducats for some drawings to be sent to Germany for an armor for the prince; AGS *Casa y Sitios Reales*, legajo 36, fol. 1/113r. Diego del Arroyo also is thought to have executed the designs on a set of wood and leather pageant saddles in the Royal Armory (Madrid, Real Armería F 60–61). The designs on these saddles feature hunting scenes in red and gold, imitating low reliefs in bronze. See Crooke y Navarrot, *Catálogo historico-descriptivo de la Real Armería*, 178; and Ruíz

Figure 2.5 Desiderius Colman, portions of an armor for the joust of Prince Philip of Spain ("strapwork" garniture), 1544. Madrid, Real Armería, A190. Used by permission.

of several years, with additional pieces added later in 1546 and 1549. The jousting harness was delivered to Philip in person by master Desiderius, who was summoned to Valladolid by the emperor in 1545.[41] Philip also owned a fancy-dress armor in antique style, said to have been worn in the tournaments at Valladolid in 1544, though this interesting armor has not survived.[42]

Prince Philip was never allowed to settle down and enjoy a normal married life. In 1545, María Manuela of Portugal died four days after giving birth to Philip's firstborn son, Don Carlos. Philip, it was rumored, had become distant from his wife and may have been seeing the first of several Spanish mistresses before her death.[43] The death of the Princess of Portugal also left Philip the most politically eligible bachelor in Europe again, and the emperor immediately began exploring new marriage possibilities for his son.[44]

In 1548 Philip was summoned by Charles V to Brussels.

Alarcón, "Sillas de montar de Diego de Arroyo, Real Armería."

[41]Desiderius was summoned to Valladolid for six weeks by the emperor in a letter from Worms dated 29 July 1545. Exchange pieces were made later for the garniture over a period of several years. Portions of an armor for war from the same garniture are preserved in Vienna, the couters stamped with the date 1546. The dates of the pieces in Madrid and Vienna suggest that the earlier parts of this armor were made for the tournaments in Valladolid and Guadalajara in 1544 and 1546. A tonlet armor and embossed pageant pieces were added in 1549. The war harness was eventually given by King Philip II to his cousin, Archduke Ferdinand II of the Tyrol, along with pieces of another armor formerly belonging to the emperor. Another pair of gauntlets from Philip's garniture were identified by the Conde de Valencia in the former Riggs collection in Paris, after they were acquired at an auction of the estate of Lord Londesborough held in London in 1888; Crooke y Navarrot, *Catálogo historico-descriptivo de la Real Armería*, 68–74, 69.

[42]Crooke y Navarrot, *Catálogo historico-descriptivo de la Real Armería*, 65.

[43]Grierson, *Two Worlds*, 22; and Kamen, *Philip of Spain*, 19–20.

[44]Loades, *Mary Tudor*, 132.

The emperor planned a grand tour of the European dominions of the Habsburgs for Philip, which would culminate in their attendance together at the imperial diet in Augsburg in 1550, where the imperial succession would be finally decided. Charles, of course, wished for Philip to succeed him, but the emperor's brother Ferdinand was pressing for the succession of his own son, the archduke Maximilian. In the festivals planned for his travels, Philip would be cast in the mold of the ideal Renaissance prince described by Castiglione and Erasmus. The prince would also be called upon to demonstrate all the old medieval prerequisites for kingship: skill in the martial arts, courtesy and generosity to his equals, and fairness and justice. The religious climate of the Reformation and subsequent Catholic Reformation also had an effect on the image of the ideal Christian prince. In addition to his martial prowess, Philip would have to demonstrate his potential as a chaste and virtuous husband, viewed as part of his fitness to rule a Christian people. Philip left Spain the same year, headed first for the imperial dominions in Italy. The prince was accompanied by the young gentlemen of his court, the court artist Diego del Arroyo, his guitar teacher, and the requisite number of officials and priests.[45] To keep in shape for the upcoming tournaments, the prince brought along his Spanish fencing teacher, Master Gaspar.[46] A record of the prince's travels was kept by Juan Cristóbal Calvete de Estrella, master of the prince's pages and official chronicler of the journey.[47]

The prince arrived in Milan in December 1548. Philip's visit coincided with the nuptials of Hippolita Gonzaga and Fabrizio Colonna, which united two of the most important noble houses of Italy (the Gonzagas were also important allies of the Habsburgs and were related to the imperial house). Tournaments on horseback and foot and a cane game were held in honor of the Princess of Malfetto, who was also staying in Milan at the time. The jousting was so furious on one occasion that two horses were killed from the shock of the collision, falling dead in the middle of the tiltyard. The knights involved left the field alive, though "somewhat abused from the encounter." A comedy was presented to the prince after the tournament.[48] On New Year's Day, the prince was invited to dinner by Ferrante Gonzaga, who maintained a palace in Milan. The decorations for the feast had military overtones: the table service was shaped like miniature cities, with statuettes of fearsome halberdiers holding the napkins. After the first dance, desserts were brought

---

[45]For Philip's entourage, see Kamen, *Philip of Spain*, 36.

[46]AGS, *Secretaría de Estado*, libro 71, fol. 36r. A *cédula* mentioning the back pay owed to Philip's fencing teacher is dated Antwerp, 17 September 1549. Master Gaspar, like several others in Philip's party, had to wait nearly a year before receiving any payment for their services.

[47]AGS, *Secretaría de Estado*, libro 71, fol. 36r.

[48]Calvete de Estrella, *El felicíssimo viaje del muy alto y muy poderoso Príncipe Don Phelippe*, 1:71–73.

to Philip by a line of handsome pages. Calvete remarks there were more
than a hundred pages, whose concerted movements reminded him of the
undulating coils of a vast serpent. The banquet, dances, and masques
lasted all evening, and the guests did not retire until the third hour
after midnight. On St. Silvester's Day, the prince participated in a tournament on foot at the barriers. The princess and her ladies entered the
courtyard in gilt triumphal cars, clad in their finest clothes and jewels.
Calvete notes all the ladies were watching Philip, who fought with particular vigor and skill against the Duke of Sessa. A dance closed the celebrations, lasting until well after midnight.[49]

The Italian poet Albicante tells a somewhat different account of
the feast and tournament at Milan. The poet's version, told in *ottava-
rima*, is rich in classical allusions and poetic hyperbole. According to
Albicante, the viands were served by no less than three hundred
Milanese youths of perfect birth. After the feast, squads of armored
knights and soldiers tramped into the hall. Suddenly a troop of golden
centaurs appeared, galloping into the chamber and taking up their posi-
tions at the entryways, darting fierce glances at the guests. At this a
strange masquerade commenced, which seemed to Albicante more like a
battle than a dance. The masques and galliards lasted until daybreak,
when the contestants prepared for the tournament. Philip and the Duke
of Sessa were armed by the Roman gods of war:

> Arma del Re Marte, la sua persona,
> Di propria mano, e la spada li cinge,
> S'arma il Duca di Sessa da Bellona,
> Com'un Diomede, che valor non finge,
> Et cosi attenti con sua voglia bona,
> Gli elmetti in capo, e l'arme, ogn'un si stringe,
> E'n aspettando, quivi hor bassi, hor alti,
> Braman d'incominciare, I fieri assalti.[50]

> [Armed by King Mars, the god himself,
> With his own hand, and the god girds his sword,
> While the Duke of Sessa is armed by Bellona,
> Like a Diomedes, whose valor's unfeigned,
> And so attended with the goodwill of the gods,
> Helms on their heads and arms donned, each draws close,
> And in waiting, there now the low, now the high,
> Eager to begin the fiercest of fights.]

Italian festivals differed from their Spanish and northern counterparts mostly in their abundant use of imagery derived from Greek and

[49]Calvete de Estrella, *Felicíssimo viaje*, 1:77–86.
[50]Albicante, *Al gran Maximiliano d'Austria granduca*. The text is not paginated.

Roman mythology. The appearance of the golden centaurs in the poet's version of the wedding feast is doubtless a reference to the story of the Lapiths and centaurs. In the Greek legend, the monstrous centaurs were invited by the Lapiths to the wedding feast of Hippodameia. The centaurs became drunk and tried to abduct the bride. A horrific battle ensued in which the Greek warriors were nearly overcome, but the Lapiths were assisted by the heroes Hercules and Theseus, who turned the tide against the centaurs. As representations of the animal nature of man, the lustful centaurs symbolized the forces of barbarism against civilization and its hallowed customs. Albicante flattered Philip by comparing the prince to the god of war, but the appearance of the centaurs reminded everyone of the consequences of violating a host's hospitality. Albicante also mined the chivalric legends of Charlemagne for suitable heroic metaphors. He compares the ladies at the tournament to Marphisa and Bradamante, warrior-maidens from the romances of Boiardo and Ariosto. The male competitors are described as so many Gradassos and Rogeros, shouting their war cries and vying for the attentions of their beloved.[51]

A list of expenses for Philip's entire voyage, loosely bound in vellum, is preserved among the state papers in the Spanish royal archives at Simancas. This document records payments for a variety of luxury items, including monies paid out for armor and other tournament equipment. Especially interesting is a note of payment for a pageant car and a panoply of helmet and shield, dated Milan, 3 January 1549:

> Domingo de Vrbea mi Criado yo Vos mando que de qualesquier dineros de Vuestro Cargo pagueys a don antonio de Toledo nuestro Cauallerizo mayor mill y doçientos setenta escudos son para Vn Carro y otras obras que hauemos mandado hazer y doçientos escudos para pagar a Vn Armero Vna Rodela y Vn morrion que del mandamos comprar....[52]

> [Domingo de Orbea my servant, I command you to pay, from those monies that are in your charge, 1,270 escudos to our grand marshall Don Antonio de Toledo, for a car and other things that we have ordered made, and two hundred escudos to pay an armorer for a shield and helmet that we are purchasing from him....]

Cars like the one mentioned in Philip's account book certainly played a role in the festivities at Milan, though the helmet and shield mentioned in the documents are difficult to track down with any certainty. Later on Philip's journey, the same list of expenses mentions

---

[51]Albicante, *Al gran Maximiliano d'Austria granduca.*
[52]AGS, *Secretaría de Estado,* libro 71, fol. 11r.

payments to Francesco Negroli of Milan, for embossed and inlaid armor and a large quantity of gold.[53]

The prince left Milan on 7 January 1549.[54] Before his departure for the north, Philip stopped briefly in Mantua, where he was entertained by Federigo Gonzaga in the old ducal castle. The prince also visited the duke's fantastic pleasure house on the outskirts of the city, the Palazzo Tè, which Calvete compared to the Cretan Labyrinth.[55] Philip hurried on to Trent, where his attendance was required at the religious councils being held there. From Trent, Philip crossed the Alps and headed for the reunion with his father in Brussels.

After meeting with Charles, Philip spent the remainder of the year on a tour of the Low Countries, where his succession was confirmed by the estates of all the principal cities of the realms. After the obligatory round of visits through the Netherlands and Flanders, the prince returned to Brussels in October, exhausted from his travels.[56] The emperor, meanwhile, spent the winter preparing for the upcoming meetings at Augsburg. Free for a while from the pressure of political appearances, Philip set about organizing festivals and tournaments. These spectacles were strictly for the entertainment of the ladies and their theme was to be the all-encompassing power of love.

Early in the spring, a knight arrived at the imperial court, complaining grievously of the pains and abuse he had suffered at the hands of the god of love. The Sorrowful Knight posted a cartellino at the gates of the palace, inviting all comers to a passage of arms for the service of the ladies and the exercise of chivalry, so he could avenge himself on Cupid for the injuries he had received. The rules of the tourney were thus:

> On Shrove Tuesday in the palace park, the god of love will be placed in the midst of a stairway of nineteen steps, with a gibbet at the top of the stairs. The Sorrowful Knight will wait at the end of the barrier, armed at all points for the joust with a barred shield. Those knights who would serve their ladies, for whom Love receives this insult, will be obliged to defend him in battle, armed likewise at all points.
>
> The Sorrowful Knight will defend from one in the afternoon until nightfall. The adventurers will each run four courses against him with the lance. If the adventurer is judged

---

[53]AGS, *Secretaría de Estado*, libro 71, esp. fol.75v. Francesco Negroli (active 1526–50) was a member of the famous Negroli family of armorers who were based in Milan and specialized in the embossing of armor in the antique style. Francesco, however, is mentioned in our documents only as a *dorador* or gilder of armor.

[54]Calvete de Estrella, *Felicíssimo viaje*, 1:86–88.

[55]Calvete de Estrella, *Felicíssimo viaje*, 109. The emperor was splendidly entertained here on his own visits to the city in 1530 and 1532.

[56]Kamen, *Philip of Spain*, 43.

the winner, Love will be lowered one step away from the gibbet, and the adventurer will receive a plume, which he will present to his lady in honor of the god. If the adventurer is vanquished, Love will be raised one step closer to the gibbet, and the adventurer must surrender a plume in token of his foolishness at having defended Cupid. If at the end of the day Love is closer to the gibbet than he is distant from it, let him be hanged for the insults he has done to his followers.

The victors in the joust will also win prizes, which they will present to their ladies.

He who drops his lance, or otherwise gives a poor account of himself, loses the prize, and cannot run again; nor will any adventurer, having run his courses against the challenger and been judged, run against the challenger a second time.[57]

On the day of the joust, the emperor and the queens took their seats in the windows and galleries, which were on the lower story of the palace looking out across the park. When the guests had assembled, a triumphal car in antique style, covered all in black velvet, was wheeled slowly into the park. The covering was embroidered with emblems showing Fortune hanging by her feet from a gibbet, which bore the inscription Por Mvdable (Changeability). In the middle of the car was a throne as tall as a man and shrouded all in black. Seated on the throne was Cupid, the god of love, impersonated by a real naked boy fitted with a pair of wings, blindfolded and carrying his darts and bow. In the car rode about twelve personages in various costumes, some like kings, others like philosophers, still others like religious men—all followers of love.[58] The car was pulled by four white horses, their manes and tails tied with twists of black silk. The driver was dressed in a long gown of black satin and next to him sat an executioner, with figures of Fortune hanging by their feet from a little gibbet on three columns. Going before the car were twelve warhorses in rich caparisons, ridden by twelve pages. Behind came eight trumpeters wearing gowns of black satin embroidered with the emblems of Fortune, one in front and another behind. The banners hanging from their trumpets bore the same device and their broad hats and plumes were black. After the trumpeters came fourteen seconds in black velvet, all gentlemen of rank.

Then the Sorrowful Knight (who was Don Alonso Pimentel) appeared in full armor riding on a mighty Spanish warhorse. Over his armor, he wore a skirt of black velvet strewn with roses of black thread

---

[57]Calvete de Estrella, Felicíssimo viaje, 2:389–90. I have expanded on the original text here for clarity.

[58]Unfortunately Calvete does not identify these figures for us.

with the same emblems of Fortune embroidered on it. Over his panache was a crest like a little gibbet on three columns with Fortune hanging from it upside down. Thus he entered in great pomp, taking two turns about the field, and presented himself to the judges. The judges' box was covered with rich tapestries and in front of the box in the middle of the barrier was a gibbet like the one Don Alonso bore as his device, though full-sized. In an architrave above the noose was an inscription in Spanish:

> Aquí puesto aun no padece,
> Con mucho lo que merece.[59]

> [Here placed, yet he does not suffer,
> Much though he deserves it.]

Alongside the gibbet was a flight of nineteen steps, wide and spacious. The god of love was situated on the tenth step with a knave standing next to him who played the part of executioner, raising or lowering the boy as ordered.

When the Sorrowful Knight had taken his place at the end of the barrier, the adventurers began to arrive, wearing diverse colors and fantastic trappings. The first to come was the prince of Spain, and with him the prince of Piedmont, Count of Egmont, and Don Diego de Acuña. Over their armor they wore skirts of white satin with flowers of murrey velvet scattered over them, and their horses were covered in the same material with plumes in the same colors. Twelve trumpeters and their seconds preceded them, dressed in white and murrey satin. Philip ran his courses against Don Alonso so valiantly that the god of love was lowered a step. Then the prince's companions jousted, each of them lowering the boy further from danger. It was no small consolation to Cupid to see the favor the adventurers did him, especially considering the prowess of the one who sought to condemn him.

The jousting continued until sixteen knights had run their courses, some winning, others losing. As the day drew to a close, the Sorrowful Knight began to have trouble urging on his exhausted steed, and seeing how many knights still waited to joust, he asked the Count of Egmont to assist him. Together they continued the battle against the adventurers, Love bobbing continually up and down the while. In the end, in spite of the number and valor of the comers, who were some of the best knights at court, the Sorrowful Knight was judged the winner, and Love was hanged from the gibbet. Later the little statue of Fortune was burned. It was fashioned with a fire-apparatus inside and when put to the torch, it exploded, hurling sparks all around.

---

[59]Calvete de Estrella, *Felicíssimo viaje*, 2:392.

That night the prince held a regal banquet for the queens and their ladies in the grand salon of the palace. Afterwards the judges, having first consulted with the ladies, announced the prizewinners. The prize for best man-at-arms went to the Count of Egmont. Then a herald strode into the court and read aloud a letter in the name of Ruy Gómez de Silva, who was one of the prince's knights:

Ruy Gómez de Silva announces that he will defend himself, this coming Sunday at the barrier in the park, from one in the afternoon forward, against all those knights who for the service of the ladies wish to joust, armed at all points and with barred shield. Each of the adventurers will run four courses, the winner of the first three receiving the prize, which will be some jewels, worth from ten to a hundred escudos. The adventurer will also place in the hands of the judges the amount he wishes to wager on his courses. The remaining course will be for the pleasure of the ladies. These are the conditions of the tournament:

The adventurer who drops his lance, or strikes the barrier or his opponent's horse, will win no prize, and he who gives a poor account of himself in any other way forfeits that course.

He who breaks the most lances in the first three courses will be judged the best man-at-arms, and the night following of the tournament will be given a diamond ring of great value.

To him who breaks the best lance of the ladies, a medal of gold.

To him who breaks the best and most lances in the mêlée, a golden plume.

And to him who makes the most gallant entry will go a ruby finger-ring.[60]

After the letter was read, a masque arranged by Ruy Gómez was performed before the company. Eight maskers entered the chamber, walking slowly and dressed in monks' habits. They wore tunics and scapulars of white satin with little caps of tawny velvet lined in white satin, and held burning tapers of white wax in their hands. Behind them came six singers with scapulars and caps of the same material, holding burning tapers like the friars. At the end of the procession came two sacristans wearing surplices of white taffeta, carrying between them a funeral bier covered in rich brocade. In the bier lay the dead god of love, dressed in red cloth of gold with silver tassels, his head

---

[60]Calvete de Estrella, *Felicíssimo viaje*, 2:393–94.

lying on pillows of brocade. The monks entered singing in low voices as if they were praying, chanting some lines from a poem by Boscán:

> El que sin tí vivir ya no quería,
> Y ha mucho tiempo que morir desea,
> Por ver si tanto mal se acabaría.[61]

> [He who lives without you won't want to,
> And is a long time in dying,
> Waiting to get it over with.]

In the middle of the room they stopped, and set down their burden before the queens. Laying the corpse on a cloth of rich brocade they began to sing, in place of a response, these stanzas by Garcí Sánchez de Badajoz:

> Perdoname, Amor, Amor,
> Que mis días no son nada,
> Pues al fin de la jornada
> Me tratas con disfavor.
> Dime qué cosa es el hombre,
> Porque tanto le engrandeces,
> O porque le favoreces
> Con las sombras de tu nombre.[62]

> [Pardon me, Love,
> Make my time worthwhile,
> Since at the end of the journey
> You treat me with disdain.
> Tell me, what is a man
> That you shower him with such honors?
> Or why you favor him
> With the shadows of your name?]

As they sang, Philip and five companions entered dressed as ancient gods, masked and wearing short tunics in the antique style. Their tunics were of red cloth of gold, with brown and white scales, and half-length sleeves of red-gold. From the elbow downwards, the sleeves resolved into fantastic serpents' mouths, also of cloth of gold. They wore hats in the same style, with scales and plumes of red and white, and long mantles of cloth of silver. Six young Spanish knights dressed like nymphs entered with the gods, wearing masks and skirts of red cloth of gold; the fronts and backs of their skirts were painted with the same pattern of scales, with fringes of cloth of silver. On their heads, they wore high head-

[61]Calvete de Estrella, *Felicíssimo viaje*, 2:394.
[62]Calvete de Estrella, *Felicíssimo viaje*, 2:394–95.

dresses filled with curling locks of hair and they carried bows and arrows in their hands. They entered the salon together, dancing a slow allemande while the musicians played. Drawing near where the body of Cupid lay, the leader of the gods and one of the nymphs passed their hands over him and taking him up in their arms they revived him, to the great joy of all. Then Cupid loosed an arrow at Madame de la Thuloie (in whose honor the pageant had been arranged) and taking her by the hand he danced gracefully with her. The rest of the company joined in, gods, nymphs, and friars, each taking a lady by the hand. The better part of the evening was taken up by these festivities and eventually the company retired to bed, everyone praising the inventiveness of Ruy Gómez' masquerade.[63]

The imagery chosen for the Tournament of Love at Brussels is interesting from a number of standpoints. Many of the young bachelor-knights of Philip's court were preparing to take their leave of lovers they had met in the Low Countries[64] and thus the symbolism of Love hanged on a gibbet must have seemed particularly apropos. The color black was not only a mourning color but also the color of true lovers, who suffered the most in their steadfastness. The masque following the tournament, in which Love is revived by the gods, suggests that the lovers ought not to despair, for they may be united again. Finally, the figure of the Sorrowful Knight, Don Alonso Pimentel, also deserves attention. Here and elsewhere in the narrative, Calvete sets up Don Alonso as a comic foil to Prince Philip. In the Tournament of Love at Brussels, Don Alonso is judged the winner of the contest, though he insults Love while Philip and his knights defend him. The image of Don Alonso urging on his tired steed while Love rises and falls renders the knight ridiculous, and doubtless appealed to a Renaissance sense of humor. Later on in the story, in the first round of the tournaments held at Binche in 1549 (discussed in chapter 4), Don Alonso embarrasses himself before the emperor when he enters the combats with a helmet that is too small for him and he is immediately overthrown by the Marquis of Berghes. Philip, however, is able to defeat the marquis.[65] Examples of comic counterparts to the hero are found in both classical and medieval literature, including such characters as the abusive Thersites in the *Iliad* and the inept Sir Dynadan in Malory's *Morte d'Arthur*.[66] In the Renaissance cycle of *Orlando Innamorato* and *Orlando Furioso*, the good-humored paladin Astolpho of England, though able to charm the ladies, is unlucky at jousting until he accidentally obtains the magic

[63]Calvete de Estrella, *Felicíssimo viaje*, 2:390–95.
[64]Kamen, *Philip of Spain*, 44.
[65]Calvete de Estrella, *Felicíssimo viaje*, 2:10–20.
[66]Malory, *Works*, ed. Vinaver, esp. 311.

lance of Argalia.[67] By using similar literary devices, Calvete shows Prince Philip to his advantage against the other knights in the Tournament of Love, emphasizing the prince's persona as hero of the episode.

Ruy Gómez's joust took place on the first Sunday of Easter, again in the park in front of the palace. Adjoining the judges' box was a set of sideboards, laden with all manner of gold and silver plate: basins, cups, jars, chains, medals, jewels, and rich golden rings set with precious stones. The jousting ended with a *mêlée*, with lances flying in fragments all around. Afterwards, the winners delivered the prizes they had won to their ladies. That night, after the queens and the prince had dined together, the judges consulted with the ladies, who announced the winners of the various categories in the jousting that day. Don Antonio de Toledo was chosen the best man-at-arms, though the Prince of Piedmont was judged to have run the best lance for the ladies. The most gallant entry was made by Don Luis de Carvajal, and Jacques de Herbaix carried away the palm for the *mêlée*. Then twenty Spanish knights entered the chamber, wearing masks and long Turkish robes of cloth of silver, with murrey velvet galloons and fancy edging of silver and murrey braid. Over these they wore Turkish-style gowns, open at the front with long sleeves hanging as far down as their feet of silver and murrey gold cloth, lined with white satin with edgings of murrey and silver. They wore tall turbans of cloth of silver and gold, with red and white plumes. While the musicians played, the Turks danced a stately allemande, carrying burning tapers of white wax as they entered. They took a turn about the salon then, setting their tapers aside, each took a lady by the hand and continued the dance. This masquerade was arranged by Philip, and the prince and his nobles spent the rest of the night dancing with their ladies.[68]

The last of the martial festivals in Brussels was a skirmish on horseback held in the palace park on Sunday, 11 May. Forty knights skirmished against forty others, with participants from Spain, Flanders, and the Kingdom of Naples. The teams were led by Garcilaso Puertocarrero and Don Alvaro of Portugal, Count of Gelves, each of whom wore the favor of his lady in the combats. Garcilaso's standard was embroidered with a Y, the initial of his lady, the Mademoiselle de l'Isle. The Count of Gelve's standard bore the letter V, the initial of his own lady, the Countess of Waldeck. The battle continued thus for the remainder of the day, followed by feasts and dances lasting until long after midnight.[69]

Philip returned to Spain following the decision of the imperial diet at Augsburg, which did not favor his succession of Charles V as Holy

[67]Ariosto, *Orlando Furioso*, ed. Nardi, 8.17–18, passim.

[68]Calvete de Estrella, *Felicíssimo viaje*, 2:395–400. Calvete does not say if Philip was one of the "Turks."

[69]Calvete de Estrella, *Felicíssimo viaje*, 2:400–409.

Roman Emperor. With the emperor still in the north, Philip began negotiating a second marriage with a Portuguese princess on his own behalf. These plans were dropped in 1553 with the death of the young King Edward VI of England and the ascent of Mary Tudor to the throne. Mary was appropriately Catholic and the emperor also saw a last opportunity to renew the old Anglo-Habsburg alliance against France. Philip was to marry the queen of England instead. The Portuguese princess was hurriedly married off to Philip's nephew Alessandro Farnese[70] and in 1554 the English ambassadors arrived in Spain to escort Philip to his new bride.

Philip prepared to sail for England in the summer of 1554, accompanied by an enormous entourage that included six thousand soldiers and sailors. The prince's advisers, concerned that such an expedition might seem like an invading army, persuaded him to settle for a more modest escort.[71] The trip began inauspiciously. The crossing from La Coruña was stormy, and Philip and several important Spanish gentlemen became violently seasick. The first few days on the English coast were spent in wind and pouring rain. Philip was met by the Earl of Arundel at Southampton, who presented him with a membership in the Order of the Garter. As the prince stepped ashore, the guns of the port boomed a salvo in welcome.[72]

Philip and Mary were wed in Winchester Cathedral on 25 July 1554. The prince was escorted to the ceremony by the Earl of Pembroke and a company of gentlemen in black velvet, along with a squadron of English archers wearing the yellow and crimson livery of Aragon.[73] The stormy crossing all but forgotten, the Spaniards were excited by the change of scenery. England, after all, was the legendary home of Arthur and Amadís of Gaul.[74] In Winchester castle, the Spaniards were solemnly shown the Round Table of King Arthur.[75] The newlyweds then proceeded to London by royal barge. The prince and his company spent the rest of the summer at Hampton Court. Mary and her consort prepared for a round of tournaments to celebrate their marriage and introduce Philip to his new subjects.

The English and their guests soon began to grate on each other's nerves, however. The queen was somewhat older than Philip had been led to believe. The Spaniards found the English quarrelsome and complained that their celebrations consisted of nothing but eating and drink-

---

[70]Kamen, *Philip II*, 54.

[71]Kamen, *Philip II*, 56.

[72]Grierson, *Two Worlds*, 43.

[73]Grierson, *Two Worlds*, 44.

[74]Despite having been born in France, most of Amadís' adventures took place in Britain.

[75]Tree-ring analysis has shown that the Round Table at Winchester was built in the middle of the thirteenth century, probably for King Henry III. Christina M. Waugh (graduate student, University of Michigan–Ann Arbor), personal communication, 6 August 1997.

Whitehall Stairs

Figure 2.6 Anthonis van den Wyngaerde, *Whitehall*, ca. 1558. Pen and ink, Oxford, Ashmolean Museum. Used by permission.

ing. The jousting champions at Brussels, moreover, stood little chance against the London pickpockets. Concerning the English, Ruy Gómez de Silva wrote that "there are great thieves among them and they rob in broad daylight." Other incidents occurred, and the Spaniards were afraid to go out at night. Several Spanish gentlemen complained to Philip, who ordered them to remain silent about the matter. It was not in His Majesty's interests, they were told, to allow their complaints to reach the ears of the queen. "We are in an excellent land, but among the worst people in the world," wrote the courtier Muñoz. "Some say they would prefer to be in the slums of Toledo rather than in the meadows of Amadís."[76]

That fall, the tournaments began in earnest. The sites of the festivities were recorded in a series of drawings from 1554 to 1558 by Anthonis van den Wyngaerde, a Dutch artist in the employ of Prince Philip.[77] The drawings are in a matter-of-fact style, though Wyngaerde made certain the tiltyard was visible in each of his views of the English palaces. In mid-October, Philip and some Spanish knights held a cane game before the queen and her guests at Whitehall (fig. 2.6).[78] In November, Lord Strange and several Spanish knights issued a challenge to all comers to fight on foot at the barriers. The combats took place on 4

[76]Kamen, *Philip of Spain*, 58.
[77]Young, *Tournaments*, 76.
[78]Loades, *Mary Tudor*, 232.

Figure 2.7 English (?), Lord Strange fights a Spanish knight at the barriers with a sword, ca. 1554. Pen and ink drawing, London, British Library (87/14169 DSC). Used by permission.

December, Philip winning a brooch for "the fairest and most gallant entry" and first place in the combat with swords. Another set of drawings, probably by an English artist, was made to record these events (fig. 2.7). The English knights and their guests are shown on an equal footing, with no attempt to aggrandize the Spanish knights. A "grett tryumph" was held in Greenwich later that month, followed by a tourney on foot with spears and swords in which Philip and some Spanish knights participated (fig. 2.8). Another tournament was held at Whitehall in January 1555, which Philip probably attended. A joust and tourney on horseback with swords was held to celebrate the marriage of Lord Strange and Lady Cumberland, followed by another cane game. On Lady Day (25 March), "as gret justes as youe have seen" took place in the Whitehall tiltyard. The challenge had been issued by a Spanish knight and Sir George Howard, whose men entered wearing surcoats trimmed in white, with horse trappings of similar material. Philip and his company entered wearing blue and yellow with blue and yellow plumes nodding from their helmets. With them came other retainers dressed in Turkish costume.[79] On this occasion, the colors worn by Philip and the other Spanish jousters were probably intended as a compliment to Queen Mary and also as a statement of Philip's right to rule England as her lawful husband. Blue and yellow were not the usual Spanish colors, nor were they part of the elaborate color symbolism of love, but they were part of the livery of the House of Tudor. Another tournament was held at Easter at Westminster, with Philip and his companions jousting, again in blue, against the English knights (fig. 2.9).

[79]Young, *Tournaments*, 31–32nn200–201.

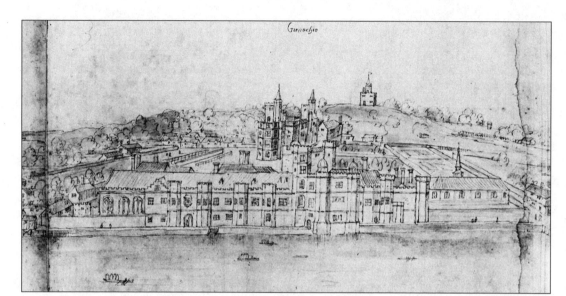

Figure 2.8 Anthonis van den Wyngaerde, *Greenwich*, ca. 1558. Oxford, Ashmolean Museum. Used by permission.

Figure 2.9 Anthonis van den Wyngaerde, *Westminster*, ca. 1544–45. Oxford, Ashmolean Museum. Used by permission.

Philip stayed in England a little over a year. The following summer, it was determined that hopeful rumors of the queen's pregnancy were false. The queen was barren, though Philip's enemies in England seized the opportunity to spread reports of his impotence.[80] With war brewing again in Europe, Philip hastily left England in September for Brussels.[81] Queen Mary died childless in 1558. Once again, the dynastic strategies of Charles V had suddenly evaporated. Philip's third marriage, to Isabel de Valois, was not until January of 1560, eighteen months after the emperor's death.

A fine armor for war and the tournament was made for the prince around 1554, the year of his journey to England (fig. 2.10). This garniture, called the "waves" or "clouds" garniture from the curvilinear decorative patterns adorning its surfaces, was probably destined for the wedding tournaments in England and required the labor of two German armorers, Wolf of Landshut and Franz Grosschedel, to complete it on time. This garniture is the largest and most complete set of armor owned by the prince. The massive jousting cuirass and barred shield for this armor alone weigh close to one hundred pounds and would have been endurable only for the short time necessary to run three or four courses with the lance.[82] The decoration is indistinguishable from the patterns found on luxury textiles from the period, completing the transformation of Renaissance armor from actual combat gear into a kind of formal dress wear.

As king of Spain, Philip II continued to attend tournaments and other martial spectacles, though tournaments at the western Habsburg court seem to have gradually tapered off in the second half of the sixteenth century. Mock battles were held at Toledo in 1560 to welcome the king's new bride, Isabel de Valois, and again at Bayonne in 1565 when the queen visited her mother in France.

Few tournaments at the Spanish court are mentioned towards the end of the sixteenth century, due in part to the failing health of the king. Philip's son Prince Philip III, while an avid hunter and an accomplished marksman, had little interest in the military arts. As a boy, he read book 1 of *Amadís of Gaul*, but quickly lost interest and was unable to finish the remaining books.[83] Tournaments, however, were an obligatory part of the marriage celebrations of Philip III to Margaret of Austria in 1599. The wedding took place in Valencia, lasting eight days and featuring bullfights, tournaments, cane games, royal jousts, *alcancías*, processions, and other activities.[84] A more formidable round of spectacles

[80]Grierson, 49.
[81]Kamen, *Philip of Spain*, 62–63.
[82]Crooke y Navarrot, *Catálogo historico-descriptivo de la Real Armería*, 83–86.
[83]Bustamante, *Felipe III*, 36.
[84]Bustamante, *Felipe III*, 69–70.

Figure 2.10 Wolf of Landshut and Franz Grosschedel, armor for war and the *Freiturnier* of Philip of Spain ("waves" or "clouds" garniture), 1554. Madrid, Real Armería, A243. Used by permission.

was held to celebrate the birth of Prince Philip IV at Valladolid in 1605. The festivities were attended by Charles Howard, Count of Nottingham and admiral of England, and included night masquerades, bullfights, cane games, tournaments, troop reviews, and shows with triumphal cars. The poet Góngora penned a sonnet on the festivals, claiming a million ducats were spent in fifteen days and that the banquets following the entertainments were worthy of the Roman emperor Elagabalus.[85] In spite of Góngora's lavish description, the festivities at Valladolid in 1599 and 1605 were really an epilogue to the art of the tournament in Renaissance Spain. Spectacular martial entertainments continued at the Spanish Habsburg court until well into the seventeenth century, though never again on the pan-European scale of the age of Charles V.

[85]Bustamante, *Felipe III*, 81.

Chapter 3

A SOLDIER OF CHRIST
The Prince as Crusader and Defender of the Church

THE CHRONICLER LAURENT VITAL presents the tournaments held for Charles of Ghent at Valladolid in 1518 as preparation for the real business of holy war. A colossal effigy of a Turk was burned as part of the closing ceremonies of the tournaments. During the king's stay in Valladolid, the sons of the Muslim ruler of Tlemcen arrived at the Spanish court asking for aid against the Barbary pirate Barbarossa, who with the aid of the Turks had captured the city and slaughtered its inhabitants. Against the wishes of his advisors, Charles decided to send Spanish soldiers to Tlemcen. Wearing a gorget, cuirass, and demigreaves beneath a golden surcoat, holding a commander's baton, and surrounded by his archers and halberdiers, the king reviewed his troops in person on the outskirts of Valladolid. Over a thousand men-at-arms passed before the king, their lances so numerous they seemed like a dark forest. Although Charles did not actually accompany his army to Africa, by July the Spanish were victorious and Barbarossa's forces were driven from Tlemcen. One of the Barbarossa brothers was killed; his head was hoisted on a lance and displayed from a tower in the city.[1]

In the sixteenth century, few people would have identified themselves as belonging to a nation in the modern sense. Renaissance Europeans

---

[1] Vital, *Viaje de Carlos I*, 349–51. Vital claims that Barbarossa himself was killed. There were, in fact, two famous pirates called by this name, Khayr ad-Din Barbarossa and his brother, who was killed in 1518.

identified themselves as Christians, especially in relation to non-European peoples, and this shaped their understanding of the world around them. Outside of Christendom lay the forces of Islam, generally regarded by the west as hostile to Christianity. The foremost threat was represented by the Ottoman Turks, whose powerful empire lay astride the eastern approaches to Europe from Istanbul, and whose navy dominated the eastern half of the Mediterranean. The Christian coastline of southern Europe was also menaced by Muslim corsairs from North Africa, whose strongholds in Tunis and Algiers were ideally situated for raids along the coasts of Italy, southern France, and Spain. In addition to the threat posed by the Turks and corsairs, the indigenous peoples of the Caribbean and the Americas, newly encountered by Europeans, were regarded by many as dangerous heathens, and consequently presented another problem for Christianity.

The old medieval idea of the crusade was also very much alive in sixteenth-century Europe.[2] European rulers still dreamed of the eventual reconquest of Jerusalem, lost to Christian control since the expulsion of the crusaders by Saladin in the twelfth century (except for the brief occupation of the city by Emperor Frederick II). Contemporary realities, however, placed serious practical limits on any plan for a crusade to free the Holy Land. The Christian west was mostly on the defensive against Islam in the sixteenth century. On the eastern front, the Habsburg monarchy struggled to hold Hungary and the Austrian territories of the Holy Roman Empire against the Ottomans, whose armies appeared before the walls of Vienna in 1529. Christian military expeditions were sent against the corsairs in North Africa in the sixteenth century, though with limited success. On more distant frontiers, one of the objectives of early European colonialism in equatorial Africa and the Far East was to locate the legendary kingdom of Prester John, a lost Christian principality rumored to lie somewhere in Asia or Africa, whose aid against Islam was hoped for by many in the west. In the New World, military expeditions against non-Christian peoples were regarded as an extension of the crusade.

Crusader ideology was a mainstay of Habsburg foreign policy in the sixteenth century. As dukes of Burgundy, the western Habsburgs held the hereditary position of Grandmaster of the Knights of the Order of the Golden Fleece, a brotherhood of chivalry founded by the Duke of Burgundy whose ultimate goal was the recapture of Jerusalem. As king of Spain, Charles V was also master of no fewer than four Spanish crusading orders: the Orders of Santiago, Calatrava, Alcántara, and Montesa. As heir of the Catholic Monarchs, Charles inherited the duty to carry on the crusade against the Turks and the Moors in North Africa. When the pope crowned him Holy Roman Emperor, Charles also swore

[2]Tracy, *Emperor Charles V,* 133.

to defend the Roman church. A good Christian knight was expected to be a stout warrior, and defense of the church was seen as one of his moral obligations. Writing around 1150 AD, John of Salisbury affirmed the purpose of the knight "to defend the church, assail the infidel, venerate the priesthood, protect the poor, and pacify the province."[3] Christian-imperial imagery was a mainstay in art, arms, and armor made for Habsburg princes as emperors-elect. These artworks reminded the prince that his empire was sacred and was bound to uphold the church against all its enemies.

Of all the chivalric emblems associated with the Habsburg monarchy, none occurs with greater frequency than the "potence" or necklace of the Order of the Golden Fleece. The transformation of an ancient talisman into a symbol of the holy crusade was enormously complex, though a synopsis of this process is vital to understanding the image of the emperor in Habsburg art. To the syncretic mentality of the Renaissance, the life-giving properties of the golden ram of Phrixus were likened to the miracle of the Christian resurrection, and thus the golden fleece of the mythical ram came to stand for the mystical Lamb of God. The pelt of the ram or *toison* was adopted as the emblem of the Knights of the Golden Fleece, an order of chivalry founded by Duke John the Good of Burgundy in 1429. The purpose of the order was to gather the flower of Christian chivalry under the military leadership of the duke, who planned a crusade to liberate the Holy Sepulchre from the infidel occupying Jerusalem. Like the Greek hero Jason, the duke was to go on a second quest for the new Golden Fleece. The messianic destiny of the duke was codified in a treatise written by the chancellor of the order, Guillaume Fillastre, who traced the duke's ancestry to the kings of Troy, themselves related to the Argonauts who sailed with Jason in quest of the Golden Fleece. In Juan Bravo's *History of the Golden Fleece and Order of the Toison*, published around 1546, the Golden Fleece was further identified with the ram of Gideon, whose pelt performed a miracle when the Israelites demanded proof that God supported their cause.[4] This intertwining of pagan and Christian mysteries comes as no surprise, since it was an integral part of Renaissance culture.[5] When Maximilian I married the childless Mary of Burgundy after the death of Charles the Bold in 1477, sovereignty of the order (and its obligations) passed directly to the Habsburg imperial house.[6]

Artworks honoring Habsburg princes nearly always include the emblems of the Golden Fleece. In the anonymous marriage portrait of

---

[3]Edge and Paddock, *Arms and Armor of the Medieval Knight*, 40.

[4]Gómez, *Arte y espectáculo en los viajes de Felipe II*, 119.

[5]Vale, *Chivalry*, 40.

[6]Tanner, *Last Descendant of Aeneas*, 146–61. For Habsburg imperial emblems and images, see also Yates, *Astraea*, 1–28.

Figure 3.1 Flanders, detail, armor of Philip I, ca. 1490–1500 (shown in fig. 2.1). Madrid, Real Armería, A11. Used by permission.

Philip of Burgundy and Juana of Castile discussed in chapter 2, the necklace of the Golden Fleece is prominently displayed, draped over the king's shoulders with the fleece hanging in front of the heraldic surcoat worn over his armor. The image of the fleece was also transferred to actual armors made for the Habsburgs (fig. 3.1). By incorporating the Golden Fleece into the decoration on his armor, Philip was reminded of his duty to carry on the crusade for Jerusalem, and was protected by the apotropaic emblem without risking the actual necklace in battle or the tournament. From this point onwards, the image of the necklace of the order was typically added to the fancy decoration on suits of fine armor made for Habsburg princes and other members of the order. The potence of the order is clearly visible on the breastplates of armors subsequently made for the young emperor Charles V and Prince Philip of Spain.

Other symbols of holy crusade are also found on armors made for the Habsburgs. More interesting from an iconograpic standpoint is the crest of a helmet made for Philip of Burgundy by an Italian armorer working in Flanders (fig. 3.2). The crest is in the form of a life-size pomegranate, splitting open to reveal the seeds inside. The pomegranate is raised over a twisted knop shaped like a turban, and ribs arranged to suggest a crown. The pomegranate (*granada* in Spanish) was the emblem of the kingdom of Granada, the last Muslim outpost in Spain, recently conquered by Ferdinand and Isabella and now part of Philip's Spanish inheritance through Juana of Castile.[7] As a symbol of the successful conclusion of the Reconquista, the pomegranate was a direct reminder of Philip's rightful authority over both Christian Spanish and Morisco subjects. The pomegranate was also part of the family crest of Philip's

[7]Godoy, "Royal Armory," 108.

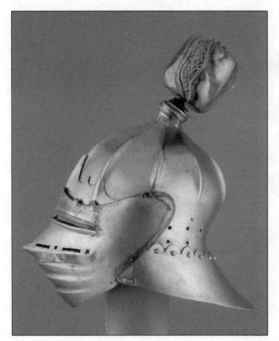

Figure 3.2 Flanders, sallet of Philip I, ca. 1496–1500. Madrid, Real Armería, D14. Used by permission.

Figure 3.3 Probably Italian [Negroli?], sallet decorated in Hispano-Moresque style, ca. 1500. Madrid, Real Armería, D12. Used by permission.

father, Emperor Maximilian I, and thus was a dual reference to Granada and the Habsburg imperial house. The pomegranate, moreover, had additional Christian connotations in Renaissance art. The multiple seeds of the fruit symbolized the multitudes embraced by one church,[8] and the opening of the husk suggested the spreading of Christ's word to the whole world. As an emblem of Christian unity, a pomegranate is shown being held by the Christ child in paintings by Fra Filippo Lippi and Sandro Botticelli. The pomegranate on Philip's helmet thus represented both the kingdom of Granada and the continuing crusade against the Muslims, which the Christian world expected to be carried from Granada to North Africa and beyond. The symbolism of the pomegranate, as we shall see, appears again in church festivals held for the visit of Prince Philip of Spain to Trent in 1548. In addition to the pomegranate helmet, Philip of Burgundy also owned two helmets decorated in a hybrid Hispano-Moresque style (fig. 3.3). These helmets might have been used for cane games played in Moorish costume. Philip's chronicler, the Seigneur de Montigny, notes that Philip wore a Moorish costume for a cane game held before the Catholic Monarchs in Toledo.[9]

[8]Ferguson, *Signs and Symbols in Christian Art*, 37.
[9]Crooke y Navarrot, *Catálogo historico-descriptivo de la Real Armería*, 143–44.

Philip's successor, however, commanded real expeditions against the enemies of Christendom. As emperor, Charles V eventually got his chance to personally lead a Christian army against the forces of Islam. Having signed a peace treaty with France, the emperor headed for Italy for his imperial coronation by the pope, scheduled for the winter of 1530 in Bologna (Rome was still recovering from the notorious sack by imperial troops in 1527). In the summer of 1529, Europe received the alarming news that a Turkish army led by the Sultan Suleiman himself had appeared before the walls of Vienna. The emperor sent an army to Austria and the sultan, who had overextended his supply lines, abandoned the siege without offering battle, only to return two years later with another army. Charles, meanwhile, continued his ceremonial progress through northern Italy. The emperor and the pope signed the Treaty of Barcelona in June. In return for papal support against the Turks in Hungary, Charles agreed to recognize papal claims to several important cities in central Italy and Sicily, and Charles was formally invested with the kingdom of Naples.[10] Tournaments were held in Bologna to celebrate the imperial coronation and the retreat of the Turks. Masses were sung in the presence of the Knights of the Golden Fleece and the Order of Santiago, another crusading order originally from Spain.[11] The Turks invaded Hungary and laid siege to Vienna again in 1532. Faced with frustrating delays by the imperial diet, the emperor eventually headed to Austria with an army of German landsknechts, sailing down the Danube to meet the sultan with an enormous flotilla of warships. Suleiman had already withdrawn from the city for the second time, but troops sent by the emperor's brother Ferdinand caught what was apparently the rearguard of the sultan's army near the town of Güns. The Turkish irregular cavalry were mauled, and Suleiman continued his retreat from Austria. The relief of Vienna was part of an ambitious project to attack the Turks on all fronts. From the sea, the imperial admiral Andrea Doria led an attack on Turkish forces in Greece.[12] The retreat of the Turks from Vienna was regarded as a divine miracle, though Charles was politely honored as the leader of the west against the armies of Asia.[13]

In 1528 or 1529, the German painter Albrecht Altdorfer painted an epic battle scene showing the pursuit of King Darius of Persia by Alexander the Great (fig. 3.4). The painting was commissioned by Duke Wilhelm of Bavaria in an effort to drum up support for the emperor against the Turkish invasion. Altdorfer updated ancient history by transposing the scene to contemporary Europe. Troops dressed as Turks and

[10]Strong, *Splendor at Court*, 85.
[11]Jacquot, "Fête chevaleresque," 422–23.
[12]Tracy, *Charles V*, 138–44.
[13]von Habsburg, *Carlos V*, 155–56.

Figure 3.4 Albrecht Altdorfer, *Battle of Alexander,* 1528–29. Oil or tempera on panel, Munich, Bayerische Staatsgemäldesammlungen, Alte Pinakothek (688). Used by permission.

Figure 3.5 Parmigianino, *Allegorical Portrait of Emperor Charles V*, 1530. Copy of lost original. Oil on canvas, private collection (formerly in Vienna, Kunsthistorischen Museum).

sixteenth-century knights in armor wage war in an allegorical landscape of Austrian cities. The historical battles are elevated to cosmic proportions, with the sun and moon presiding over the scene. The painting was accompanied by a multivolume history penned by a German scholar, Johannes Aventinus, who describes Alexander's defense of the Danube frontier against the Persians and his subsequent victory over Darius on the banks of the river Issus. The analogy with the Habsburg emperor's impending campaign against the Turks is obvious.[14] Classical precedents for current events were readily supplied by Renaissance artists, and Altdorfer's epic retelling of ancient history was also a plea for the final expulsion of Islam from Europe and the continuance of the crusade to the east.

During Charles's stay in Bologna, an allegorical portrait of him was painted by Parmigianino, who supposedly painted the emperor's likeness from memory after watching him dine.[15] Charles is shown in full knightly armor, resting his military staff on the globe in token of his triumph over his enemies (fig. 3.5). His left hand is wrapped around the hilt of his sword, though the blade is held firmly in its sheath. In

[14]Janzen, *Albrecht Altdorfer*, 32–33.
[15]Campbell, *Renaissance Portraits*, 162–63.

honor of his victories, Fame offers the emperor a palm branch and a sprig of laurel (symbols of spiritual and temporal victory), and the infant Hercules hands him the globe.[16] The painting is in the elegant and sophisticated style of the Italian *maniera*, though Parmigianino's portrait is surprisingly old-fashioned in one respect: the map shows only the Old World, with the location of Jerusalem suggested in its traditional medieval position at the center of the map. The central position of the Holy Land on Parmigianino's map indicates that the original objective of the Crusades was once again an attainable goal, perhaps during the emperor's lifetime. The iconography of the painting is fully in keeping with the events surrounding the imperial coronation at Bologna: the retreat of the Turks from Vienna and the consolidation of the emperor's authority in Italy. Control of Italy and a decisive victory over the Turks, it was hoped, would reopen the way to Jerusalem, and the fulfillment of the divine destiny of the emperor. As we shall see, northern portraits of Charles V as a young man suggested an imperial destiny in a manner that was still essentially Gothic. Parmigianino's portrait of the emperor as a victorious crusader combined classical and chivalric elements in a fully developed Renaissance style, and carried a more complex message about his role in sacred history.

While Renaissance painters celebrated the military achievements of Charles V in different modes, Italian armorers were busy reviving armor in classical style. The epics of Homer and Virgil describe panoplies of helmet and shield, manufactured by the gods and illustrated with marvelous scenes. In classical mythology, divine armor had magical qualities and was bestowed on favored mortals by the gods. This type of heroic armor was revived in the Renaissance by the armorers of Milan and was worn by princes and military leaders for ceremonial entries and fancy-dress tournaments. The twin cults of pagan antiquity and Christian chivalry were blended in a decorated panoply of pageant armor made by Filippo Negroli for Charles V in 1533 (fig. 3.6). The Golden Fleece and imperial emblems occur together on this armor, which was presented to the emperor by the Duke of Mantua.[17] There can be no doubt that this armor was made specifically to honor Charles, since it is decorated with direct references to the emperor. The helmet fully encloses the wearer's head and is embossed to resemble the idealized features of Charles, his gilt curls bound by a slender fillet of laurel leaves, an ancient token of victory. The collar of the Order of the Golden Fleece is embossed around the gorget, imitating the actual pendant worn by members of the

---

[16]Freedberg, *Parmigianino*, 112.
[17]The helmet and companion shield are signed and dated by Filippo Negroli in 1533. The panoply is mentioned as part of a gift of etched armor from the Duke of Mantua in the *Relación de Valladolid*, an inventory of the emperor's armors made around 1557, the year before the

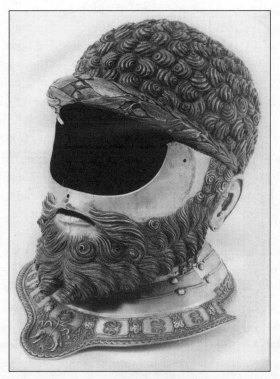

Figure 3.6a and b Filippo Negroli, panoply of Charles V, 1533. Madrid, Real Armería, D1, D2. Used by permission.

order. The necklace is formed by joined firesteels and flints, the heraldic devices of the house of Burgundy. At the nape of the helmet is a medallion with the Pillars of Hercules and the imperial crown, supported by a pair of eaglets. The pillars and heraldic motifs are repeated on the rim of the companion shield, along with the double-headed imperial eagle, or *Reichsadler*. The centerpiece of the shield is the head of a fantastic hybrid beast, perhaps the Nemean Lion, whose invulnerable pelt was worn by Hercules, or the ram of the Golden Fleece itself (there are tiny ram's horns in place of the lion's ears). The armor's allusion to a victorious hero and the Golden Fleece are especially interesting since Hercules was one of the Argonauts, the legendary band of warriors led by Jason to the East in quest of the pelt of the magical ram. Hercules was frequently associated with Charles V in Habsburg-sponsored art, and the quest for the Golden Fleece was transformed into an archetype of the crusade with the foundation of the Order of the Golden Fleece in the fifteenth century. Helmets with embossed decoration resembling curly hair and lifelike face-guards were made in ancient times for Sumerian kings and Roman cavalry officers, and it is certainly possible an actual antique was the inspiration for Charles's magnificent helmet. The emperor had heard a glowing report about a similar helmet made by Filippo Negroli for the Duke of Urbino and was eager to possess one of his own.[18] The date of Charles's panoply suggests the armor was commissioned for him by the Duke of Mantua to commemorate the emperor's successful campaign against the Turks the previous year, and the iconography is fully in keeping with Charles's crusade to the East.

Allusions to the Golden Fleece occur again on a bard, or horse armor, made for Charles V sometime after 1519 (fig. 3.7). On the chamfron or face-plate are a pair of embossed ram's horns, which can be added or removed at pleasure from the armor by turn-pins under the ears. With the ram's horns in place, horse and rider were transformed into a living representation of the magical ram ridden by Phrixus, the Argive youth who brought the Golden Fleece to Asia. Parts of the armor may originally have been gilded, which would have made the resemblance to a golden ram even more striking. The crupper is etched with scenes showing David against Goliath and Samson battling the Philistines. David and Samson defended God's chosen people against the enemies of Israel, and thus to the Renaissance mind were precursors of

emperor's death; AGS, *Casa y Sitios Reales*, legajo 134 n° 351, fols. 5r, 11r. The same helmet and shield are shown along with a different suit of armor known as the palm-branch armor in the *Inventario iluminado*, an illustrated inventory of the emperor's armors and related possessions made around 1544; Pyhrr and Godoy, *Heroic Armor*, 254. The lower plates on the visor and neck guard of the helmet do not fit together precisely and are embossed with different decorative motifs, suggesting that a second, nearly identical helmet and visor were also made for the emperor.

[18]Pyhrr and Godoy, *Heroic Armor*, 128–30.

Figure 3.7a *above*, German, armor and bard of Charles V with ram's horns, after 1519. **b** *left*, detail of crupper. Madrid, Real Armería, A37. Used by permission.

modern holy warriors. David was also one of the mythical ancestors of Charles V, and was frequently identified with the messianic destiny of the Habsburg imperial house.[19] The peytral of the horse-armor bears a pair of embossed lion's heads between hammered festoons, imitating the actual fancy cloth mantling worn by horses in tournaments. Like Hercules, Samson was a lion-fighter, and the lion's masks are probably an allusion to the superhuman strength of the Old Testament hero. The bard is unsigned and undated, though the presence of the imperial eagle on a little shield in front of the plume-holder suggests a date after the emperor's coronation in 1530 or at least after his election in 1519. The iconography of Samson as a lion-fighter and hero of Israel echoes the decoration on another fine bard in the Royal Armory, which illustrates the deeds of Samson and Hercules. Samson was considered the biblical equivalent of the Greek hero, whose labors were also accomplished with divine aid. The other bard, though inherited by Charles V, was probably made for his grandfather Maximilian I in 1517 or 1518.

Following the retreat of the Turks from Vienna, Charles V pursued a policy of active aggression against Islam, personally leading his troops against the Muslim states of North Africa. This time the blow against the Turks would be struck at Tunis, the stronghold of the Barbary pirate Khayr-ad-Din Barbarossa. Barbarossa, himself a renegade Christian, was an enormously successful warlord who had recently been appointed admiral of the western seas by the Turkish sultan. A Turkish garrison stiffened the defenses of Tunis, and Barbarossa used the city as a base from which to raid the coasts of Sicily and southern Italy. Charles mustered his German, Italian, and Iberian troops at Barcelona in 1534, though the destination of the expedition was kept secret. Hunts and tournaments were held while the imperial fleet was prepared.[20] The seriousness of Charles's crusading ideals was shown by his response to events in Germany at this time. During the emperor's absence from the north, the Schmalkaldic League seized the opportunity to invade the Habsburg territory of Württemberg. Charles, however, refused to abandon his preparations for the Tunis campaign. The pope had urged Charles to head straight for Istanbul, though the emperor wisely rejected this idea.[21] In the spring of 1535, Charles launched his assault on Tunis. The immediate goals of the emperor's crusade were to restore the Tunisian ruler Mulay Hasan to the throne and to free the large numbers of Christian captives being held in the city. The assault was aided by escaped Christian slaves, who stormed the city's arsenal as Charles's

[19]Pizarro Gómez, *Arte y espectáculo en los viajes de Felipe II*, 132.

[20]The chronicler Johannes Secundus, writing probably from Barcelona in 1535, mentions the emperor's cane games; Horn, *Vermeyen*, 26.

[21]Tracy, *Emperor Charles V*, 147.

troops neared the city. According to the chronicler Santa Cruz, Charles himself took to the battlefield, carrying a lance and taking the same risks as a common soldier.[22] The emperor's campaign was successful, and Tunis was taken and pillaged by imperial troops on 21 July 1535. Close to two thousand Christian captives were freed and the victors seized large amounts of booty in the form of clothing, cash, and slaves. The emperor's conquest of Tunis was short-lived and its historical importance is debatable, but the emotional impact of his victory over the Muslims in the Christian west was profound.

Charles returned to a hero's welcome in Italy. A triumphal entry in Roman style, complete with temporary theaters, arches, colossal statues, and other *apparati*, was held at Naples to celebrate the emperor's arrival. Charles entered the city on a warm sunny morning on St. Catherine's Day, 25 November 1535. The emperor was accompanied by his men-at-arms and preceded by the Marqués del Vasto, who bore a naked sword. Out of Christian humility, Charles himself wore no armor on this occasion. As he approached the gates, the emperor dismounted and was greeted by the assembled clergy of the city bearing a great silver cross, which Charles knelt to adore. Remounting and passing beneath the gates, the emperor saw statues representing African river gods and trophies of Moorish arms, along with a colossus comparing him to Scipio Africanus, the Roman conqueror of Carthage (modern Tunis). Other statues were strategically placed along Charles's route to the center of town, including colossi representing Jupiter, Neptune, Hercules carrying the pillars, winged Fame with her trumpet, and Faith. The most impressive *apparatus* was a fountain in the shape of a vast mountain, with huge statues of the giants who made war on heaven. An artillery blast sounded as the emperor entered the *castello*.[23]

Charles's entry was followed by jousts, cane games, bullfights on horseback, and a carrousel. The festivities continued for two and a half months, taking advantage of the pleasant weather in Naples at that time of year. An arena of ample space was set up in the Piazza di San Giovanni di Carbonara, so the spectacles could be viewed from the windows of the many palaces and townhouses that surrounded the square. The emperor participated in the games wearing Moorish dress in honor of his victory at Tunis.[24] The games culminated in a bullfight in which teams of local Italian nobles and Spanish grandees, all in Moorish costume, took turns killing six fierce bulls in the arena. Tensions between the noble cavalry and the German soldiers erupted during the cane games that followed the bullfights, however. The end of the games was to be signalled by the entry of the emperor's German bodyguard, but the horsemen refused to stop their maneuvers, and several Germans were trampled and dragged. The Germans retreated from the arena and the cavalry continued their skirmish.[25]

Charles's road back north passed through Rome. In 1536, the emperor was fêted as a returning hero by Pope Paul III in the Eternal City. Charles was granted a real Roman triumph, his route into the city taking him past the ruins of the triumphal arches of the soldier-emperors of Rome. In sight of the Capitoline Hill, actors dressed as ancient senators hailed the return of the new Caesar as *miles christi* and a handsome page presented Charles with an embossed shield.[26]

Encouraged by the success of his Tunisian campaign, the emperor mounted another expedition to North Africa in 1541. The goal of the emperor's second African campaign was the corsair stronghold of Algiers, where Barbarossa had taken up residence after being driven from Tunis. This time, however, the imperial fleet was wrecked by an autumn storm while weighing anchor near Algiers and the emperor was unable to disembark his troops. Some soldiers caught in the water were killed by the Algerians and Charles decided to withdraw.[27]

The emperor's first African campaign was meticulously recorded for posterity eleven years later in a series of twelve tapestries known as the *Conquest of Tunis*, woven between 1549 and 1554 in the workshop of Willem de Pannemaker in Brussels. The tapestry cartoons by Pieter Coecke van Aelst were based on sketches drawn from life by the Flemish artist Jan Cornelisz Vermeyen, who accompanied the emperor to Tunis in 1535.[28] Most of the scenes are concerned with the infantry assault on the fortress of La Goletta and the subsequent capture of the city. In the second panel of the tapestries, Charles is shown reviewing his troops on parade at Barcelona prior to his departure for Tunis (fig. 3.8). The emperor sits astride his horse in the center of the scene as his German bodyguard reports to the quartermaster, but the vista is dominated entirely by the emperor's knights, who revolve counterclockwise around Charles with all the pomp and circumstance of Renaissance chivalry. The procession is watched by three knights in gleaming armor who stand apart, one of whom raises a battle standard blazoned with an image of the Virgin and Child, as if the Virgin herself were presiding over the muster of the Christian soldiers.[29] The actual battle for

[25]Sala, *La triomphale Entrata de Carlo V*, fols. 31r–35r.

[26]Forcella, *Tornei e giostre*. For Roman festivals and tournaments in the Renaissance, see also Centro de Studi Storici (Narni), *La civiltà del torneo*; Pastor, *Storia dei papi dalla fine del medioevo*, vol. 5, *Paolo III*; and Tosi, *Il torneo di Belvedere*.

[27]Tracy, *Emperor Charles V*, 176.

[28]Carretero, "Renaissance Tapestries from the Patrimonio Nacional," 75. See also Campbell, *Tapestry in the Renaissance*, 429. Vermeyen also illustrated a tourney held at Toledo in 1539, with images again apparently drawn from life; Wilenski, *Flemish Painters, 1430–1830*, 1:130.

[29]Horn, *Vermeyen*, 186.

Figure 3.8 Willem de Pannemaker after Jan Vermeyen & Pieter Coecke van Aelst, *Conquest of Tunis*, panel 2, 1549–54. Tapestry, Madrid, Palacio Real, PN. S.13/2. Used by permission.

Tunis was won largely by the emperor's German and Italian infantry, but in the visual record of the preliminaries at Barcelona, pride of place is still reserved for the knightly class.[30]

The emperor owned a number of fine armors for war and the tournament from this period, but most of these are fragmentary and all are difficult to connect precisely with historical events. These include an armor for war said to have been worn by the emperor on his victorious campaign to Tunis in 1535, though only portions of this armor have survived.[31] The "Tunis armor" is attributed to Caremolo Modrone, and was made around 1530 to the exact measurements of the emperor.[32] An illustration of the Tunis armor from the *Inventario Iluminado*, an illustrated inventory of the emperor's armors made sometime between 1556 and 1558, shows that the surfaces of the Tunis armor were hammered smooth and covered entirely in gold. This is probably the armor depicted in a drawing by Vermeyen for panel eleven of the Tunis tapestries, where Charles is shown at the head of his troops on the march to Rada. This armor, however, clearly is not the one Charles is wearing for the preliminaries at Barcelona in the second panel of the tapestries. In the second panel, Charles is shown wearing an armor decorated with vertical bands of gold. The emperor, it turns out, owned several different armors with decoration of this type, and it is impossible to determine which of these is illustrated in panel two of the Tunis tapestries.[33]

Other armors made for the emperor from this period are decorated with motifs alluding to victory and the crusade. These armors all date between about 1534 and 1545, the span of years that encompassed the emperor's campaigns against the Barbary states. A fine German armor bearing a prominent etching of the Virgin and Child on the breastplate was made for the emperor in 1538; called the broad-bands armor, it is presumably the work of the imperial armorer Desiderius Colman (fig. 3.9). This is perhaps the handsomest armor owned by the emperor, and combines decorative elements of the earlier Maximilian style with structural features characteristic of later sixteenth-century armor. This armor is decorated on the breastplate with a large etching of the Virgin and Child, surrounded by an oval radiance or glory called a mandorla. An

---

[30]Many years later, a set of prints by Maerten van Heemskerck was published illustrating the battle of Tunis and other military victories of the emperor. Van Heemskerck was not an eyewitness to these events, and his illustrations show the battles in an elevated epic style, with imaginary antique armor worn by the combatants on both sides. Van Heemskerck's prints were published in 1555–56; Pinson, "Imperial Ideology in the Triumphal Entry into Lille of Charles V and the Crown Prince."

[31]The *Relación de Valladolid*, an unillustrated inventory of the emperor's armors made in 1557, lists an armor taken by the emperor to Tunis; AGS, *Casa y Sitios Reales*, legajo 134 n° 351, fols. 7v, 8r.

[32]Pyhrr and Godoy, *Heroic Armor*, 251.

[33]Of these armors, at least two could also conceivably have been worn on the emperor's campaign to Tunis: the "hunt" garniture and the "horns-of-plenty" garniture, both by Colman Helmschmied and dating to about 1524–26 and 1525–30.

image of the Virgin was cus-
tomarily carried before Christian armies in the Renaissance,
and this practice is illustrated
in Austrian folk paintings of
crusading knights from the
early sixteenth century. The
emblem on Charles's breastplate
also echoes the holy image on
the banner raised by the
emperor's knights in the second
panel of the Tunis tapestries.
The Virgin and other religious
emblems are common on
armor from this period and
were a kind of personal devo-
tional image for soldiers to
wear into battle.[34]

The emperor also owned a
complete armor by the Negroli
from this period, the "masks"
garniture, signed by the Negroli
brothers in 1539. This armor is
more or less intact, and was
decorated on the breast and
backplate with gold appliqués
representing the Virgin and St.

Figure 3.9 Desiderius Colman (attr.), breastplate of Charles V
("broad-bands" armor), 1538. Madrid, Real Armería, A129. Used
by permission.

Barbara. Figurative appliqués like this are somewhat unusual on armor,
though they resemble the metal badges of saints carried by pilgrims to
Christian holy places. In a military context, the image of the Virgin was
a crusading emblem, but the image of St. Barbara was believed to protect those in need of spiritual strength or who risked a violent death.
This pair of images nearly always occurs on the emperor's armors after
about 1531.[35] A second inventory of the emperor's armors made around
the time of his death notes that pieces of another armor in the Royal
Armory belonged to an armor lost on the campaign to Algiers. One of
the breastplates made for this armor is also decorated with an oversized
image of the Virgin, with St. Barbara on the backplate. A second breastplate that apparently belonged to the same garniture is decorated with
an image of Santiago Matamoros (St. James the Moor-killer), the patron
saint of crusading Spain. The history of this particular armor, however, is

---

[34]Krenn and Karcheski, *Imperial Austria*, 85.
[35]Crooke y Navarrot, *Catálogo historico-descriptivo de la Real Armería*, 61.

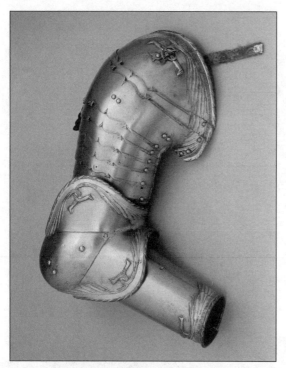

Figure 3.10 Caremolo Modrone (attr.), portions of an armor of Charles V ("palm-branch" armor), ca. 1536. Madrid, Real Armería, A114. Used by permission.

extremely difficult to untangle.[36] Images of the Virgin, saints, and other holy emblems on Christian armor performed an apotropaic function, and protected the wearer from physical harm, as the head of Medusa had protected heroes in ancient times. Warrior-saints like Santiago, St. Maurice, St. Sebastian, and St. George were also considered exemplars of Christian chivalry in the Renaissance, since they performed miraculous feats of valor and died in the service of God.[37]

Another fragmentary armor from this period, the "palm-branch" armor (also attributed to Caremolo Modrone), was embossed with the motif of crossed palm branches and damascened borders in pseudo-Kufic script (fig. 3.10). In Renaissance art, pseudo-Kufic script was used to decorate the costumes of Old Testament heroes like David, who was shown wearing a short tunic bordered with pseudo-Kufic script in the well-known sculpture by Andrea Verrocchio from about 1475. The palm branch was a symbol of victory inherited from the decorative vocabulary of classical art, though it also had Christian connotations,[38] especially when the branches are shown crossed (as a sign of victory in Christ, a palm branch is typically held by holy martyrs in Christian art). The palm-branch armor was completed around 1536, but again only tantalizing portions of this armor have survived.

In the triumphal entry at Naples, the emperor's victories were compared to the African campaigns of Scipio Africanus, the Roman general who led the armies of the Republic to victory at Carthage. Romans and Carthaginians do battle on a pageant panoply of helmet and shield preserved in the Royal Armory in Madrid, presumably made in remembrance of the African campaigns of Charles V (fig. 3.11).[39] That the city

[36]Crooke y Navarrot, *Catálogo historico-descriptivo de la Real Armería*, 52-54; and Godoy, "Royal Armory," 136-37.

[37]Vale, *Chivalry*, 54.

[38]Freedberg, *Parmigianino*, 112.

[39]Crooke y Navarrot, *Catálogo historico-descriptivo de la Real Armería*, 135. The Conde's assertion that the panoply belonged to Charles V is based on the Carthaginian theme on the shield, though the armor is not mentioned in the inventories of the emperor's possessions. Godoy has recently

in the background is Carthage is confirmed by the little banderole in the
upper register of the shield, which is
inscribed CARTHAGINE. The central
figure on the shield was lifted verbatim from scenes of the Trojan War
painted by Giulio Romano in the
Sala di Troia in the ducal palace at
Mantua.[40] The connection is interesting and suggests the panoply may
have been commissioned by the Duke
of Mantua, an important ally of
Charles V who also commissioned the
Hercules helmet and shield for the
emperor in 1533. The Trojans were
among the mythic ancestors of
Charles V, and this might explain the
selection of a Trojan warrior for a
panoply honoring Charles's expedition
to Africa (Carthage was also one of
the stopping places of the hero
Aeneas following his flight from
Troy). Compared with the Tunis tapestries, the evocation of the emperor's
victory here is purely an academic
one, with no attempt to portray the
actual battle.

Figures 3.11a and b Italian, pageant panoply, after 1535
or 1560–65. Madrid, Real Armería, D3, D4. Used by permission.

Undoubtedly one of the finest
pieces of armor owned by the
emperor is an embossed and damascened helmet signed by Filippo and
Francesco Negroli in 1545 (fig. 3.12).
The crest of the helmet is embossed
with the likeness of a captive Turk,
whose moustaches are gripped by
winged figures of Fame with her trumpet and Victory holding a palm
branch. The front of the helmet bears an inscription hailing Charles as
unconquered Caesar. This helmet, with its overly optimistic image of a
subjected Islam, may originally have been planned as a trophy for
Charles following his second African campaign in 1541.

---

challenged the association with Charles V, dating the panoply on the basis of style to circa 1560–
65. Godoy and Leyde, *Parures triomphales*, 439.

[40]The decorations in the Sala di Troia were also copied by the printmaker Diana Scultori.

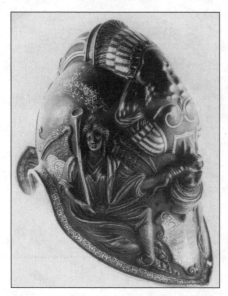

Figure 3.12 Filippo and Francesco Negroli, helmet of Charles V, 1545. Madrid, Real Armería, D30. Used by permission.

In addition to defending the church from enemies outside the Christian frontier, as Catholic monarchs, Charles V and his successors were also obliged to defend the church from within. In 1531, the Protestant princes of the Schmalkaldic League formed an alliance against Charles V. The emperor's struggles with the Protestants were temporarily resolved at the Battle of Mühlberg in 1547, when imperial forces resoundingly defeated the armies of the League and took the Elector of Saxony prisoner. Charles personally led his troops again at Mühlberg, and the emperor's victory was immortalized in a painting by Titian, his court painter (fig. 3.13). The artist traveled through the Alpine snows from Venice to Augsburg in the winter of 1548 specifically to paint the emperor's portrait from life.[41] The painting duplicated the emperor's appearance and equipment at the battle in detail, as confirmed by Don Luis de Avila y Zúñiga, the imperial chamberlain and an eyewitness to the event.[42] The armor worn by the emperor in Titian's painting is part of a large garniture that survives intact in the Royal Armory in Madrid (fig. 3.14), along with the wheel lock pistol carried at his saddlebow.[43] The proportions of the cuirass have increased, reflecting the emperor's heavier build as a middle-aged man. In the painting, the emperor is equipped as a light cavalryman, wielding a long spear and protected by a sallet, gauntlets, and cuirass, with mail protection only for the lower arms. Charles wears the transverse sash of a field commander in the red color of the Catholic party, with a band of the same color wrapped around his helmet in Spanish style and the pendant of the Golden Fleece hanging from his neck. The Mühlberg armor in Madrid is etched on the breastplate with an image of the Virgin (barely visible in the painting) and with an image of St. Barbara on the backplate. The emperor favored these images during his years of crusade, and they were reused on the armor the emperor chose for the battle against the Protestants. The emperor's pose in the painting, mounted on a rearing charger with his lance held out at his side, recalls Hellenistic sculptures of Alexander the Great on Bucephalus and the myriad Roman imitations of them. The emperor actually carried a smaller javelin into battle at Mühlberg, but as a symbolic weapon the spear has many additional

---

[41]Wethey, *Complete Paintings of Titian*, 2:35.
[42]Crooke y Navarrot, *Catálogo historico-descriptivo de la Real Armería*, 61.
[43]Schalkhausser, "Peter Peck, the Emperor's Gunsmith."

Figure 3.13 Titian, *Charles V at Mühlberg*, 1548. Oil on canvas, Madrid, Museo Nacional del Prado (410). Used by permission.

Figure 3.14 German, armor of Charles V ("Mühlberg" armor), 1544. Madrid, Real Armería, A165. Used by permission.

connotations in western art. The spear was an emblem of absolute authority in ancient Rome and is shown in this context on ancient coins and medals. The hilt of a knight's sword resembled the cross and was of course a Christian symbol, but many contemporary writers regarded the lance as the proper weapon of chivalry. A lance or spear, for example, was the archetypal weapon of the perfect Christian knight in Erasmus' *Miles Christianus*.[44] Titian's equestrian portrait of Charles V wielding a spear also recalls Renaissance images of the first Christian emperor, Constantine, wielding the Holy Lance. In a fresco painted between 1521 and 1523 by Giulio Romano in the Sala di Constantino in the Vatican, Constantine is shown on a rearing horse with the Holy Lance defeating the pagan army of Maxentius.[45] The imagery used on the Mühlberg armor and the allusions suggested in Titian's painting underscored the emperor's role as Christian warrior and defender of the church, in the ascendant again after the victory at Mühlberg.

As a counterpart to Charles's victories on the battlefield, tournaments were held during this period too, but they are sparsely documented, due, perhaps, to the emperor's real military commitments on all fronts. The tournaments held for Charles's son and heir, Prince Philip of Spain, are better understood. Philip's future identity as defender of the faith was set in motion in childhood. In 1531, Philip was admitted *in absentia* to the Order of the Golden Fleece, the arch-brotherhood of chivalry dedicated to the recapture of Jerusalem.[46] At the age of sixteen, Philip was given a pageant shield embossed with an allegorical scene of the Ship of Humanity guided by the nude figure of Fortitude (fig. 3.15). The shield is light and small, ideal for a slender teenager whose muscles were still developing. The shield is etched and embossed

[44]For the iconography of the lance *see* Panofsky, *Problems in Titian*, 85–86. This painting and the emperor's role as conqueror and Christian knight are also discussed by Wethey (*Titian*, 35).

[45]Romano's paintings were widely known in the form of prints by Marcantonio Raimondi and Diana Scultori, and could have been studied by Titian.

[46]Foronda y Aguilera, *Viajes de Carlos V*, 358.

in the German style and signed by Matteus Frauenpreis, armorer of Augsburg. The ship's sail is torn and she is tossed about on stormy seas, but Fortitude pilots her with a steady gaze, guided by the compass of Religion and protected by the shield of Faith. In Renaissance art, Fortitude was a standard virtue applied to military men, but Fortitude was also a Christian virtue, especially when shown in a religious context. The shield of Faith also recalls the symbolic armor of a good Christian described by Paul in the Epistle to the Ephesians, who were told to put on the armor of God.[47] The allegorical scene here is very much like the emblems or *imprese* carried by Elizabethan courtiers on their shields and performed the same function of analogical self-identification at tournaments.[48] Philip's decorated shield may have been given to him shortly after the games and pageants held at Valencia to celebrate his acceptance as the emperor's heir in Spain.

Figure 3.15 Matteus Frauenpreis, shield of Philip II, 1543. Madrid, Real Armería, D68. Used by permission.

Following the emperor's victory at Mühlberg, it was safe for Philip to travel abroad and the emperor summoned his son to the meeting of the imperial diet at Augsburg in 1550, where the matter of the imperial succession had still to be decided. In addition to presenting Philip as an ideal royal husband, the imagery at tournaments held on the prince's European tour alluded to Philip as the perfect Catholic monarch, especially in cities with major religious festivals. Essential to Philip's acceptance by the church was the assurance that the prince would carry on his father's role as defender of the faith. A more solemn type of imagery generally prevailed in tournaments held in conjunction with religious events, emphasizing the serious nature of the prince's religious obligations and his duty to carry on the crusade against all enemies of the church. Images of courtly love were set aside, replaced by elaborate symbolic tableaux pointing to the alliance of emperor and pope and, ultimately, to the triumph of the church. As a sign of the times François de la Noue, a Calvinist soldier, complained that romances like *Amadís of Gaul*, in

[47]Ephesians 6:16 (DRV).
[48]For more on *impresa* shields, see "Curious Devices," in Young, *Tudor and Jacobean Tournaments*, 123–43.

addition to encouraging outdated military doctrine, contained references to sorcery and black magic.[49]

From a religious standpoint, by far the most important stop on Philip's tour was the city of Trent, the site chosen for the reforming councils summoned by Pope Paul III in 1548. Philip's visit to the city on his way to the imperial diet was a perfect opportunity for a strong show of mutual support by the Habsburg monarchy and the Roman church. The conciliar city was packed with cardinals, bishops, and other important people when Philip arrived in the winter of 1549. After a brief stop in Mantua, where he was met by the Duke of Ferrara and the Venetian ambassador, the prince arrived in Trent on a Friday in late January. A particularly splendid series of festivals and tournaments awaited Philip at Trent. The entertainments staged for the prince took advantage of the city's spectacular location in the foothills of the Alps and were remembered as the most elaborate festivals ever seen in Italy.

Philip's *adventus* and the tournaments that followed are described in detail by Calvete de Estrella and Michelangelo Mariani.[50] Mariani reports that a mock skirmish of foot soldiers and arquebusiers took place immediately after Philip's arrival, which is said to have greatly delighted the prince. Afterwards, Philip was greeted by salvos of artillery and was met by his host, the Cardinal-Bishop Madruzzo, who presented him with a fine courser. Philip and the cardinal then entered the cathedral to hear Mass.

During the ceremonies in the cathedral, an entire mock castle with moving parts was erected in the main square in front of the palace.[51] Illustrations of tournament castles from the sixteenth century are extremely rare, though the castle at Trent probably resembled similar structures designed by Renaissance artists for the theater. A castle sketched by Inigo Jones for a play at the Stuart court, for example, featured working gates and a mechanical drawbridge. These would have been operated by devices like those illustrated in a set of drawings of sixteenth-century stage machinery from the Teatro Farnese preserved in the Biblioteca Palatina in Rome. The backstage views of the Teatro Farnese show machines operated by windlasses and complicated arrangements of weights and pulleys. The mock castle at Trent must have been erected from prefabricated sections, otherwise it is difficult to explain Mariani's claim that the structure was set up in the time it took the prince to perform his devotions.[52]

---

[49]O'Connor, *Amadís de Gaule and Its Influence on Elizabethan Literature*, 14–15.

[50]Mariani wrote his account over a century after the events and relied extensively on earlier sources, especially Calvete de Estrella.

[51]Mariani, *Trento con il Sacro Concilio et altri*, 358–61.

[52]Mariani, *Trento con il Sacro Concilio et altri*, 358–61.

Calvete describes the spectacular events that followed the service in the cathedral. As darkness fell, two great wheels of fireworks shaped like spinning stars were set into motion on top of a snow-capped mountain on one side of the city. As the wheels spun faster and faster, diverse shapes and figures appeared in the center. This display was answered by a third volley of fireworks from a steep precipice on the other side of town. The smokes and lights continued for almost an hour and a half, until it seemed that all the mountains were on fire.[53] The mysterious castle in the piazza remained dormant, however, awaiting the next round of festivities.

The following evening, a strange combat was enacted in the main square. An artillery barrage from the castle announced the beginning of the spectacle, which was answered by a thunder of guns from the palace and other parts of the city. Suddenly the gates of the castle sprang open. Four centaurs and a squad of soldiers dressed like Turks issued from the interior and made a turn around the castle. Then, four giants dressed as fearsome savages emerged from a cave at the opposite end of the piazza. According to Calvete, the cave represented hell. A colossal figure of Hercules was placed near the entrance, dragging Cerberus from the underworld on a giant chain. Next, eight men-at-arms entered from another side of the square. Each bore a helmet on his head, with a crest in the form of Hercules strangling the Nemean lion. The lions spouted sparks and tongues of flame from their mouths, though Calvete is at a loss to explain this marvel. The men were armed with hollow pikes filled with gunpowder, which shot sparks like thunderbolts over the heads of the crowd. The men-at-arms now took a turn about the castle and battle was joined with the giants of the cave, who were armed with fire-spitting trumpets. But just as the giants were about to be overcome, the centaurs galloped from the castle to their aid, each armed with a flaming lance. The four centaurs clashed with four of the men-at-arms, while the others struggled to keep the giants at bay. At the end of the combat, the first of three wheels of fireworks set on the corners of the castle was set aflame, showering the piazza with a cascade of lights.[54]

The combats continued on into the night. The men-at-arms now assaulted the castle of the centaurs, who defended with javelins and fire-arrows. A third and final combat had the giants attacking the besiegers. At the end of each round, the two remaining wheels on the mountains were lit.

The next day, on Sunday afternoon, a combat at the barriers took place in the piazza. Following a banquet and dance, the prince and his

[53]Calvete de Estrella, *Felicíssimo viaje*, 1:134.

[54]Calvete's description of the castle is unclear at this point. He describes the plan as *cuadrado* ("squared"), but says that the wheels were placed *a las tres esquinas dél* ("on the three corners of it"). Mariani, *Trento con il Sacro Concilio et altri*, 134–35.

retinue descended to watch the tournament. The four challengers entered in order wearing shining armor, with crests on their helmets in the form of phoenixes burning in flames. This was the device of the Cardinal of Trent, and was accompanied by the motto "Vt Vivam" (That You Might Live). The combatants precessed around the field, preceded by halberdiers with gleaming weapons. Then the comers arrived, wearing various liveries. A volley of guns began the combat, which proceeded quickly from pikes to swords. The comers were defeated and retired, and the challengers crossed the field to the noise of tambors, fifes, and trumpets. Seeing that no other comers arose, the challengers returned to their stockade. Suddenly, the four centaurs who had defended the mysterious castle the night before burst onto the scene, accompanied by many warlike persons dressed as Turks. All bore targets and maces of iron, and one great centaur carried a lance in his hand. They entered the castle, which in addition to the three firewheels now bore a colossal pomegranate on the summit of the tower.

A second night of fantastic combats now began. This time, the centaur who bore the flaming lance fought a malformed and hideous giant. The giant was killed, but before the centaur and his army could return to their castle, a host of devils jumped from the infernal cave. Some devils dragged out an ass, which spouted rays of fire from its nostrils, ears, and behind. The ass bore a mask on its head, surrounded by a marvelous fire. The horns of the devils and their weapons also spouted flames. The devils tried to load the body of the giant onto the ass, but now a huge and frightening serpent emerged from the castle. The serpent had vast wings, each carrying five fires. Above the serpent was mounted a disk or garland, surrounded with flames, and thunderbolts spouted from its mouth and tail. The serpent tried to bear away the body of the giant and battle was joined. Eventually the serpent was driven off and the devils returned to the cave with the body of the giant. Calvete remarks that the whole spectacle seemed of diabolic rather than human invention, reminding him of a vision of hell.[55]

Then, fifty arquebusiers who had lain in ambush sallied forward with banners flying and laid siege to the castle. The tambors sounded the charge and an even more furious battle began. The Turks and centaurs defended the castle valiantly, but eventually the gunners seized the castle and raised their banner on the ramparts. Finally, the new castellan emerged from the castle. With a burning mace in his hand, he ran towards the mouth of hell. Incendiary devices were placed close together in the entrance, and when the castellan touched the first bomb with his torch, explosions engulfed the cave. The three heads of Cerberus spouted fire, and Hercules menaced the dog with a flaming club. The

---

[55]Mariani, *Trento con il Sacro Concilio et altri*, 139.

pomegranate atop the castle was also ignited and burst asunder, showering the onlookers with sparks like so many seeds. At the close of the
festival, the soldiers discharged their guns in the air, and retired to their
quarters. A dance and German-style masquerades followed the spectacle,
lasting until dawn. The cardinal entertained Philip for the rest of the
following day, and the prince departed the next morning.

Martial festivals held by the church placed a greater emphasis on
religious symbolism than their secular counterparts. The spectacles held
for Prince Philip at Trent were doubtless laden with complex allegorical
meanings, though the descriptive nature of Calvete's account makes their
interpretation elusive. The forms of the temporary architecture and other
decorations at Trent were probably derived from the *Hypnertomachia
Poliphili*, an illustrated book about the migration of the soul from lower
to higher things.[56] The *Hypnertomachia* was based on the Hermetic doc-
trines of a shadowy ancient mystic known as Horapollo, and was first
published in Italy in the fifteenth century. The *Hypnertomachia* included
emblems and illustrations of fantastic architectural backdrops in pseudo-
antique style similar to the mock-ups erected for Philip's entry described
by Calvete. The Cave or Maw of Hell, filled with demons and other
damned souls, was a stock motif in northern painting of the late Middle
Ages and Renaissance, and commonly occurs in paintings showing the
Last Judgment. The imagery chosen for the tournaments at Trent is also
reminiscent of Dante's morally ordered vision of the cosmos begun in
the *Inferno*, which was still regarded by the church as an authoritative
vision of hell. A Dantean connection is also suggested by the inscriptions on the temporary arches erected for the scenery, which bore hieroglyphs praising the prince along with inscriptions lifted from Dante's
main source, the poems of Virgil.[57] Centaurs, giants, and other weird
monsters occur as fearsome denizens of hell in Virgil and in Dante's
Christian version of the Virgilian underworld. In western art, giants and
centaurs represented the forces of chaos and barbarism, and giants are
shown in this context elsewhere in Habsburg art.[58] Jupiter or Jove, king
of the Olympian gods and the heavenly father of Hercules, was a mythic
counterpart of the Habsburg emperor. The battle between Jove and the
giants for dominion over Olympus was likened to the emperor's struggles
against the Turks, Protestants, and other powerful forces that threatened
the unity of the Christian empire.[59]

[56]Jacquot, "Fête chevaleresque," 444.

[57]Checa, *Felipe II*, 76.

[58]The Giants are shown being cast down by Jupiter on the reverse of a large medal of
Charles V in armor by Leone Leoni, struck around 1550. Hill mentions the reverse of the Leoni
medal as a reference to the emperor's victory over the Protestants at Mühlberg; Hill and Pollard,
Renaissance Medals, 81.

[59]Tanner, *Aeneas*, 116. For an analysis of the monsters at Trent, see Pizarro-Gómez, *Arte y espectáculo en los viajes de Felipe II*, 23.

Prior to the council of Trent, King Francis I of France, encouraged by news of the emperor's defeat at Algiers, had formed alliances with both the Turks and the Protestant princes of Germany, orchestrating attacks on the Habsburg territories from all directions.[60] In the spectacles at Trent, the monsters probably represented the many enemies of Charles V, with the flaming trumpets of the giants symbolizing a kind of infernal fame. The winged serpent represented heresy, a more pervasive menace that threatened both the church and the Habsburg empire. Charles V's struggles against his enemies were also likened to the Labors of Hercules in Habsburg art, and Hercules imagery also appeared in the tournaments at Trent. The Hercules emblem worn by the men-at-arms who fought against the monsters and Turks probably indicated that the men represented Habsburg soldiers. At the end of the spectacle, Hercules' capture of Cerberus, the Hound of Hell, may have been a hopeful allusion to the final victory of the Catholic emperor. Finally, the number three is a recurring motif in Calvete's description of the festivals. Three was the number of the Holy Trinity and probably stood for the divine guidance of the reforming councils at Trent. The shape of the temporary castle erected at Trent was triangular, the standard form of an artillery bastion in the sixteenth century, though the fortress's triangular shape also suggests the Trinity, and thus by extension was a symbol of the guardianship of the Christian faith. The pomegranate surmounting the castle, as we have already seen, was a dual emblem representing both Spain and the triumph of Christianity.

Tournaments celebrating the courtship and marriage of Renaissance princes relied heavily on festive and chivalric imagery, as we have seen. The symbolism of the martial spectacles at Trent, however, addressed the increasingly complex relationship between church and state in the sixteenth century, and thus spoke to their audience in a different type of visual language. The tournaments at Trent, of course, were intended to appeal to the young prince initially on a far more immediate level. The hope was that through his enjoyment of the spectacle, Philip would eventually come to understand the Habsburg triumph as part of a higher plan.

After his reception at Trent, Philip headed directly north across the Alps. Philip rejoined his father in Brussels, who had scheduled a meeting of the Flemish estates to decide the matter of Philip's succession in the Low Countries prior to the imperial councils at Augsburg. A magnificent round of tournaments and combats at the barriers were held to celebrate the reunion of father and son.[61] On the Sunday after

---

[60]Tracy, *Emperor Charles V*, 7.

[61]The main source for the tournaments and other festivities attended by Philip in the north is Calvete de Estrella. A roster of the competitors and their prizes at Brussels in 1549 was also published by Bartholomaeus Clamorinus in 1591, with woodcuts illustrating scenes of jousts and

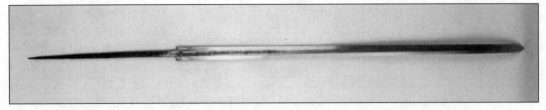

Figure 3.16 Italian, pontifical sword, ca. 1550. Madrid, Real Armería, G7. Used by permission.

Ascension Day, the emperor and the prince watched a procession in honor of Our Lady of the Sablon. This procession took place every year, winding through the main streets of Brussels.[62] The pageant began with a solemn parade of over two hundred men-at-arms and pages, followed by the leading guilds of the city and triumphal cars representing the holidays of Christ and the Virgin. The mood changed abruptly in the middle the procession, however: a cavalcade of grotesques appeared, including children dressed as wild animals, dancing bears, monkeys, and a boy playing an "organ" with live cats hidden in the sound box. The tails of the cats projected from holes in front of the box, and as the boy tugged on their tails, the cats yowled on different notes. A comedy was presented to Charles and Prince Philip afterwards.[63]

The tournaments and festivals held at Brussels were a prelude to serious political discussions between the emperor and the Estates of Flanders. Calvete claims that the Estates initially rejected the succession of Philip as overlord of Flanders.[64] During the discussions, however, a papal envoy arrived in Brussels and delivered a ceremonial sword and bonnet to the prince while he heard Mass in the cathedral.[65] This sword is preserved in the Royal Armory in Madrid, along with nine other pontifical weapons sent to the kings of Spain from the fifteenth through the seventeenth centuries (fig. 3.16). The sword sent to Philip is decorated with the arms of Paul III accompanied by golden images of the apostles Peter and Paul.[66] As tokens of the secular power theoretically granted to the state by the church and ultimately by God, the papal swords sent to

---

other combats. The woodcuts are generic, however, and no attempt was made to illustrate the actual events.

[62]There is a painting of a similar procession in the Place du Grand Sablon at Brussels by Anthonie Sallaert in the Galleria Sabauda, Turin, dated ca. 1620.

[63]Calvete de Estrella, *Felicíssimo viaje*, 1:204–11.

[64]Calvete de Estrella, *Felicíssimo viaje*, 1:211.

[65]Calvete de Estrella, *Felicíssimo viaje*, 1:211, 215.

[66]The Conde de Valencia identifies this sword as the one sent to Philip in Brussels in 1549. The sword is also mentioned in an inventory of Philip's swords and jewelry made in 1567, though the richly decorated hilt described in the inventory is now missing. The conde notes there were originally thirteen pontifical swords in the Royal Armory; Crooke y Navarrot, *Catálogo historico-descriptivo de la Real Armería*, 191.

Philip and his successors were potent reminders of the church's support of the western Habsburg monarchy. The majority of Flemings were still Catholic in 1549 and the chronicler Calvete gives the impression that this splendid token of papal approval shifted the balance in Philip's favor at a critical point in the negotiations. According to Calvete, further discussions confirmed Philip as the emperor's legal heir in Flanders.

With affairs in Brussels settled for the time being, the emperor and his son continued their tour of the Flemish cities.[67] Following the prince's entry into the emperor's hometown of Ghent, the prince was formally accepted as heir to the county of Flanders in a solemn ceremony in the abbey church of St. Peter. As Philip knelt to adore the cross, the abbot girt the prince's sword around his waist. After the ceremony, the king of arms and his heralds tossed gold and silver coins to the crowd. The obverse of the coins bore a nude figure of the prince, while on the reverse were the royal arms and an inscription in praise of virtue.[68] A commemorative medal by Leone Leoni bearing the same inscription on the reverse has survived, and can probably be associated with this period of Philip's travels (fig. 3.17). Leoni's medal shows Philip in a classical cuirass on the obverse, with an emblematic reverse depicting Hercules choosing Virtue over Vice.[69] Hercules was the classical hero most frequently associated with Charles V and his successors in Habsburg art, but Leoni's allegorical emblem also had religious implications to the Renaissance mind. The story of Hercules choosing virtue over vice (or duty over pleasure) is of ancient origin, but like other pre-Christian legends it had taken on a Christian meaning in earlier medieval and Renaissance art. To medieval Christians, the hero's battles against monsters and evil-doers essentially represented moral struggles, in which he counted on divine assistance. Hercules was also an Argonaut and one of the heroes who sailed in quest of the Golden Fleece, which was transformed in the late Middle Ages into a symbol of the Resurrection. Leoni's profile portrait of

Figure 3.17 Leone Leoni, portrait medal of Philip of Spain, ca. 1549. London, British Museum (A229-906-11-3-135). Used by permission.

---

[67]Calvete de Estrella, *Felicíssimo viaje*, 1:216.

[68]Calvete de Estrella, *Felicíssimo viaje*, 1:305. The inscription on the reverse reads "Colit Ardva Virtus." The sense of the inscription is basically, "Virtue lies in difficult things."

[69]Cano, "Leone y Pompeo Leoni, medallistas de la casa de Austria," 180–81. The story of Hercules at the Crossroads dates from antiquity, and is mentioned by Plato in *The Socratic Dialogues*.

Prince Philip in a classical cuirass duplicated the format of ancient imperial coins, and thus suggested the transfer of legitimate authority from the old empire to the new. By showing Hercules on the reverse, an ontological connection was established between Philip and the moral strength of the hero. Interestingly, Hercules was also believed to have founded several cities in Spain and Gaul, and was numbered among the mythical ancestors of the Spanish Habsburgs.

In November, news arrived from Rome of the death of Pope Paul III. The conclave to choose a new pontiff lasted until February 1550, when Giovanni Maria, Cardinal del Monte, was elected Pope Julius III. Julius hastily dispatched a brief reaffirming papal approval of Philip as imperial successor, hailing Philip as the foremost prince in all the world.

Prince Philip's marriage to Mary Tudor in 1554 was also arranged partly for religious reasons. Many hoped that, among other things, an alliance between the houses of Habsburg and Tudor would halt the spread of Protestantism in England. Initial plans to have Philip marry the Princess Elizabeth were dropped, due at least in part to Elizabeth's Protestant beliefs. As queen of England and a steadfast Catholic, Mary Tudor was settled upon as the better candidate. Philip viewed his journey to England as a holy crusade.[70] Several important Protestants were burned at the stake during Philip's stay, with the prince's full approval, though Charles had expressly warned his son against alienating the English with an excess of fanaticism.[71] As the new king of Spain, Philip visited Mary in England again in 1557, though only to ask for money and English troops for the war against France. On 10 August 1557, the king's Spanish and English troops defeated the French at the Battle of St. Quentin. The city was defended by Admiral Coligny, the future Huguenot and leader of the French Protestant cause. Philip was not present at the battle, though he rode into camp the next morning in glittering armor to inspect the prisoners and pay his respects to the wounded men. Philip did take part in the storming of the town after the battle. The king was unable to control his German mercenaries, however, and the surrender of the town turned into a brutal spectacle of fire, murder, and rape, quite unlike the poetic tournaments of Philip's youth. Philip is said to have found the scene profoundly distressing, but he wrote proudly to his father afterwards, informing him of his first military victory.[72]

In 1551, the armorer Wolf of Landshut completed an equestrian armor for war for Philip as prince of Spain (fig. 3.18). This armor, known as the "Burgundy-cross" armor, is covered with a repeating pattern

---

[70]Grierson, *Two Worlds*, 43.
[71]Grierson, *Two Worlds*, 47–48.
[72]Grierson, *Two Worlds*, 62.

Figure 3.18 Wolf of Landshut, armor of Philip II for man and horse ("Burgundy-cross" armor), 1550. Madrid, Real Armería, A263. Used by permission.

based on the St. Andrew's cross. The X-shaped cross of St. Andrew was one of the heraldic emblems of the house of Burgundy, which was part of Philip's northern inheritance and directly explains the use of this motif on Philip's armor. The cross of St. Andrew, however, was also a potent reminder of the spread of early Christianity in the north. St. Andrew brought Christianity to the Low Countries, and as defender of the northern Habsburg patrimony and crusader against the Protestants, Philip must have felt a special affinity with the Apostle of the North. Medieval crusaders, as Philip no doubt was aware, had worn the emblem of the holy cross over their armor. Philip owned dozens of armors and armor garnitures, but wears the Burgundy-cross armor almost exclusively in his portraits from the 1550s to the 1570s. Philip II chose the Burgundy-cross armor for his portrait by Antonis Mor in 1557, painted shortly after the Battle of St. Quentin, the king's first significant military victory in the North (fig. 3.19).[73] This painting was doubtless intended as a parallel to Titian's famous portrait of Charles V at Mühlberg. Philip is said to have found Titian's painterly style unsatisfactory, and the more precise approach of northern painters like Mor may have appealed to him. Like Charles, Philip is shown wearing his favorite armor, quite probably the same one he wore at the storming of St. Quentin. Philip, however, is shown standing, even though he wears a half-armor with a lance rest and high boots for light cavalry use. The image of the Virgin appears again on Philip's breastplate. The king holds a plain commander's baton in his hand and the pendant of the Golden Fleece hangs from his neck on a soft silk band.

As king of Spain, Philip's commitment to support the Catholic Church deepened on all fronts. In the Americas, it was clear that the evangelization of the Indians was incomplete and Philip strongly supported the spread of Christianity by force of arms in Chile, Peru, northern Mexico, and the Philippines. At home in Spain, Philip was faced with a rebellion of the Moriscos in 1568, which ended in the expulsion of the Moriscos from Granada and their forced resettlement in other parts of Spain. By far the most serious problem faced by the Spanish crown, however, was the revolt of the Protestants in the Netherlands, which was still unresolved at the beginning of the seventeenth century. The Turks also posed a serious threat to Spanish naval power in the Mediterranean Sea. Decisive blows were struck against the Ottomans at Malta in 1565 and at Lepanto in 1571. A combined Spanish and Italian fleet led by Philip's half-brother Don Juan of Austria defeated the Turkish navy in the Battle of Lepanto, effectively closing the door against Ottoman expansion into the western Mediterranean. Significantly, Don Juan's flagship was named *Argo*, the ship of the heroes of the Golden Fleece.[74] The triumph of the Christian fleet was celebrated in a painting by Titian from around 1571 (fig. 3.20). Although Philip was not present at the actual battle, he is shown in armor as the symbolic leader of the Christian fleet, offering his son in thanks to God for his victory while a captive Turk lies before him. Philip raises his son in a gesture that recalls the elevation of the host at Mass, casting the king in a role that is both military and sacerdotal.[75] Philip's ceaseless efforts

[73]Philip is shown wearing the same armor again in a portrait by Sofonisba Anguissola from about 1570.
[74]Tanner, *Aeneas*, esp. 5.
[75]Tanner, *Aeneas*, 217.

Figure 3.19 Anthonis Mor, *Portrait of Philip II*, 1557. Oil on panel, El Escorial. Used by permission.

Figure 3.20 Titian, *Allegory,* after 1571. Oil on canvas, Madrid, Museo del Prado (431). Used by permission.

against paganism, heresy, and Islam from 1568 to 1572 have been called the Years of Crusade.[76]

The crusading ideals of Habsburg Spain are summed up in the decoration on a magnificent pageant shield presumably made for Philip II sometime in the late sixteenth century (fig. 3.21).[77] This object is among the most remarkable in the collections of the royal house of Spain. The shield is an *adarga* or light-cavalry shield of typical Iberian

[76]Parker, *Philip II,* 96–116.
[77]Crooke y Navarrot, *Catálogo histórico-descriptivo de la Real Armería,* 161–63.

Figure 3.21 Mexican, feather shield of Philip II, after 1571. Madrid, Real Armería, D88. Used by permission.

type, though the decoration in this case is a mosaic of tiny multicolored feathers from tropical birds. This type of decoration was a specialty of the Amantecas of Mexico, whose featherwork skills were exploited by the Aztecs and later by the Spanish-colonial rulers of New Spain. Shields decorated with brightly colored feathers called *chimallis* were used in war by the Aztecs, and trophies of Indian feather shields and armor are mentioned in the inventories of Charles V and Philip II. Philip's feather shield was doubtless designed with these shields in mind, though the illustrations in this case represent important events from Spanish history. Beginning at upper left are shown four major victories of Christian

Spain over Islam: the defeat of the Almohads by Alfonso VIII, the conquest of Granada by the Catholic Monarchs, the victory of Charles V at Tunis, and the Battle of Lepanto. In the frame on the lower right, Don Juan of Austria is shown offering palms of victory to Philip II, who is shown seated on a throne of colossal proportions straddling the map of eastern Europe. The various scenes on the shield are tied together by the image in the central medallion, an emblem showing two cranes wearing royal crowns defeating a winged reptile. The emblem was lifted from a book by Piero Valeriano, and alludes to the struggle against evil by the servants of God, with the winged serpent representing heresy.[78] The emblem leaves no doubt as to the sacred duty of the Habsburg dynasty and elevates the military triumphs of Spain to a cosmic level. The cranes might refer to Charles V and Philip II, or perhaps to Philip II and his own son Philip III, as the inscription in the banderole suggests only one hope remains to advanced old age.[79] The emblem on Philip's feather shield resembles the *imprese* on tournament shields from the fifteenth and sixteenth centuries, which were likewise accompanied by brief inscriptions (often cryptic), though it seems unlikely that the delicate decoration on this particular shield would have been risked in tournament combat. Whatever the original purpose of the shield, it was a splendid diplomatic gift from America to the King of Two Worlds.

The program of tournaments attended by an older Philip II also alluded to the king's struggles against the enemies of Christendom. Mock assaults and a *naumachia*, or sea battle, representing the Siege of Malta (raised by the arrival of the Spanish fleet), greeted the king at Valencia in 1586. Near the end of his life, Philip had himself shown at prayer with his family in the funerary sculpture by Pompeo Leoni in the chapel of San Lorenzo in the Escorial. Once again, Philip is wearing the Burgundy-cross armor. In Leoni's funerary sculpture, the context of the armor is both Christian and dynastic. The king kneels reverently at the head of his family with his gaze directed at the high altar, awaiting Judgment Day as a soldier of the cross.[80]

[78]Checa, *Felipe II*, 173. For more on Habsburg emblems, see Pizarro Gómez, *Arte y espectáculo en los viajes de Felipe II: La iconografía*, 89-145. A pair of cranes standing over a serpent was also a symbol of Concord; ibid., 139.

[79]The inscription reads "Serae Spes Una Senectae."

[80]Real armors and pieces of armor were used in the funeral processions of sixteenth-century nobles; Kavaler, "Being the Count of Nassau," 32-33.

Chapter 4

THE EMPIRE REBORN

The Prince as Heir Apparent and Divine Deliverer

THE YEAR 1500 WAS A PORTENTOUS ONE for Christendom. For many, the midpoint of the millennium marked the beginning of the last days described in the book of Revelation, culminating in Christ's return and the end of the world. The awesome event would be preceded by portents and signs, which could be correctly interpreted by those who understood the divine mysteries. Among these signs would be the appearance of the Last World Emperor, the Christian successor of Caesar Augustus and the last descendant of Aeneas, who would arise before the Apocalypse and crush the forces of the Antichrist. Then the hosts of the Christian Caesar would reenter Jerusalem, and the emperor would fall to his knees and adore the Holy Cross in the sepulcher of Christ. The reign of the new Augustus would usher in a second golden age, an era of peace and prosperity immediately preceding the end of days. Little of this was taken verbatim from the Bible, of course, but was part of the vast corpus of medieval prophecy, saintly visions, and folklore that had accumulated around the writings of the apostles.[1] For most people, the sixteenth century remained an age primarily of belief, and lack of historical credibility did little to slow the spread of an attractive idea.

---

[1] Marie Tanner treats the legend of the Last World Emperor at length in her study of the imperial myth of the Habsburgs. Though difficult to pin down historically, the idea of the apotheosis of the Christian emperor took shape during the reign of Theodosius in the writings of Lactantius and Prudentius, which were based in turn on the prophecies of the Tiburtine Sybil. Tanner, *Aeneas*, esp. 121.

In an effort to explain an increasingly complex world, astrologers and prognosticators searched the heavens and combed ancient history for signs charting the course of events. Charles of Ghent was born in 1500, a year fraught with occult possibilities. Charles's birth sign, moreover, was Capricorn, the same as that of Augustus. Court genealogists, meanwhile, traced the Habsburg emperor's descent from Charlemagne to the mythic heroes of Troy, and through the house of David all the way back to Noah and Adam.[2] The early sixteenth century was the age of Machiavelli, but at the same time was obsessed with legitimacy and the divine right of princes. Charles V and his successor, Philip II, stood at a pivotal point in the development of a new type of royal persona in which individual achievements were matched with heavenly destiny. The Habsburg formula for sacred monarchy proved uniquely effective, and was imitated and improved upon by the rulers of Christian Europe for the next two hundred years.

The need for a compelling new imperial identity was especially urgent in the years following the death of Emperor Maximilian I in 1519. Maximilian had already presented himself as a virtuous ruler protected by God in his biography *Der Weiss Kunig* (The White King) and in the *Theuerdank*, a semiautobiographical tale in which a good young knight is tested by a series of moral adventures.[3] As defenders of the eastern marches against the Turks, the archdukes of Austria traditionally held the title of emperor, but the Holy Roman Empire was still in theory an elective monarchy and the young King Francis I of France also claimed the imperial title. Charles of Ghent, the emperor's grandson and now king of Spain, was only able to secure his election as Holy Roman Emperor with a massive payoff to the German princes, borrowed from the Fugger bank in Augsburg. The battle between Habsburg and Valois had begun in Italy in 1494 and was not resolved until the Battle of Pavia in 1525, a decisive victory for imperial troops that resulted in the capture of the French king. Charles's troubles, however, were far from over. In addition to the European claimants to the imperial title, the Ottoman sultans, as rulers of Istanbul (ancient Constantinople), were also technically Roman emperors. The new sultan, Suleiman the Magnificent, clearly had imperial ambitions in the West.[4]

Portraits of Charles from this period abound—in fact, there are probably more surviving portraits of Charles V than any other Renaissance monarch (with the possible exception of Elizabeth I). These portraits were not simply likenesses of the emperor, but were carefully

---

[2]Tanner, *Aeneas*, 113.

[3]Hale, *Artists and Warfare in the Renaissance*, 98.

[4]The Ottoman-Habsburg rivalry is treated at greater length in Necipoglu, "Suleyman the Magnificent and the Representation of Power."

Figure 4.1 German, *Emperor Charles V as a Boy*, ca. 1515. Oil or tempera on panel. Vienna, Kunsthistorisches Museum, Gemäldegalerie (PG5618). Used by permission.

crafted presentations of the imperial persona, designed to appeal to an audience already familiar with the visual rhetoric of sacred empire. Many of these portraits show Charles in knightly armor, including an early portrait of Charles as adolescent archduke (fig. 4.1). In this portrait, Charles is shown wearing a full suit of armor in the rippled and fluted Maximilian style. The earliest examples of armor in this style are from the imperial workshops and were often sent as gifts to allied princes. The armor shown in this painting may be one of the suits ordered for

Charles by his grandfather Maximilian from Augsburg in 1512–14.[5] In his right hand, Charles raises a long sword held point upwards. A cross-shaped sword or scepter was part of the standard trappings of imperial authority in Western art and swords appear in this context in Carolingian and Ottonian manuscripts from as early as the ninth century. In medieval political theory, the emperor's sword represented the second of two swords ordained by God to dispense justice and defend his people—the Sword of the Church and the Sword of State. Writing in the twelfth century, Etienne de Fougères says Christ granted two swords to Peter, one for the clergy and the other for the Christian knight.[6] Charles's pose with upraised sword also recalls medieval and Renaissance illustrations of the Nine Worthies, a select group of historical personages whose chivalry and moral conduct were considered exemplary.[7] The roster of Nine Worthies included such strange bedfellows as Charlemagne, King David, and Hector of Troy, traditionally shown armed and holding the tokens of their office. As leader of Christian knights and defender of the imperial peace, Char-lemagne was the prototype and model for the later Holy Roman Emperors.

Figure 4.2 Albrecht Dürer, *Charlemagne*, 1512–13. Oil or tempra on panel. Vienna, Kunsthistorisches Museum, Treasury (GG2771). Used by permission.

The portrait of young Charles V holding a sword echoes the pose of his famous namesake, to whom he was frequently compared in contemporary literature (fig. 4.2).[8] Though not yet emperor, Charles is shown in

---

[5]Campbell, *Renaissance Portraits*, 234n254.

[6]Oakeshott, *Archaeology of Weapons*, 184–85.

[7]The Nine Worthies are the subject of a series of sculptures in Cologne Cathedral. Henry VIII once had himself illustrated as the Tenth Worthy; Strong, *Art and Power*, 15.

[8]For more on Charles V as the second Charlemagne, see Yates, "Charles Quint et l'idée d'empire," 57–62 and esp. 80–88, 97. Ariosto's fantastic tales of chivalry, set in the age of Charle-magne, were dedicated to Charles V.

Figure 4.3 Colman Helmschmied, armor of Charles V ("KD" garniture), 1515–25. Madrid, Real Armería, A19. Used by permission.

his early portraits with an iconography that clearly looks forward to an imperial destiny.

Actual armors, of course, were made for Charles as Duke of Burgundy and Count of Flanders; a fine boy's tonlet armor now in the Waffensammlung, Vienna, was made by the imperial armorer, Konrad Seusenhofer. The decoration on this armor, however, is limited to the heraldic badges of the house of Burgundy, with no allusions to the imperial office. The beginnings of an imperial identity are hinted at in the decoration of an armor garniture made for Charles sometime between 1515 and 1525, years in which first Maximilian and then Charles V were at war with the king of France. This armor, known as the KD garniture for the initials embossed on the left pauldron of the harness for war, was probably made by the imperial armorer, Colman Helmschmied of Augsburg (fig. 4.3). The initials "KD" are puzzling, but could stand for Karolus Dux, Charles's title as the Duke of Burgundy.[9] The initials, however, could also stand for Karolus Divus or Divine Charles, one the accolades later applied to Charles V as Holy Roman Emperor.[10] Still more interesting are the small etched designs on a jousting shield made to accompany the armor (fig. 4.4). The etching is attributed to Daniel Hopfer, a German artist known to have decorated armors made by the Helmschmieds. The etched decoration on Renaissance armor is often quite generic, but the decoration on this shield is more illustrative, showing an eaglet surrounded by cocks and cranes, all in aggressive postures. Birds of various kinds were a common motif in emblem books published in the Renaissance, and eagles and cranes in particular were associated with the Habsburg dynasty. As the bird of Jove, the eagle had been a symbol of the Roman Empire since ancient times, and was

---

[9]This armor may be the same one shown in the great seal of the Counts of Flanders from 1515, on which Charles's official titles at that date are listed; Crooke y Navarrot, *Catálogo historico-descriptivo de la Real Armería,* 16–21.

[10]Godoy, "Royal Armory," 124.

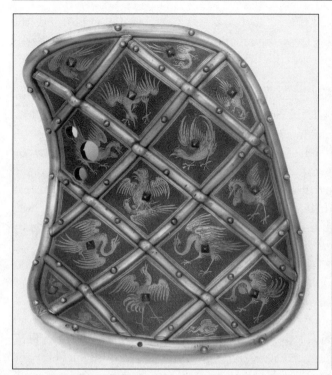

Figure 4.4 Colman Helmschmied, jousting shield with birds, 1515–25. Madrid, Real Armería, A27. Used by permission.

Figure 4.5 Matteus Frauenpreis, shield of Francis I, ca. 1525. Madrid, Real Armería, M6. Used by permission.

a standard part of the imperial coat of arms in the Middle Ages and Renaissance. The fighting cock, on the other hand, was traditionally associated with France. The eaglet on Charles's shield is shown dominating a cock-chick, an allusion, perhaps, to the hopeful outcome of the contest between the young Habsburg and Valois rulers. The compliment was returned on an unusual embossed shield in Turco-Hungarian style made for a light cavalryman, said to have belonged to Francis I, and part of the trophy of arms from the Battle of Pavia now in the Royal Armory in Madrid (fig. 4.5).[11] Here the Gallic cock chases a German soldier, who flees the battlefield with a comic expression of terror.

Charles's victory over France in northern Italy opened the way to Rome. Control of the papacy did not come so easily, however, and eventually imperial troops appeared before the walls of the Eternal City. Against the emperor's wishes, Rome was plundered by his unpaid German mercenaries in 1527. Rome was still recovering from the disaster

[11]Crooke y Navarrot, *Catálogo historico-descriptivo de la Real Armería*, 359. The shield is atypical in several respects. Wing-shaped shields like this were used by light cavalry in the Balkans and eastern Europe. At the Battle of Marignano in 1515, the king of France employed mercenary cavalry from the Balkans known as Stradiots against imperial troops.

when Charles entered Italy for his coronation by the pope, and the site of the ceremonies was diplomatically removed to Bologna. Charles already held the imperial title in Germany, but in accordance with a long-standing tradition he had also to secure the approval of the church and an official coronation by the pope. Following the first withdrawal of the Turks from Vienna, the emperor was received by Clement VII in Bologna in November of 1529, and prepared for his imperial coronation. Charles made a triumphal entry into the city on horseback, dressed in full armor and surrounded by his knights and infantry. The emperor was met at the Porta San Felice by twenty cardinals and four hundred soldiers of the papal guard. The emperor was preceded by three hundred light horsemen, followed by Spanish grandees bearing banners and three hundred knights in armor with red plumes on their helmets. Ten huge cannons mounted on their trunnions followed the knights, escorted by fourteen companies of German *landsknechts* playing martial music, their banners rippling in the wind. More squadrons followed this, drawn from all over the emperor's dominions to emphasize the international scope of his authority. Then the emperor himself arrived, with a golden crest on his helmet and surrounded by his imperial bodyguard, with four armored knights walking beside him to hold his parasol. Before the gateway were dancing putti and a triumph of Bacchus and Neptune, showing that the emperor's sway extended over both land and sea. The gate itself was decorated with medallions of Caesar, Augustus, Trajan, and Vespasian, along with equestrian statues of Furius Camillus, Scipio Africanus, and other illustrious Romans whose generalship protected the boundaries of the ancient empire. The emperor's route took him along a triumphal way decorated with arches in the antique style, whose inscriptions described the emperor's earthly role in relation to the pope.[12]

Several visual records of Charles's entry have survived, the most interesting being a series of prints now in the Albertina in Vienna. The emperor is shown in full armor on horseback and surrounded by a crowd of diminutive pages, whose tiny scale in relation to Charles emphasizes the importance of the imperial majesty. Charles's helmet is surmounted by the Roman eagle and in his right hand the emperor raises a mace or scepter, an ancient symbol of absolute authority that has its origins in the distant art of Old Kingdom Egypt. The emperor is preceded by his men-at-arms, led by the Marquis of Astorga, whose horse is fitted with a set of ram's horns like the horns on the real armor made for Charles's horse around the time of his coronation, an allusion to the Knights of the Golden Fleece who served the emperor (fig. 4.6).

[12]Strong, *Splendor at Court*, 86–87.

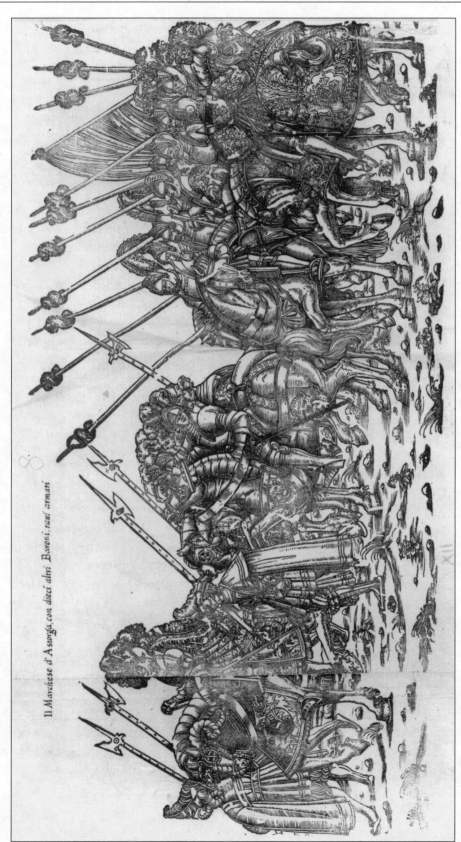

Figure 4.6 Venetian, print from series, *Entry of Charles V into Bologna*, 1529. Vienna, Albertina, GS. Used by permission.

Charles V was finally crowned Holy Roman Emperor by Pope Clement VII in Bologna in a solemn ceremony in February 1530. Despite the tense atmosphere following the sack of Rome, martial imagery and tournaments figured prominently in the emperor's meetings with the pope. Tournaments were held in Bologna following the imperial entry in 1529 to celebrate the emperor's arrival and the birth of his nephew, though these tournaments are not described in detail. In January of the following year more festivities, including tournaments, were held to celebrate the New Year and news of the surrender of Florence to imperial troops.[13] More tournaments were held for the emperor's visit to Mantua the same year, and possibly upon his second visit to the city two years later, though again few details about these events survive.[14] *Apparati* erected by Giulio Romano at Mantua emphasized the heavenly origins of the emperor's power and presented Europe as a single entity united by the Christian faith, controlled and defended by the emperor.[15]

Between 1519 and 1533, Spanish conquistadors claimed a new world in the Americas in the name of Charles V. Flocks of converts were brought to Christianity by the efforts of the monastic orders in Mexico and Peru. In the Old World, the rival faith of Islam, though unconquered, was held at bay until the middle of the century by the emperor's victories at Vienna and Tunis. According to the legend of the Last World Emperor, in the last days the word of Christ would spread to all corners of the globe and it seemed the prophecies were on the verge of being fulfilled.[16] Portraits of the emperor at the height of his power celebrated Charles V as lord of the world, and his image appears in this context on arms and armor made for him as well.

The apotheosis of Charles V is the subject of an embossed pageant shield representing the emperor's victories on land and sea (fig. 4.7). The artist is unknown, though the style and subject are certainly Italian. Charles stands in the prow of a Roman galley, wearing a muscled cuirass in the antique style. The emperor raises a battle standard surmounted by the imperial eagle, whose double heads look both east and west. Charles is crowned with laurel by a winged figure of Victory, who points to the west while Fame kneels before him, inscribing the emperor's motto, "Plus Ultra" (More Beyond), on an oval shield. The emperor's motto was part of his personal device, which showed the Pillars of Hercules and referred to the extension of imperial authority to a wider world than was known to the ancient Greeks and Romans, who believed the world ended at Gibraltar. The extension of the emperor's authority and the bringing of the Christian faith to new lands beyond

---

[13]Jacquot, "Fête chevaleresque," 22–23.
[14]Amadeo Belluzi, "Carlo V a Mantova e Milano," 47.
[15]Amadeo Belluzi, "Carlo V a Mantova e Milano," 47–48, 50.
[16]Tanner, *Aeneas.*

Figure 4.7 Italian, shield of Charles V, after 1535. Madrid, Real Armería, D63. Used by permission.

the sea were part of the legend of the Last World Emperor, whose reign directly preceded the second coming of Christ.[17] The emperor's galley sails past figures of a female captive representing Africa, bound before a pillar bearing the turban of the Turk, and a reclining river god representing the River Guadalquivir.[18] The motif of the bound captive subdued by the majesty of Caesar is an ancient one, and was adapted from reliefs celebrating imperial victories found on Roman triumphal arches.[19] Alongside the galley strides the figure of Hercules with his columns, while Neptune stands guard with his trident. The shield is bounded by cherubs and swags bearing ripe fruit, symbols of abundance and plenty, with the wonder-working talisman of the Golden Fleece at the top of

---

[17]Yates, *Astraea*, 23.

[18]Crooke y Navarrot, *Catálogo historico-descriptivo de la Real Armería*, 153.

[19]Drawings of military trophies from the Arch of Diocletian were made by Jacopo Ripanda in the early sixteenth century; Pyhrr and Godoy, *Heroic Armor*, 11.

the scene. The visual message of the shield seems to be that the emperor, guided by Neptune, sails past Africa and beyond the Pillars of Hercules, while the hero raises his pillars to plant them again on new and distant shores. The conquest of the New World by the second Augustus heralds the return of the Age of Gold and the fulfillment of divine prophecy: the world united under one emperor in Christ. The imagery on the shield repeats the iconography revealed to Charles V at his triumphal entry into Naples in 1535, while hinting that a still more glorious destiny awaits the emperor in the West.

Images of the emperor as *renovator imperii* were echoed in the rhetoric employed at the triumphs and fêtes held for Charles V at the crescendo of his power. By the middle of the sixteenth century, the visual language of courtly festival had become fairly standardized across Europe. The classical topoi of the ruler ordained by heaven reappeared in their antique guises at the Italian entries of Charles V from 1529 to 1543. At the emperor's entry into Milan in 1541, heroic statues of Hercules and Jason bearing the Golden Fleece were erected on the bridge at the Porta Ticinese, accompanied by inscriptions hailing Charles as the restorer of the Golden Age. The ceremonial progress of the emperor was described in verse by Albicante, who claims that Charles was accompanied by a thousand Spanish cavaliers, all in polished armor and magnificent surcoats.[20] Albicante explains the figures on the arches before the gate:

> Portò Giasone à Colchi il vello d'oro
> Et Carlo rinova l'età de l'oro[21]

> [Jason carried from Colchis the Golden Fleece
> And Charles renews the Age of Gold]

The inscription echoes Virgil's *Aeneid*, in which Augustus's reign is prophesied to bring back the mythical Golden Age, in which humankind lived in peace and prosperity in harmony with the gods.[22] Another pair of statues showed Jupiter and armed Mars accompanied by Capricorn, the birth sign of Augustus and Charles, with an inscription granting Charles a kingdom without end.[23] A triumphal arch was placed in the center of town at the entry to the piazza; it bore a colossal equestrian figure of the emperor in armor trampling figures dressed as Africa, the Turk, and an American Indian (fig. 4.8). The image of the Roman emperor on horseback subduing foreign nations was a mainstay of later Roman art and was revived by Leonardo da Vinci for his colossal equestrian portrait of Francesco Sforza, which, though never finished, was

---

[20]Albicante, *Trattato del'intrar in Milano di Carlo V*, 10.
[21]Albicante, *Trattato del'intrar in Milano di Carlo V*, 20–23.
[22]Strong, *Splendor at Court*, 79.
[23]Albicante, *Trattato del'intrar in Milano di Carlo V*, 20–23.

Figure 4.8 Italian, arch of Charles V at Milan, 1541. Woodcut, reproduced from Giovanni Alberto Albicante, *Trattato del'intrar in Milano, di Carlo V.C. sempre Aug. con le proprie figure de li archi...* (Milan: Apud Andream Calvum, 1541), fol. F4v. Reproduced by permission of University of Illinois at Champagne–Urbana Library.

planned to embellish the ducal palace at Milan. Inscriptions en route to the piazza praised Charles for the expulsion of Islam from the Mediterranean and the extension of the Christian empire into Peru. The final arch, erected in front of the cathedral, bore effigies of the emperor's Spanish and Burgundian ancestors. Inscriptions over the portal lauded Charles's auspicious peace, the tranquility of the church, and the liberty of Christendom.[24] Albicante notes the *apparati* for Charles's entry at Milan were designed by Giulio Romano, who made sketches of the monuments, though these have not survived.[25] Tournaments were held after the emperor's entry, though regrettably Albicante does not describe them.

The themes of sacred empire and the prince as divine deliverer were repeated in the triumphal entries and tournaments held on Prince Philip's grand tour in 1548–51, though with definite modulations. The stage was set at Genoa, where Charles himself had entered Italy in 1529 and 1533. The emperor's son, however, was welcomed with a dual imagery combining the *topoi* of a global Christian empire with the idea of succession. Philip's galley sailed for Genoa from the port of Barcelona on 18 October 1548. The prince was received in state at Genoa by the Doria and other noble families of the city. The Republic of Genoa was, for all practical purposes, a vassal state of the empire, ruled by the powerful Doria family, who held the position of admiral of the imperial fleet. Andrea Doria previously had received the emperor himself and now prepared to receive the imperial heir.[26] The decorations for the prince's entry into Genoa included a statue of a giant representing Liberty and a triumphal arch surmounted by a colossal equestrian statue of Philip flanked by Jupiter and Apollo. Encomia inscribed on the archway hailed the prince as the worthy successor of a mighty father whose conquests ranged from Africa to the New World.

Following his entry, Philip was lodged in the Fassolo palace, probably in the same rooms where Charles had stayed during his own visits to Genoa. A marvelous edifice like a triumphal arch with two gates was erected before the main portal of the palace. The arch was decorated with figures of Jupiter and Neptune (lords of the land and sea), and stories alluding to the virtue of the young prince.[27] Philip's stay in Genoa, however, was marred by rioting following a dispute between Genoese and Spanish troops quartered in the city.[28] No tournaments were held at Genoa to mark the prince's visit, perhaps out of fear of further outbreaks of violence.

---

[24]Albicante, *Trattato del'intrar in Milano di Carlo V*, 22–55.

[25]Mitchell, *Italian Civic Pageantry in the High Renaissance*, 89–91.

[26]Gorse, "Between Empire and Republic," 194–99.

[27]Calvete de Estrella, *Felicíssimo viaje*, 1:32–46. For an overview and analysis of the ephemeral art on Philip's journey, see also Checa, *Felipe II*, 70–87.

[28]The atmosphere in Genoa was already tense following the Fieschi revolt and questions concerning the loyalty of the Doria to the Habsburgs; Gorse, "Genoa," 200, 202.

The next major stop on Philip's itinerary was Milan. Philip arrived at the gates of the city on 20 December 1548. A triumphal entry, tournaments, plays, banquets, and masques were planned for his visit. Alberto de' Nobili, an eyewitness to the festivities, published a concise account of Philip's entry shortly after the events. De' Nobili glosses over the tournaments, but mentions colossal figures armed in cuirasses placed on the bridge and over the entryway of the triumphal arch at the Porta Ticinese. According to Alberto, the figures on the bridge represented Milan and the house of Austria.[29] The poet Albicante was also on hand and mentions *prospettive* erected before the façade of the cathedral depicting an orb sustained by Hercules and Atlas,[30] a trope referring to the devolution of the imperial authority from father to son that would be repeated at other stops on Philip's journey. On the third day of Christmas, Philip visited the castle, where he was greeted by an honorary salvo of artillery from the walls.

At the time of Philip's visit, Milan was ruled by a Spanish governor, who maintained a garrison of Spanish soldiers in the city. The events at Milan included a tournament on foot of Spanish soldiers, which took place in the palace square outside the fortress late in the afternoon on St. Silvester's Day. The courtyard was so packed with spectators that streets, doorways, and windows were blocked. The soldiers entered to the music of fifes and drums, and took up their places on opposite sides of the square. The skirmish began with salvos of artillery from small field guns and volleys from the arquebusiers. Combat was joined with pikes and swords, which was so fierce that a number of weapons were broken. The field marshall, however, maintained such good order that no one was hurt and the squadrons left the field in the same order they had entered. On 4 January 1549, Philip himself took part in a royal tournament on foot at the barriers. The prince's band was to fight the Duke of Sessa and his retainers. This combat was to be held indoors, in the same chamber where the banquet was held. The companies armed in the palace apartments, placed themselves in order, and descended to the great hall with their pikes on their shoulders. Philip led the teams, accompanied by four drummers and a pair of fifers. His team was dressed in jackets and hose of white velvet, with white plumes. Four seconds followed them, bearing small lances or *assegais* with white tassels. The duke of Sessa's team was all in white as well,

---

[29]De' Nobili, *La trionfale intrata del serenissimo prence de Spagna*. A brief account of Philip's visit to Milan was also published by Bugati, who essentially paraphrases de' Nobili, though Bugati notes that the celebrations for Philip, while memorable, were not as lavish as those for Charles V on his own entry into the city in 1541; Bugati, *Historia universale di M. Gaspare Bugati Milanese*, 960. A poetic account of Philip's entry and the tournaments that followed was penned by Giovanni Albicante around 1556; Albicante, *Trattato del'intrar in Milano di Carlo V*.

[30]Albicante, *Trattato del'intrar in Milano di Carlo V*.

but with white and red plumes. The fighters passed before the Princess of Malfetto to do her honor, then began the combat. After the pikes were broken, the contestants switched to swords. The chronicler notes that Philip fought especially well in the tournament, though he neglects to mention the winner of the contest.[31] The special emphasis placed on combats on foot in the tournaments at Milan reflected the growing importance of infantry on sixteenth-century battlefields. Spanish and German infantry armed with pike, sword, and shot were integral parts of the imperial armies fielded by Charles V, winning victories from Italy to the New World. Spanish infantry, in fact, were compared by Renaissance writers to the famous legions of Rome. Infantry formations were the backbone of Charles's armies and as the imperial heir, it was important for Philip to show himself an effective commander of the Spanish foot soldiers at Milan.

During his first stay in Milan, Philip had his portrait painted by Titian. This portrait is probably the one of Philip II in armor now in the Prado Museum (fig. 4.9).[32] Titian's portrait of the slender young prince is a study in Renaissance ideas of princely majesty, though the artist has carefully manipulated the proportions of the figure to give an impression of grandeur to Philip's small frame. Philip, his hair clipped short in the fashionable German military style, stands in three-quarter view, gazing proudly out at the viewer. The prince is clad in a half-armor for combat on foot, his hand resting on the crest of his helmet, which is topped by a white plume and doffed casually along with his gauntlets on a table covered by a rich scarlet cloth. A light sword with a decorated hilt hangs from a belt around his waist and the collar of the Order of the Golden Fleece is draped around his shoulders. Underneath his armor, Philip is wearing white hose and trunks of slashed white velvet and silk, and a white plume graces his helmet. According to Calvete, Philip's team wore white hose and white plumes for the royal tournament on foot at Milan in 1549. Calvete's account of the tournament thus sheds a new ray of light on the 1549 portrait, which was very likely painted to commemorate Philip's participation in the Milan combats.[33] The color white had several interrelated meanings in the

---

[31]Calvete de Estrella, *Felicíssimo viaje*, 1:71–86.

[32]Campbell, *Renaissance Portraits*, n241. Titian visited Philip in 1549 in Milan and again in 1551 in Augsburg, where he painted two copies of the original portrait. Campbell believes that the Prado portrait is the original of 1549, though others have argued for a later date for the painting. Wethey dates the Prado portrait to 1551, though he notes that Titian visited Philip in Milan in 1549; Wethey, *Complete Paintings of Titian*, 2:28n12. Brown dates the original portrait even earlier than Campbell, to 1548; Brown, *Golden Age of Painting in Spain*, 39. Records of payments by Philip to Titian from 1549 and 1551 are preserved in the Archivo General de Simancas, though details of the work performed are not specified; AGS, *Secretaría de Estado*, libro 71, fol. 18r.

[33]Philip wore white liveries later that same year at Brussels and Binche, and again at Brussels in 1550, though these combats were all on horseback, and Titian's portrait clearly shows Philip wearing a half-armor for combat on foot (the breastplate lacks the lancerest used in mounted combat).

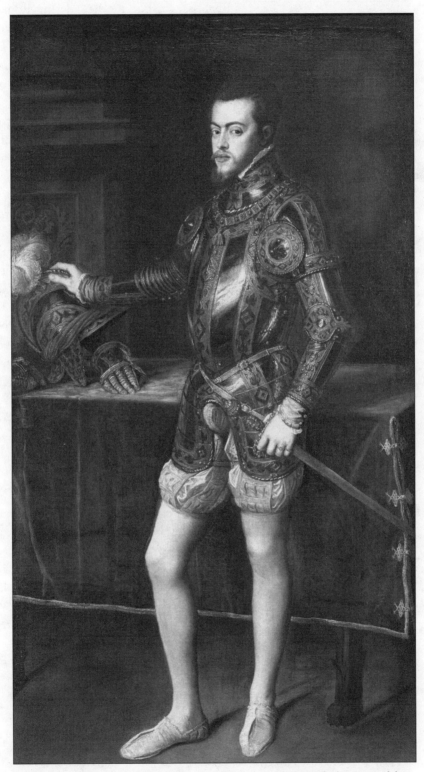

Figure 4.9 Titian, *Portrait of Philip II*, 1549. Oil on canvas, Madrid, Museo del Prado (410). Used by permission.

Figure 4.10 Desiderius Colman (attr.), armor of Philip II ("flower" garniture), ca. 1549. Madrid, Real Armería, A218. Used by permission.

Renaissance, but to the ancient Romans it was the color worn by a candidate for public office (the word candidate comes from the Latin word for white), and thus was the perfect color for one preparing to assume the mantle of imperial authority. In the dark background of the scene, a classical plinth and the shaft of a column can just be discerned behind a swatch of rich fabric. The pillar or column, of course, was one of the personal emblems of Philip's father, Charles V, but the column motif and cuirass, representing the virtue of Fortitude, are common in traditional portraits of military men.[34] In Titian's painting, the column, like the virtues of the young prince, is shown on the point of being revealed, as if in promise of greater accomplishments to come. Titian's image of the young prince as a military leader and the incarnation of Fortitude anticipates the *impresa* portraits of Elizabethan courtiers in armor, which are similar in purpose, though Titian's emblematic language is more subtle and effective. A copy of Titian's portrait was sent to the emperor's sister, Mary of Hungary, who was to play a significant role in the upcoming controversy over the imperial succession.

Like the armor worn by Charles in Titian's portrait of the emperor at Mühlberg, the armor worn by Philip in Titian's portrait of the prince is a recognizable one, parts of which survive today in the Royal Armory in Madrid (fig. 4.10). Philip's armor is in the latest fashion. The raised flutings of the old Maximilian style have now completely vanished, replaced by elegant vertical bands of etched ornament, smooth and fire-gilt, with a jet blue finish over

Philip's team is described as wearing white hose and plumes for a combat on foot only at Milan, when the prince sparred with the Duke of Sessa. A much later portrait of King Philip II in armor by Sofonisba Anguissola also shows the king with white hose and plumes. The armor in this portrait, however, has a lance rest for cavalry use. Only the Titian portrait of 1549 shows Philip wearing a half-armor for combat on foot with white hose and plumes.

[34]Fletcher mentions the column as a Habsburg *impresa* in her discussion of this painting; Fletcher, "Titian as a Painter of Portraits," 38. For the column and cuirass as attributes of Fortitude *see* Hall, *Symbols*, 247–48; and Pizarro Gómez, *Arte y espectáculo en los viajes de Felipe II*, 98.

the rest of the surfaces (Titian's portrait shows the original finish of the armor, which has worn off the surviving pieces in Madrid). The "flower" garniture derives its name from the decorative bands of leaves and lozenges running vertically along the surfaces of the armor. The flower garniture originally featured a full complement of exchange pieces for war and the tournament. The armor is attributed to Desiderius Colman and dates to around 1549, which is corroborated by the date of Titian's first version of this painting. The breastplate of Philip's armor is decorated with a figure of the Virgin, though this part of the armor is obscured by the pendant of the Golden Fleece in Titian's painting. The backplate is etched with a tiny figure of St. Barbara in the corresponding position. St. Barbara was the patron of soldiers and gunners, protecting her followers from accidents and sudden death.[35] As a holy martyr, St. Barbara was also an example of Christian fortitude, the religious counterpart of the standard military virtue. The flower garniture is illustrated again on a portrait medal of Prince Philip by Jacopo da Trezzo struck in 1555, the year following the Habsburg-Tudor alliance and the tenuous extension of Habsburg imperial power to England (fig. 4.11). Like Leoni's earlier medal showing Philip as the incarnation of virtue, Jacopo's portrait duplicates the profile format of Roman coins, but Jacopo depicted the prince wearing a modern armor he actually owned. In addition to evoking the classical past, medals were often given as tournament prizes, and the depiction of the prince in contemporary armor ties Jacopo's medal to the chivalric tradition as well.

Figure 4.11 Jacopo da Trezzo, portrait medal of Philip of Spain, 1555. Florence, Museo Nazionale del' Bargello. Used by permission.

From Milan, the prince pressed on to Trent and across the Alps into Austria, the eastern march of the empire and the ancestral homeland of the Habsburgs. Prince Philip was greeted with military pomp and circumstance just outside Innsbruck, which belonged to his uncle Ferdinand, king of the Romans. A massive regiment of German infantry and arquebusiers, splendid in their glittering armor as they marched across the snowy field, passed in review before the prince, who stopped to watch their maneuvers. They were accompanied by a squadron of men-at-arms and twenty pieces of heavy artillery. The gunners sounded a welcoming volley as the soldiers passed; Philip was then invited to put

[35]Ferguson, *Signs and Symbols*, 107.

the troops through their paces himself. Commanding them to reload, he ordered the arquebusiers to discharge another fusillade, followed by a second boom from the heavy artillery. The prince then continued on his way to the city, where he was received by the daughters of King Ferdinand and the entire council and chancellery of the Tyrol.[36]

From Innsbruck, Philip continued his journey through Austria and on into Germany. Accompanied by Duke Maurice of Saxony, the prince made a number of stops in the old imperial cities, though no grand triumphs were held until his arrival in Brussels. In Augsburg, Philip admired the work of the famous armorers and weaponsmiths of the city.[37] At Ulm, the prince was entertained by a joust between fleets of boats on the Danube (the losers were toppled into the freezing water).[38] The Grand Master of the Teutonic Knights met Philip at Vaihingen, accompanying him with a military escort as far as Speyer.[39] Philip also visited the castle of Heidelberg, where the prince was impressed by the armory and gardens of the count.[40] Some jousts were held in the courtyard of the castle and Philip probably participated in the combats.[41] The prince spent the remainder of the winter traveling slowly through northwestern Germany, not reaching Flanders until late March.

A series of especially grand pageants were held in the Low Countries to celebrate the long-awaited reunion of the emperor and his son.[42] Philip arrived in the vicinity of Brussels on 1 April, and was met first by the emperor's chief advisor Antoine Perrenot, the bishop of Arras and seigneur de Granvelle. Before making his official entry into the city, however, the prince rested from his long journey at the nearby castle of Wura, where he was welcomed by his aunt Mary, queen of Hungary and Bohemia and regent of the Netherlands. The queen of France[43] was also in Brussels for the occasion, along with her entire court and a great many princes, lords, and knights of Flanders. Philip dined with the queen of Hungary at the castle, then set out for the triumphs and tournaments awaiting him in Brussels.

[36]Calvete de Estrella, *Felicíssimo viaje*, 1:144–45.
[37]Calvete de Estrella, *Felicíssimo viaje*, 143, 150.
[38]Kamen, *Philip of Spain*, 39.
[39]Kamen, *Philip of Spain*, 39.
[40]Calvete de Estrella, *Felicíssimo viaje*, 1:156–57. Calvete has nothing specific to say about the count's armory.
[41]Kamen, *Philip of Spain*, 39.
[42]Again, the main source for the tournaments and other festivities attended by Philip in Brussels and the north is Calvete de Estrella. For Brussels, see Calvete de Estrella, *Felicíssimo viaje*, 1:166–204. A roster of the competitors and their prizes at Brussels in 1549 was also published by Bartholomaeus Clamorinus in 1591, with generic woodcuts illustrating scenes of the jousts and other combats.
[43]Calvete does not specify whether this is Eleanor, daughter of Philip the Handsome and wife of François I or Catherine de Médicis, wife of Henri II, who became king of France in 1547. Van de Put notes that Queen Eleanor was present at the festivals at Binche held a little later on Philip's tour, and this is probably the person to whom Calvete refers; Van de Put, "Two Drawings of the Fêtes at Binche for Charles V and Philip (II) 1549," 51.

Before making his entry, however, Philip paused to witness a spectacle held in a sandy field a half league from the city. A grand and sumptuous gallery was erected there, decorated with trophies of arms and an image of Minerva or Pallas bearing a shield painted with the frightful head of Medusa, whose terrifying visage was worn as protection by ancient warriors. Inside the gallery, the tenor of the imagery changed to abundance and plenty: the woodwork ceilings were painted with citrus trees pendant with fruits, with golden roses carved in relief on the walls. The opposite side of the gallery, which faced north, opened like a theater onto a parade ground replete with temporary bastions, moats, outworks, and pavilions. The stands in the gallery were filled with lords and ladies who had come from town to see the spectacle. Two armies, representing the imperial forces of East and West, faced each other across the field a cannon shot apart, already drawn up in order when Philip took his seat. The skirmish began with a flourish of banners and volleys of artillery. The costumes of some of the combatants were in a distinctly eastern European style: the light horse on both sides were dressed like hussars in long coats of satin with high plumed caps, and bore lances and painted shields in Hungarian fashion. Other troops included infantry and a squadron of mounted gunners who were equipped in the German manner. The formations described by Calvete recall the Hungarian Ordonnance of 1532, a huge array of pikemen and cavalry assembled by Charles V to drive the Turks from Vienna. This formation, designed to resist any Turkish assault, was flanked by two wings of lightly armed Hungarian horsemen.[44] The tournament in the Sandy Field at Brussels is probably the subject of a pair of panoramic drawings preserved today in the Louvre (figs. 4.12, 4.13). In these drawings, knights, mounted gunners, and plumed hussars do battle in a field overlooked by a long wooden gallery similar to the one described by Calvete. The central section of the gallery is surmounted by a seated figure of Minerva (Athena or Pallas to the Greeks), flanked by trophies of war. As an armed deity, Minerva was a patron of the military arts, but as the goddess of wisdom, her image reminded the prince that in a leader of armies, martial valor must be tempered by insight. Interestingly, in Jean Bouchet's *Panegyric du Chevalier sans Reproche*, published in 1527, an aspiring warrior is advised by Minerva.[45]

After the show, Philip entered the city of Brussels by torchlight through the Louvain Gate. The prince and his cortege passed beneath a triumphal arch decorated with portraits of his ancestors, whose deeds were compared to David against Goliath and the Labors of Hercules. Various *tableaux vivants* were also presented to the prince, in which Philip

---

[44]Miller, *Landsknechts*, 12 (illustration and caption).
[45]Vale, *Chivalry*, 70.

Figure 4.12 *above and facing page,* Jan Cornelisz Vermeyen, *Combat* (drawing 1), 1549. Pen and ink, Louvre, Paris. Reproduced from Hendrick J. Horn, *Jan Cornelisz Vermeyen, Painter of Charles V and His Conquest of Tunis* (Meppel: Davaro, 1989), by permission of the publisher.

Figure 4.13 *above and facing page,* Jan Cornelisz Vermeyen, *Combat* (drawing 2), 1549. Pen and ink, Louvre, Paris. Reproduced from Hendrick J. Horn, *Jan Cornelisz Vermeyen, Painter of Charles V and His Conquest of Tunis* (Meppel: Davaro, 1989), by permission of the publisher.

was compared to wise King Solomon, successor to the warrior King David.[46] The long-awaited reunion of Philip and his father, however, was tense at first. The emperor seems to have had detailed knowledge of certain events that had occurred before and after the prince's departure. Charles castigated Philip for having become cold to his wife before her death. The prince also came home late from hunting, and wasted an inordinate amount of time getting out of bed and dressing in the morning. Philip, moreover, had treated the Italians with contempt, in particular the Duke of Ferrara and the Venetian ambassador, who had come to pay their respects to him at Mantua. An English observer of the festivities there remarked that Philip's behavior had earned him a reputation for insolence throughout Italy.[47] Charles and his son were soon reconciled, however, and Philip's arrival was celebrated a week later with a series of splendid jousts and processions.

On the morning of 2 April, two *cartellinos* were found posted on the gates of the palace, one in Spanish and another in French:

> Four gentlemen of rank and arms will hold a joust with barred shields against all comers, from one o'clock in the afternoon until sunset, in the main square before the town hall of Brussels on the coming Sunday, for the service of the ladies. The comers will be obliged to touch with their lances three plumes borne by the ladies; those who do not wish to touch all three must at least touch one of the plumes, declaring which of the knights they will fight so that their names may be registered.
>
> He who enters most gallantly and in best order will win a circlet of gold worth not less than three hundred escudos.
>
> He who runs the best course with the lance for three jousts wins a diamond worth a thousand escudos.
>
> He who runs the best lance for the ladies wins a ruby worth at least five hundred escudos.
>
> He who wins the *mêlée* will have a medal, four hundred escudos in value.
>
> The prizes will be given by the ladies, and the jouster who gives a poor account of himself will win no prize.
>
> The lances will be provided by the challengers, and the comers cannot joust with any other lances.
>
> In the case that Fortune abandons a competitor, so that he may no longer run his courses, let him put in his place

---

[46]Calvete de Estrella, *Felicíssimo viaje*, 1:166–89. See also Checa, *Felipe II*, 81.

[47]Parker, *Philip II*, 20–21. Parker cites Bratli for his quotation of John Elder's account of Philip's reception in Mantua.

one who seems able to complete the three courses, at the discretion of the judges.[48]

The timing of the celebrations conflicted with Lent, however, so the jousts were postponed until Quasimodo Sunday, after Easter. In the meantime, a great rectangular stockade was erected in the town square. Gates were placed at the ends of the stockade, surmounted by architraves and pedestals. Over the gates were carved golden lions holding shields emblazoned with the arms of the city, while the pedestals were carved with the imperial eagle. A row of pillars in the antique style ran around the top of the stockade, carved with an alternating pattern of vases and golden seraphs. The seraphs held gilt rings in their mouths, from which hung festoons of fruit and other symbols of plenty. A long cordon was passed through the rings, girdling the entire enclosure. Rows of actual trees were planted at the base of the stockade, with green branches like a miniature forest.

Galleries were built around the stockade for the more important spectators. The judges, carefully chosen to represent each of the different nations competing that day, sat in a separate elevated box on one side of the stockade. The box was lined with rich tapestries and painted on the outside with the arms of the emperor and prince, the queens of France and Hungary, and the arms of Brussels and Brabant in blue and gold. The balcony was decorated in the center with four shields that bore the arms of the four challengers. On the cornice were carved eight figures in bold relief: on the right were Philip, the queen of Hungary, Emperor Maximilian I, and Duke Charles of Burgundy. On the left were Emperor Charles V, his wife, Isabella of Portugal, her sister Beatrice, and Mary of Burgundy, Emperor Maximilian's first wife. In front of a building called the House of the Horn, a gateway like a freestanding triumphal arch was erected, where the challengers were to gather. The arch was topped by another box, raised on four pillars of false jasper. A standard flew from the box, with a black eagle on a golden field bearing the arms of Spain, Austria, Burgundy, and Flanders. Two additional standards bore the arms of Brussels and Brabant. In front of the arch ran the cloth barrier to separate the jousters, stretching from one end of the enclosure to the other.

The remaining galleries were strictly divided according to sex and social rank. On one side were seated the ladies of the court and the gentlewomen of Brussels. The other side was divided into three separate sections: one for the royal ambassadors, another for the lords and knights of the court, and a third section for the burgomasters, judges, counselors, preceptors, pensioners, and gentlemen of the town. The

[48]Calvete de Estrella, *Felicíssimo viaje*, 1:189–90.

Gothic buildings surrounding the square were adapted with window boxes to accommodate the most important spectators, who were covered with awnings to protect them from the sun. By tradition, four windows on the Tower of St. Michael were reserved for the princes of Flanders when they attended jousts in the square. Calvete is vague at this point, but it is safe to assume that the emperor and his guests would be seated here.

On 5 May, the spectators finally assembled in the spacious square, which was so jammed with people that even the windows of the surrounding buildings were blocked (fig. 4.14). The day of the joust dawned bright and clear. After hearing an early Mass, the emperor, the queens, and the Duchess of Lorraine took their seats in the tower. At seven o'clock in the morning, two gentlemen on horseback entered the enclosure, accompanied by the heralds of the challengers. The challengers entered to a blast of trumpets and took a turn about the stockade, accompanied by their musicians and more than seventy other knights, all clad in the same livery of cloth of silver and gold, with broad-brimmed hats of the same material with white and yellow plumes. Their horses were richly adorned with caparisons, collars, and peytrals of the same stuff. A large number of lackeys and armorers also came with them, all in jackets and caps of the same colors. The challengers themselves were clad in shining armor, with short skirts of cloth of silver and gold; the skirts were tricked out with scallops of red velvet, and their plumes were white and yellow. Each was followed by four pages, mounted on fine horses and clad in the same livery. The cavalcade paused before the emperor to do him honor, then gathered under the triumphal arch to await the comers.

The first band of adventurers entered the stockade led by the count of Meghen. All were well equipped, with gowns over their armor of brown velvet with the letter M embroidered in gold, with caparisons and plumes of the same colors. Their attendants and pages were clad in the same livery. The adventurers took a turn around the stockade and touched the plumes of the ladies, then presented themselves to the judges. They ran their courses with each of the challengers, in the same order they had entered.

Before they had finished their courses, however, a mysterious knight, all in black velvet with a black mask and plumes, thundered into the arena to the blast of a trumpet. The knight was accompanied by a postillion in the same livery, who bore a black satchel on the crupper of his horse.[49] The knight took a turn about the enclosure and presented himself to the judges, revealing himself as Don Hernando de Lanoy.

---

[49]Calvete de Estrella, *Felicíssimo viaje*, 197. Calvete does not specify the contents of the mysterious satchel.

Figure 4.14 Flemish, a tournament at Brussels (?), illumination from *Les Heures de Notre Dame*, sixteenth century. London, British Library (f88/0302DSC). Used by permission.

Don Hernando ran his courses and left the arena at the same speed he had entered. A number of Flemish and German knights jousted after Don Hernando, accompanied by their retinues and clad in various colorful liveries. After these had jousted, two bands of Spanish adventurers entered the lists. They jousted well with the challengers, who had stood their ground valiantly all afternoon.

Then Prince Philip of Spain, entered the lists, accompanied by Emmanuel Philibert, Prince of Piedmont, and many other leading knights and lords of Flanders. Their seconds wore skirts of scarlet velvet and cloth of gold, with high caps like stradiots of the same material embellished with gold, with plumes of red and yellow and bands of red and yellow taffeta. Their lackeys wore jackets, hose, and caps with plumes of the same colors. The prince and those knights who rode with him wore skirts of deep red velvet over their armor, all embroidered with gaudy ornaments of cloth of gold, silk twists, and trimmings. The skirts were sewn with big rosettes carved in relief, with fluted buds like diamond points. Their horses were richly adorned with panaches of red and yellow.[50] Everyone watched as they entered so gallantly, in precise order like proper cavalrymen. Having taken a turn around the arena and paid their respects to the emperor and the queens, they presented themselves to the judges and prepared to joust. The first to put himself at the barrier was the Prince of Spain. He jousted with the Count of Mansfelt and broke his lances very well. Their encounter was breathtaking, shattering the prince's lance in pieces in the air. After this, his companions ran their courses and all performed well.

When the last of the jousters had run his courses, minstrels placed over the gate near the judge's box began to play and the knights drew apart into two large groups. At the sound of the call to arms, they began the *mêlée* with fury, breaking their lances in their encounters. The battle continued until seven o'clock in the evening, when the trumpets sounded again, signaling for the knights to retire. Defenders and adventurers left the square with the same pomp as when they had entered. After the jousts, the competitors dined with the emperor, Prince Philip, the queens, and the Duchess of Lorraine.

After the feast, a knight-errant dressed all in green arrived at the door. His armor hung about him all in pieces, and he rode a tired and dispirited horse. The knight rode straight into the royal hall, and with downcast countenance threw himself on his knees before the emperor and handed him a letter. When His Majesty had read the letter, the knight begged leave to be allowed to fix a *cartellino* to the gates of the imperial palace. Charles kindly bade him rise and answered that, God

[50]Red and yellow were the colors of the arms of Aragon, one of Philip's hereditary possessions in Spain.

willing, he would go in person to the palace at Binche, and see for himself the strange things and difficult adventures recounted in the letter. Consoled by the generosity of the emperor, the knight left the chamber and posted the *cartellino* to the gate. The prince and all the knights of the court were astonished at what they had seen and were eager to try their prowess in the adventures at Binche.

Then the musicians began to play softly and the judges announced the prizes won that day. For the Lance of the Ladies, the Prince of Spain won a rich ruby. The Prince of Piedmont was awarded the gold circlet when his entry was judged the most impressive and gallant. Count of Egmont won the medal for having been foremost in the *mêlée*, and Francis de Lambert gained the diamond for having run the best three lances. After the announcements came more music and dessert, accompanied by fountains rigged to spray scented waters on the guests. A round dance followed, then the prince and his knights danced separately with the ladies. During the dance, three or four bands of masqueraders entered, some dressed as Turks with silver robes, others like Stradiots in long gowns and high hats of white satin. Among them came four maskers dressed like Venetian senators, with brocade gowns and long sleeves that hung to the floor, with little hats of cloth of gold. The masques lasted until ten o'clock, when the guests spilled out into the palace square to watch a display of fireworks. The fireworks were so bright it seemed like day. The displays especially pleased the common folk, who danced through the streets tossing sparklers in the air. The emperor and his guests retired at midnight. Philip, however, stayed up to entertain a particularly important visitor, Adolf of Schönburg, archbishop of Cologne and Prince Elector of the empire. Before the emperor and Philip left Brussels, two Spanish knights held another round of jousts in a park near the palace.[51]

A grand triumphal entry and more festivals awaited Charles and Philip in the emperor's hometown of Ghent. The program of the entry was organized by a small army of humanists under the command of Aegidius Theodorius, who ransacked biblical, classical, and medieval sources for appropriate examples of the transfer of power from father to son. The first arch at Ghent was decorated with scenes showing David granting the scepter to Solomon, Philip of Macedon giving his heart to Alexander, Vespasian leading his son in triumph to the senate, Charlemagne crowning Louis, and Thierry of Alsace devolving authority to his son before his departure for Jerusalem.[52] Cane games in Moorish costume were held on the afternoon after Philip's arrival, in which the

[51]Calvete de Estrella, *Felicíssimo viaje*, 1:190–202.
[52]Calvete de Estrella, *Felicíssimo viaje*, 217–305; and Checa, *Felipe II*, 82–83. For an analysis of the iconography of the entry at Ghent and the humanists and artists who worked on the program, see Lageirse, "L'entrée du prince Philippe à Gand," 302, 305.

prince participated. Later, Philip and his companions joined the emperor for dinner at the house of the governor of Ghent. There they were treated to a variety of dances and pleasures, highlighted by a curious masque arranged by Don Juan Pimentel. Ten Spanish knights dressed like landsknechts with short cloaks and yellow and black livery entered the imperial chamber and danced with the ladies, who also wore German-style outfits. The knights danced with tall white tapers[53] in their hands and with German swords and daggers fitted with hilts of embossed silver at their sides, their hair pulled up under feathered caps like imperial soldiers. For the amusement of his guests, the governor also maintained a menagerie in the palace, which included lions, bears, and other wild animals. The emperor and Philip left Ghent the following day.[54]

Tournaments held in the north differed from their Italian counterparts in several significant ways. Antique imagery at the festivals held for Philip in Italy emphasized the divine descent and authority of the prince. The classical topoi chosen for the festivals and triumphs at Brussels and Ghent, however, stressed the virtue of wisdom.[55] The figures of Minerva/Pallas, David, and Solomon that appeared in the decorations of the parade ground at Brussels and the triumphal arches at Ghent underscored the necessity of wisdom and discretion for a young prince preparing to assume the role of military leader. Calvete's description of the tournament held in the town square at Brussels also placed special emphasis on heraldry and other chivalric trappings of the knightly class. By the inclusion of the arms of the Flemish knights who jousted at Brussels, visiting princes were reminded of the hereditary rights and privileges of the local nobility. The heraldry at Brussels also included the arms of the city alongside the family arms of Charles V. In showing the arms of the city conjoined with the arms of the empire and Flanders, the merchant nobility of Brussels announced themselves as a corporate authority whose political identity, though separate from the empire, was united with it in a common interest. This more collective type of political imagery was typical at chivalric events in northern cities, and was used to establish a symbolic dialogue between the city and visiting rulers.[56] The divine destiny of the prince, however, would be reaffirmed in the upcoming festivals at Binche, in the most splendid festivals ever seen in the north.

[53]Calvete says the knights danced holding *hachas blancas* in their hands, which can be translated as either white torches or battle-axes. Illustrations of Renaissance dances often show the participants holding outsized wax tapers and this is presumably Calvete's meaning here; Calvete de Estrella, *Felicíssimo viaje*, 1:311.
[54]Calvete de Estrella, *Felicíssimo viaje*, 305–11.
[55]Kavaler, "Nassau," 31. Exempla of wisdom were presented to Charles upon his entry into Bruges as the Duke of Burgundy in 1515.
[56]The subject of the triumphal entry in Flanders is treated at greater length by Smith, "Venit nobis pacificus Dominus."

The emperor and Philip arrived at the town of Binche in the province of Hainault on 22 August 1549. Charles's sister Mary, dowager queen of Hungary and Bohemia and regent of the Netherlands, had established her residence here after the defeat and death of her husband at the hands of the Turks at the Battle of Mohacs in 1526. The queen had become an important part of the Habsburg network in the north, governing in her brother's name during his lengthy absences from their ancestral domains. The queen received the emperor and his son in her splendid new palace, which was still under construction, at the southernmost end of town.[57] Not to be outdone by the Italians, the queen planned a grand series of magnificent entertainments for her guests, completed by a spectacular *tournois à theme*. As at Trent, a fantastic drama was set to unfold over a number of successive days and nights, including tournament combats, feasts, and masques. In Italian festivals of the sixteenth century, most of the imagery was drawn from the world of Greek and Roman myth. At Binche, however, the tenor of the festivities was closer to the tales of northern chivalry and this time the prince was to play the leading role.[58]

At dusk the imperial party approached the gates of Binche, where they were met by the governor, the burgomaster, and various gentlemen of the town. A salvo of artillery was sounded as they entered, and torches were placed in the streets to light their way to the palace. At the entrance to the palace, a temporary triumphal arch in the Ionic style was erected. The arch was decorated with figures of Mars, Pallas, Hercules, and Mercury, with a dedication to Charles V on the frieze in

[57]According to Calvete, the palace was begun a little more than four years before the emperor's visit and was still under construction in 1549; Calvete de Estrella, *Felicíssimo viaje*, 2:3. The palace at Binche and a smaller castle at Mariemont were designed by Jacques du Broecq of Mons (ca. 1500–1584). Both buildings were destroyed when Henri II invaded the Low Countries in 1554; Van de Put, "Fêtes at Binche," 49.

[58]There are a number of sources for the tournaments at Binche, as they were one of the principal festivals of the sixteenth century. The main source for the festivities, of course, is Calvete de Estrella. A shorter account in Spanish was published by Don Hieronymo Cabanillas in 1559. Fray Pedro de Sandoval, secretary and official historian of Charles V, also discusses the festivals at Binche in his itinerary of the emperor's journeys, though Sandoval relied on Calvete for everything regarding Philip's voyage to the Low Countries. A brief account in French was written by Jean Vandenesse, comptroller to Charles V and Philip II. Another French version is found in the encyclopedic history of the princes of the Franche-Comté and Burgundy published by Loys Gollut in 1592, which was reprinted in the seventeenth century. An anonymous Italian writer described the festivities at Binche in his correspondence of 1559, though he admits to having consulted "a French author" for details of the events. For the other Spanish, French, and Italian writers on Binche, I am indebted to Daniel Devoto's notes in his article "Folklore et politique au Château Ténébreux," nn326–27. An anonymous account of various northern tournaments was also published in German in *Thurnier, Kampff, unnd Ritterspiel* sometime around 1549, illustrated with prints depicting various episodes of the tournaments at Binche and Mariemont. Another brief account and roster of the competitors at Binche and other tournaments was printed by the Frankfurt publisher Sigmund Feyerabend in 1566, with generic woodcuts of sieges, feasts, and jousts by Jost Amman. Clamorinus also provides a roster of the competitors at Binche and their prizes in his tournament book of 1591.

large golden letters. The arch also bore paintings of the emperor's military triumphs on land and sea, with eagles representing the flight of the Turks from Hungary and the defeats of the king of France, Duke John Frederick of Saxony, and Philip, landgrave of Hesse.

The queen's palace had been planned specifically to accommodate important visitors and their large retinues. The guest wing was already completed, and arranged so that the comings and goings of the royal households would not inconvenience one another. The antechamber had a chapel at one end and was hung with rich tapestries illustrating scenes from Roman history, the punishment of those who rose against the Olympian gods, and a procession of the Vices and their slaves. The windows were of stained glass and opened onto a fragrant garden with paths arranged like a labyrinth. Calvete assures the reader that the fireplaces in the antechamber were made of jasper, surmounted by medallions with busts of Roman caesars famed for their virtue. The coffered ceiling was of solid oak, carved and inlaid in the German manner. The prince's chamber was especially luxurious and was decorated with tapestries illustrating the victory won by his father's army at Pavia.[59] The seigneur de Brantôme, writing about the palace at Binche after its destruction by the French in 1554, compared it to the seven wonders of the ancient world.[60]

The queen of Hungary's chamber and the galleries above opened directly onto a large courtyard, some forty paces long and nearly the same distance across. A palisade for the first round of tournaments had been constructed in the midst of the courtyard, with a railing decorated with military trophies and other decorations appropriate to the event. Two gates faced each other across the enclosure. To the right and just outside the palisade, two small arches had been erected. The arches were supported by four balusters, upon which hung four shields in the antique style. On the first shield was painted a pike and a sword; on the second was a javelin and a tremendous broadsword. The third shield was decorated with a war-spear and its ferrule, while the fourth bore a battle-axe. A small gallery for the judges was joined to this structure, with a pavilion set up alongside.

At the main entrance to the courtyard were posted two *cartellinos*, one in French and the other in Spanish:

> On the day following the entry of the emperor into Binche,
> six gentlemen of rank and arms desire to hold a tournament,
> on foot without a barrier, against all comers of knightly rank,
> from ten o'clock in the morning until nightfall. To whit:
> Three blows with the pikestaff and five with the sword,

---

[59]Calvete de Estrella, *Felicíssimo viaje*, 2:1–10.
[60]For Brantôme on Binche, see Devoto, "Château Ténébreux," 311.

three blows of the spear and three with the ferrule, one cast of the javelin and seven blows with the two-handed sword, and nine blows with the axe. The adventurers will be obliged, upon entering the arena, to touch a plume, borne by Mademoiselle Sierstein as her token. After this, the adventurers will indicate by touching the shields which combats they desire (with weapons of equal size and weight, which will be supplied by the challengers).

The gentleman who loses his weapon, though he might be provided with another until the required number of blows were completed, will win no prize.

He who strikes a foul blow, or hits his opponent below the belt, also wins no prize.

Those adventurers who are defeated prior to the combat with battle-axes are to surrender their helmets and will be ejected from the lists, nor may they compete for the remainder of that day's combats.

The prizes will be as follows:

For the best contestant with the pikestaff, a golden pike worth at least a thousand escudos.

For the combat with swords, a golden sword worth no more than four hundred escudos.

For the spear, a golden spear worth at least a thousand escudos.

For the javelin-cast, a javelin of gold worth at least five hundred ducats.

The adventurer who gives the best account of himself with the battle-axe will win a diamond worth five hundred escudos, given by the hand of whichever lady he may choose.

Finally, after the single combats, all the contestants will engage in a *mêlée* with pikes and swords. The best among the challengers in the *mêlée* will also win prizes: The challenger who fights best with the pike will be given a rich circlet, while he who fights best with the sword will gain a ruby worth at least four hundred escudos.[61]

The tournament began on St. Bartholomew's Day. The guests rose early to hear Mass before the tournament, then took their seats in the windows and galleries of the courtyard, resting on cushions of fine brocade. The judges entered and took their places, accompanied by the kings of arms and other gentlemen. Then, the six challengers entered with great pomp. Attending the challengers were fifers and drummers,

[61]Calvete de Estrella, *Felicíssimo viaje*, 2:12–13.

armorers and pages, with twelve knights carrying batons who served as their seconds. All were clad in jackets of slashed red satin over white, with fringes of silver. The challengers took a turn about the palisade and paid homage to the emperor and the queens, then took their places before their tents and pavilions to await the comers.

The first of the adventurers to enter was the Prince of Piedmont, with nine chosen knights. They entered two by two, dressed in shining armor and accompanied by their fifers, drummers, and seconds. They touched the plume of Mademoiselle Sierstein, then chose the contests they desired at the shields. The first band of adventurers wished to try their skill with pike and sword, save for Gaspar de Robles, who touched all the shields. The adventurers declared their names before the judges and took a turn around the arena. The first to enter the field was the Prince of Piedmont, who fought with vigor and skill. Juan Quijada distinguished himself with the sword and Robles fought dexterously with all arms, especially the javelin-cast.

The combats continued until nightfall and the challengers stood their ground valiantly against all comers. As the day wore on, the dress of the adventurers and their presentations became increasingly outlandish. One band of knights entered dressed as humble pilgrims in brown habits, preceded by four little pilgrims wearing hair shirts who sang in the German manner. Another pair of knights were accompanied by servants dressed as huntsmen with baskets and hounds. After the knights announced their names to the judges, the boys blew their horns and released a number of rabbits and cats into the arena, who jumped about pursued by the barking dogs, to the great delight of the audience.

The chronicler also records an embarrassing incident that occurred in the combats that day. Don Alonso Pimentel entered the lists with pike and ferrule, but as Calvete sourly notes, his helmet was so small and poorly lined that it could not have withstood a blow from the lightest staff, still less from the ferrule of the heavy spear. The massive marquis of Berghes knocked Don Alonso to the ground, though to his credit the Spanish knight sprang to his feet without losing his weapon and returned to the combat. Calvete blames the incident on Don Alonso's carelessness, but says that otherwise he was a brave and sturdy fighter.

Towards the end of the single combats, an *apparatus* like a giant serpent spouting flames and sparks from its mouth was wheeled into the enclosure. As the serpent drew near the galleries, two knights dressed like savages with ivy draped over their armor leaped from within its hollow body. They fought valiantly with the comers, especially in the combat with two-handed swords. In the heat of competition, however, one of the adventurers forgot he had also elected to fight with the axe and had to be ordered to return to the combat. This knight was André de

Busanton, who fought so skillfully with his battle-axe that he was called the Valiant Savage.

Finally, Prince Philip entered the lists with his squadron. They entered with great pomp, wearing jackets of crimson murrey velvet over their harness, embroidered with wavy stripes in golden thread. Their trunk hose were of murrey velvet, slashed over yellow, with fringes of silver and yellow satin. Their lower hose were stitched with yellow silk, with yellow shoes, scabbards, tabards, and plumes. The prince and his party touched each of the shields, signifying their desire to fight in all the combats, and declared their names before the judges. Philip paid homage to his father, then fought ardently with pike and sword against the marquis of Berghes.

As the afternoon drew to a close, the combatants drew apart into two teams for the *mêlée*. A barrier was erected to separate the teams, who came together with a tremendous clash of pikes, shattering their weapons in many pieces. Having broken his pike, the prince's hand flew to his sword and he dealt strong strokes on left and right, wounding many. Nightfall put an end to the tournament and the competitors withdrew to their lodgings.[62]

A complete armor for combat on foot was completed for Prince Philip around the date of the first tournament at Binche (fig. 4.15). The tonlet armor is part of the strapwork garniture begun by Desiderius Colman in 1544, though the additional pieces of exchange for combat on foot were not finished until some time in 1549.[63] The lower lame of the tonlet skirt is decorated with an embossed and gilt design of flints, fire-steels, and gryphons, emblems of the houses of Burgundy and Habsburg.[64] This type of armor was designed specifically for single combat on foot in the *champ clos* with sword, pike, javelin, or pollaxe. Philip participated in just such a combat at Binche when he fought the Marquis of Berghes with pike and sword.[65] The left gauntlet is of standard type, but the right gauntlet is a locking gauntlet with a finger-plate that can be hyperextended and locked to the bottom of the cuff by a little turnpin, thus ensuring that the contestant can never drop his weapon.[66]

A set of pageant pieces was also completed for this armor (fig. 4.16). The helmet and shoulders of the pageant suit are covered with a

[62]Calvete de Estrella, *Felicíssimo viaje*, 10–20.

[63]Crooke y Navarrot, *Catálogo historico-descriptivo de la Real Armería*, 69. The *Conde* is unclear about the date of armor for combat on foot, but notes that pieces were added to the armor in 1546 and 1549.

[64]Gryphons are shown pulling a triumphal car in Burgkmair's prints of the Triumph of Maximilian I.

[65]The conde was certain that the prince wore this armor in the August celebrations at Binche; Crooke y Navarrot, *Catálogo historico-descriptivo de la Real Armería*, 69n3.

[66]Locking gauntlets like this were banned from some tournaments and are called "forbidden" gauntlets by some writers; Clephan, *The Tournament*, 49, 106. Young, however, notes that by the reign of Henry VIII, locking gauntlets were permitted in English tournaments; Young, *Tournaments*, 16.

Figure 4.15 Desiderius Colman, tonlet armor of Philip of Spain ("strapwork" garniture), ca. 1544–49. Madrid, Real Armería, A189. Used by permission.

Figure 4.16 Desiderius Colman, portions of an armor and pageant pieces of Philip of Spain ("strapwork" garniture), ca. 1544–49. Madrid, Real Armería, A191. Used by permission.

design of embossed scales, with sections of the arm and leg harness
deliberately cut away and bordered with a design like rows of dragon's
teeth, allowing the wearer to pull gathers of bright clothing through the
openings for a showy effect, or show off his mail sleeves when these
were worn under the armor. Scales are a common decorative motif on
armors from this period and may have been modeled on real scale
armor worn by the Romans, though the scales on Philip's armor also
suggest the skin of a dragon or serpent. A colossal serpent, as mentioned above, was one of the fantastic *apparati* appearing in the preliminary contests at Binche. In a Christian context, serpents generally
represented heresy and evil, but the history of the serpent as a symbol is
far more complex. Serpents were symbols of fertility to the ancients and
had healing and protective powers. In Germanic myth, dragon's blood
conferred invulnerability. Serpents also occasionally appear in a protective
role in Christian art. Moses, for example, raised a brazen serpent in the
wilderness as a protector of the Israelites. In the story of Jason and the
Golden Fleece, the magical fleece is guarded by a fearsome dragon. The
Fleece had healing powers and was transformed in the Renaissance into
a symbol of the Resurrection. Dressed in an armor of dragon-scales and
wearing the pendant of the order, Philip was transformed into the awesome guardian of the Golden Fleece. Other heroes from Greek mythology were also associated with serpents. The legendary Golden Apples of
the Hesperides were located in Spain and were protected by a dragon.
The hero Cadmus slew another dragon, sowing its teeth to create a band
of supernatural warriors. The gods persecuted Cadmus for his deed and
he was transformed into a serpent at the end of his life. Cadmus, moreover, was the mythical founder of Thebes, the birthplace of Hercules,
one of the Argonauts and the hero most often associated with the Habsburg dynasty. The sequels to the *Amadís* stories also featured dragon-slay-
ing heroes like Espandián, the son of Amadís, and Palmerín de Oliva.[67]
Among other Christian saints, Philip's namesake, St. Philip the Apostle,
was a dragon slayer in medieval legend, performing a miracle at Hierop-
olis when he caused a serpent to disappear.[68] In Renaissance emblem
books, the serpent was a symbol of prudence.[69]

After the competitors in the tournament had refreshed themselves,
they met for dinner with the emperor in the Hall of Medals. A masked
ball with many dances and other diversions followed the feast. At midnight, the King of Arms announced the winners of the tournament,
who were bidden to deliver their prizes to the lady of their choice. For
being foremost in the *mêlée*, the Prince of Spain was given a diamond,

[67]Spence, *Spain: Myths and Legends*, 141, 171-73.
[68]Ferguson, *Symbols*, 139-40.
[69]Pizarro Gómez, *Arte y espectáculo en los viajes de Felipe II*, 98.

which he sent to the Princess of Espinoy. Before the guests retired, however, the emperor was presented with a letter on behalf of all the knights assembled at Binche. This was the same letter that had been delivered to Charles in Brussels, and now he read it aloud so that all might hear:

Holy Catholic Caesarian Majesty:

As the Creator of all things has instituted the emperor to rule over the three parts of the earth, those who are oppressed may take certain and secure refuge in His Majesty. In Gallia Belgica, near the village of Binche, across the ancient causeway of Brunheault, an enchanter named Norabroch has perpetrated untold evils with his magic and diabolical arts. An enemy of all chivalry, he holds many knights and nobles in cruel captivity. Norabroch has his abode in an enchanted castle, perpetually shrouded in clouds and mists, called the Castle of Shadows. The exact location of the castle may only be surmised, though it lies somewhere on the Prosperous Isle, beyond the Perilous Tower and the Fortunate Pass. Those knights who would prove their worth will be tested by the enchantments of the place. The kindly Queen Fadada, a friend to all nobility, foreseeing evil at the birth of Norabroch, has instituted a wise and difficult quest. On the Prosperous Isle is a high rock surmounted by a pillar, in which is thrust a marvelous sword, with two tall pillars nearby bearing the following inscription in ancient letters:

"The knight who draws forth the sword from this pillar will achieve the adventure of this place, loosing the enchantments and freeing the prisoners from their cruel captivity, and finally will cast the Castle of Shadows into the abyss, moreover accomplishing many other fine deeds which, though here they may not be related, are destined and foretold.

"Many valiant knights have already tried the adventure of the sword, but all in vain; they remain in the clutches of the enchanter. The good queen also languishes under the inhuman tyranny of Norabroch, but has set up the following trials to restrain his evil will.

"Three knights have their residence before the entry to the Prosperous Isle, standing guard at the three passes: The first knight guards the Fortunate Pass, where a bridge crosses over a deep river surrounded by a mighty barrier. The knight who watches the bridge is called the Knight of the Red Gryphon. At the second pass is the Perilous Tower, where another knight stands guard, the Knight of the Black Eagle. And at the third pass is the third knight, who bars the entry to the Prosperous Isle; he is the Knight of the Golden Lion....

"...Your Majesty's knights, assembled before you at Binche, having already proven their worth across the seas in Asia, Africa, the Indies, and to the ends of the earth, do humbly beseech you to exercise your judgment and clemency, and allow us to try these strange adventures and enchantments, and punish said Norabroch for his enormous crimes. May God give Your Majesty health, good fortune, and a long life,

> "Your most humble and obedient servants,
> The knights-errant of Gallia Belgica"[70]

On the morning of 25 August, the guests ran to see the *apparati* that had been erected in the gardens below the walls of the town. All the marvels described in the letter were there: the Fortunate Pass, the Perilous Tower, and the Prosperous Isle. Behind these rose a vast and dark cloud, large enough that it could easily be seen from the windows of the palace, whose towers were built along the perimeter of the walls.[71]

The first adventure was the Fortunate Pass. A mighty barricade, nearly a hundred fifty paces long, was erected on both sides of the causeway of Brunheault, which ran between the hedge and some hillocks beyond the town walls. Two pillars stood before the entry to the barricade, with an inscription on high instructing the adventurer to read the conditions and cross over the bridge. Blocking the way was a third pillar surmounted by a herm, who bore a shield with a red gryphon on a white ground. On the third pillar was an inscription in French:

> If the adventurer conquers the Knight of the Gryphon in three courses of the lance, he may pass freely to the second pass; if not, let him be taken prisoner.

Beneath the inscription hung an ivory horn by silken cords. A little further on was a lopsided turret, with a dwarf sitting in the window. The turret was placed alongside the doors, which were the same height as the barricade and guarded by two common soldiers armed with halberds and steel caps. Once the adventurer was inside, the gatekeepers closed the doors until the next comer arrived. A secret passage ran from the

---

[70]Calvete de Estrella, *Felicíssimo viaje*, 2:20-27.

[71]The precise date of the beginning of the second tournament at Binche is difficult to determine from Calvete's account. Clamorinus says the Adventure of the Golden Sword at Binche began on 25 August 1549; Clamorinus, *Thurnierbüchlein*. It is impossible to reconstruct the exact disposition of the *apparati* for the fancy-dress tournament at Binche based on Calvete's description of the site. Calvete also notes that by the time he wrote his account, the area had been covered over by gardens; Calvete de Estrella, *Felicíssimo viaje*, 2:28.

lists all the way to the Castle of Shadows; through this conquered knights were carried off to the dungeons of the cruel Norabroch. At the end of the lists was a pavilion where the Knight of the Red Gryphon awaited his first opponent.

The second pass, the Pass of the Perilous Tower, was entered via a great arch at the other end of the causeway, which turned to the left in front of the pavilion of the Knight of the Gryphon. A box was built above the arch for the judges of the previous pass. Within the gates was a column on the right, with a shield above the capital bearing the arms of a black eagle on a white field. Below this hung a second horn and an inscription:

> The knight-errant who fails to conquer the Knight of the Black Eagle with one blow of the lance and seven with the sword will be taken prisoner to the castle, but if he conquers him, he may pass freely to the third combat.

This section of the causeway was also enclosed by a high barrier, almost two hundred paces in length, from the pillars outside the Fortunate Pass almost up to the Castle of Shadows. At the far end rose the Perilous Tower, which was like a triumphal arch with a large box on top, from which the judges could easily view the contest.

The third pass was entered through the gates of the Perilous Tower, which were opened when the Knight of the Black Eagle descended to fight or when an adventurer was admitted to the third pass. Before the Prosperous Isle was an open plain, forty paces long and eighty paces wide. On the left hand was a pyramid, with a shield on which was painted a golden lion on a blue field. Below the shield was another inscription in French:

> The knight who gives the most blows with the sword, or seems to the judges to have surpassed the Knight of the Golden Lion fighting on foot, let him pass freely to the Prosperous Isle. Otherwise, let him be sent prisoner to the Castle of Shadows.

The plain was bounded on the opposite end by a deep river, which surrounded the Prosperous Isle like a moat. The river could be crossed only in a strange barque fashioned in the shape of a red-gold dragon with oars of red and gold and a richly decorated garret on the stern. The craft was propelled by two rowers of strange aspect, clad in long robes of scarlet silk in the antique style. The path to the Enchanted Sword rose on the other side of the river, where two plain obelisks stood. Here the captain of the barque, who was dressed in the same manner as the oarsmen, noted the true name of the adventurer and guided him on the ascent to the sword, which wound steeply up a high outcropping of rock in a series of switchbacks. On the height of the out-cropping was a pillar of jasper bounded by a sward of long green grass; the unpressed grass signified how few of the knights were able to reach this far in the quest. Thrust into the middle of the pillar was a rich sword with a golden hilt embellished with precious stones of inestimable value. The prophecy related in the letter to the emperor was inscribed on top of the pillar. From the summit of the rock, the Castle of Shad-ows could almost be discerned, were it not for the immense cloud obscuring the view. The illusion of the hidden fortress was achieved by hanging broad billows of dark cloth, painted with wavy lines like clouds, over all four sides of the structure. Within the castle Norabroch and his prisoners waited. Mirroring the structure of the tournament, Calvete deliberately crafted his account of the combats that followed to read like a medieval romance, including stock devices derived from chivalric litera-ture: the knightly quest, trial by combat, various damsels in distress, enchanted swords, and a hidden fortress guarded by powerful magic.

The better part of the day had already passed when the emperor, the queens, and the prince took their seats in the main tower of the palace. At last a knight was seen approaching the gates of the first pass. His armor was embossed with black designs and he was dressed all in black, accompanied by a handsomely clad page. Arriving at the pillar he blew a note on the horn, and the dwarf, clad all in red silk, appeared at the window of the lopsided turret. The newcomer announced his name and the dwarf scurried off to warn the guardian of the Fortunate Pass to prepare for battle with the Black Knight. The gates were flung open and two lances were presented to the newcomer, who chose one and entered the enclosure. The Knight of the Red Gryphon mounted his horse, wearing full armor and a skirt and surcoat of red velvet slashed over cloth of silver. Taking up the other lance from his squire, he thundered down the lists against the adventurer, who was over-thrown. The unfortunate knight was forced to reveal his true name to the judges and was seized by two squires, who guided him along the secret passage to the dungeons of Norabroch.

The Black Knight had hardly been borne off when a beautiful damsel, richly clad and mounted on a palfrey, rode in haste to the gate of the first pass. She begged the dwarf to open the doors, saying that she had come to complain to the Knight of the Gryphon about certain insults she had received at the hands of two knights who were coming to fight with him. Tearfully the damsel recounted her plight, saying that the two knights had tried to force themselves on her. The Knight of the Gryphon, who was merciful as well as strong, promised to send the mis-creants to the enchanter.

No sooner had he uttered these words than the horn was sounded again, announcing the arrival of two knights, the Knight of the Sun and the Knight of the White Mule. The Knight of the Sun was quickly defeated by the Knight of the Gryphon, and sent prisoner to the castle. The damsel was overjoyed to see the overthrow of the Knight of the Sun, though his companion still waited at the first pass.

The second adventurer called himself the Knight of the White Mule, though his livery was all of black. He sounded a great note on the horn and the new Knight of the Gryphon came out to meet him. The Knight of the White Mule fought valiantly and overthrowing the challenger, he continued on to the second contest. Choosing his arms, he threw himself against the Knight of the Black Eagle, who was also vanquished. The adventurer dismounted and passed through the gates of the Perilous Tower, though the knight seemed a bit tired from the two battles he had already fought. The damsel was dismayed; holding little hope of seeing the Knight of the White Mule conquered, she ran from side to side, straining to see the outcome of the final contest. The adventurer paused briefly at the pyramid to read the inscription, then prepared to do battle with the guardian of the third pass. The Knight of the Golden Lion was seated before his pavilion. He wore a glittering half-armor with a jacket of slashed scarlet and yellow velvet over his harness. His jacket was decorated with twists of gold and his trunks were of scarlet velvet slashed over cloth of gold. He rose from his seat and sent the adventurer two swords, bidding him choose which he would fight with. The combat commenced, the knights hurling themselves at each other boldly and striking such fierce blows that their swords flew apart in pieces. Taking up new swords they continued the contest, fighting long and tirelessly, though neither knight was able to gain the advantage. Eventually the new weapons were also shattered and the opponents drew apart for a while to catch their breath. A third pair of swords was fetched and the combat began again. Finally, the Knight of the White Mule was overthrown and, after revealing his name, was sent to join his companion in the dungeons of Norabroch. The damsel was overjoyed. Many other adventurers still waited to try their luck in the tournament, though seeing how little daylight remained, it was decided to postpone the combats until the following day.

Then, with whimsical exaggeration, Calvete explains how the captive knights left the Castle of Shadows to spend the evening in the palace. Queen Fadada, sorry to see such knights languishing in the Castle of Shadows, decided she wished to see them attempt the adventure again. That night, aided by her wisdom and spells, she spirited the captives from their prison without Norabroch's knowledge. The knights awoke the next morning in their own beds, astonished at their freedom and determined to see if fortune would prove more favorable the second day.[72]

[72]Calvete de Estrella, *Felicíssimo viaje,* 2:28–36.

At sunrise the fields were already packed with spectators. Having breakfasted, the emperor and the queens took their seats. The jousting began and continued all day, the names and liveries of the knights becoming ever more fantastic. At midday there arrived a pair of Spanish knights dressed as Hungarians in scarlet and yellow silk, with two damsels bearing their lances. Their minstrel, Luisillo, rode with them, singing "A las armas Moriscote" as they came. The first adventurer was unable to overcome the guardian. The second Hungarian made it to the second pass and by the sword fight on horseback still had the best of it, but then he was hit with a strong stroke, smashing his gauntlet and wounding him in the hand. At this the Knight of the Black Eagle told the adventurer to either finish the combat thus disarmed or surrender himself. "This is not at all to my liking," the Hungarian replied,[73] and angrily hurled a stroke at his opponent with his wounded hand. His sword arm was still numb from the blow he had received, however, and at the impact his weapon fell from his senseless fingers to the ground, whereupon the valiant Hungarian was sent to prison like his companion.

While these combats were going on, two knights dressed like Moors in cassocks of murrey-gold cloth arrived. They were accompanied by two little Moors who rode ahead wearing nothing but gauzy cloaks thrown over their bare shoulders and fastened again below their arms. The cloaks bore the cognizances of the newcomers: Don Guilán the Watchful and Angriote de Estranaus. Seeing his companion successfully pass forward, Angriote was eager to test his own luck, but was taken prisoner at the Fortunate Pass. Don Guilán, however, made it quickly to the third pass and, after a great battle with the Knight of the Lion, he was the first of all the adventurers to cross in the barque to the Prosperous Isle. The Moor leaped ashore between the obelisks, where the captain inquired his true name. Don Guilán answered that he was Juan Quijada and the captain guided him up the steep ascent, instructing him all the while what he had to do to accomplish the adventure of the sword. Arriving at the summit, Juan beheld the pillar with the wondrous sword and, grasping it by the hilt, he pulled but he was not able to draw it forth in the slightest, not even an inch. He fell back confounded and said to the captain, "Of greater valor must be he who will finish this quest, for certain it is not I who was destined for it."

"Yet your own deeds are not unworthy," answered the captain. "Long has it been since any have arrived here and not so little is your glory in having accomplished even this."[74] And so that he would not descend from that place without some testament to his strength and valor, the captain bade him accept a rich circlet from Queen Fadada,

[73]Calvete de Estrella, *Felicíssimo viaje*, 2:38.
[74]Calvete de Estrella, *Felicíssimo viaje*, 38–39.

which was also his license to return unmolested along the way he had come. Happily the knight took the circlet and descended the rocks; bidding farewell to the captain, he returned in the barque.

At this there entered a lady, richly dressed and mounted on a palfrey. Her features were hidden by a mask and she sought battle on behalf of three knights. A beautiful youth came with her, dressed in slashed ruddy silk with puffs of silver cloth pulled through the cuts; this was the same livery in which the three knights-errant came. The first to come was the Second Knight of the Sun, so called because his device was the sun surrounded by a garland above a beautiful crest of white heron plumes; the rest of his company were outfitted the same. Running against the Knight of the Gryphon he came off bravely and also against the Knight of the Black Eagle, and so he passed on to do battle with the Knight of the Golden Lion. In the furious fight that ensued, none could guess what the outcome might be. Suddenly the Knight of the Sun received such a horrific buffet on the helmet that his head lolled forward, momentarily senseless. The onlookers gasped, but the adventurer rallied and wounded the Knight of the Lion on the shoulder and was permitted to cross in the barque. The Knight of the Stars was made captive by the Knight of the Eagle, but the Knight of the Moon crossed over in the barque. Unable to complete the adventure, however, he too received only the circlet from the captain.

As the day drew to a close, the heavens surrounding the Castle of Shadows began to move. Rain burst forth and dreadful voices were heard clamoring within the castle. None doubted the prediction of Queen Fadada that the adventure would be finished that same day, yet by sunset no new knights had come to try the adventure of the sword. There remained only the last of the adventurers, who seized the horn and sounded it with such fury that the blast was heard even within the Castle of Shadows. The dwarf appeared at the window of the turret and begged the newcomer not to be so hasty, for soon he would be answered. He had hardly finished speaking when the villeins opened the gates and the valiant Knight of the Gryphon left his pavilion. Having taken some refreshment and rested awhile, he mounted a powerful horse and cantered towards the adventurer. Everyone present noticed the fair and intrepid aspect of the newcomer, who eagerly waited to see what would come of the fight. They lowered their lances and charged impetuously to the encounter, so that it seemed all the earth trembled, and in the middle of the course the adventurer gave the Knight of the Gryphon such a blow that his lance exploded in fragments. They turned about and charged again, but this time the adventurer missed his target, and the Knight of the Gryphon's lance was sent flying at the blow. The newcomer righted himself and directed his horse again at the Knight of the Gryphon, who had taken up another lance. This time it was the

Knight of the Gryphon who missed his mark and he felt the force of his opponent's blow, which was judged the best given that day. The gates of the second pass were opened and the judges, eager to know the identity of such a knight, inquired his name. The newcomer, courteous as well as strong, replied that he was called Beltenebros.

Arriving at the column, Beltenebros paused to read what was written there and sounded the second horn. The two gentlemen and the *maréchal* came down from the Perilous Tower to offer Beltenebros his choice of weapons; having selected them, he readied himself for battle. The Knight of the Black Eagle took up the remaining weapons and spurring his horse forward, he encountered Beltenebros. In their zeal for combat, however, both knights missed their targets at the first encounter and turning their horses, they gave each other fierce blows with their swords. The skill and valor with which Beltenebros fought and the dexterity with which he turned his horse from side to side were something to see. Even before the seven blows were completed, the Knight of the Black Eagle knew himself vanquished. Leaping lightly from his steed, Beltenebros passed beneath the arch of the Perilous Tower. Everyone was certain that if this graceful young man were unable to accomplish the adventure of the sword, it would remain fixed in the pillar forever.

Now the Knight of the Lion came out to receive his opponent, who had stopped to read the inscription on the pyramid. After Beltenebros had chosen one of the two swords, the Knight of the Lion took the other and they lashed each other with fierce blows. Both fought with great spirit, parrying and moving lightly in and out in a way that was marvelous to see, but in the end the Knight of the Lion was conquered. Seeing the worth of his opponent, Beltenebros left off striking him, and the judges declared the young knight-errant the victor.

By this time, the sun was setting and night drew near. Frightful howls came from the castle and all were certain that this last knight would complete the strange adventure. The onlookers ran down from the heights, scurrying this way and that; some were even jumping the barriers and climbing the trees to see what would happen. The emperor, the queens, and their retinues pressed forward in the galleries and windows of the royal palace. Meanwhile, the barque was waiting on the near side of the river. A herald informed Beltenebros what he had to do, and at once the knight and his second boarded the boat. The weird crew rowed them in haste across the river and the adventurer disembarked on the other side between the obelisks. There he stopped and gave his true name to the captain, who was astonished and overjoyed to know what a great prince the knight was. Passing forward, the captain guided Beltenebros up the rocks, telling him along the way what he had to do to accomplish the adventure of the enchanted sword. The knight arrived at the summit and marveled at the strange decoration on the hilt and pommel of the sword. When he had read and undertood what was inscribed on the pillar, he set his hand to the hilt of the sword and with a mighty pull he drew it from the pillar. Thus Beltenebros ended the quest, which so many good knights had proven unable to accomplish.

Now the sky echoed with rolling thunders and dreadful cries were heard within the castle, but Beltenebros was unafraid. Throwing himself at Beltenebros' feet, the ancient captain said, "O fortunate prince, of such high valor and illustrious virtue, blessed is the day of your arrival. Today, through your prowess, I leave off the labors and cares that I have suffered for so many years; yet for the sake of the captives, I must detain you here no longer."[75] Thus he spoke, and presented Beltenebros with a fine scabbard, encrusted with beautiful gems and of workmanship worthy to accompany such a sword, which was the best in all the world. With the sword in his hand and the scabbard girt around his waist, Beltenebros quickly descended from the heights and, guided by the captain, found the path to the Castle of Shadows. When they arrived at the far end of the island, the clouds suddenly vanished, revealing a bridge across the river. Across the bridge they saw the castle, which up to then had been invisible. But the gates of the castle were closed. Hanging in front of the gates was a phial, with many richly armored knights drawn up before it. The cruel Norabroch, knowing that his arts would not avail him against the one who had gained the sword, had taken the knights from his dungeons and, choosing the most valiant, had stationed them there with his enchantments to defend the entrance.

But Beltenebros had been instructed by the captain how to deal with the guardians. Leaping boldly among them, he dealt strokes on left and right with his sword, and as soon as he touched them, they fell senseless to the ground. Arriving at the gates, Beltenebros hurled a mighty slash at the phial that hung there. Within the phial were all the magic forces of the enchantment and before the shards had even fallen, the gates were thrown down and the knights were roused from their slumber. Without delay, Beltenebros freed those knights who remained in the dungeon and prepared to deliver punishment to Norabroch, whose cruelty and pride well merited it. The enchanter, clad all in glittering brocade, was left seated upon his throne, but forever unable to rise from it. The prisoners were overjoyed on beholding themselves freed from such a cruel captivity and Norabroch punished as his evil works deserved. Some thanked Beltenebros, while others knelt and kissed the skirt of his harness. Taking him by the hand, they asked him who in truth he was and at that moment the knight revealed himself as Prince Philip of Spain.

[75]Calvete de Estrella, *Felicíssimo viaje*, 48–49.

That night, Philip returned to the palace for a royal feast, accompanied by all the knights who had competed in the tournament. Everyone laughed when Norabroch was at last unmasked, and revealed as Claude Bouton, the Count of Hoogstraten. After the feast the rocks, the pillar, the castle, and all the rest of the *apparati* built for the tournament were burned to the ground.

The Adventure of the Enchanted Sword at Binche was filled with the usual staples of medieval romance: haunted castles and magic swords, lovely ladies and chivalrous knights. These ideas were part of the common stock of Celto-Germanic literature, especially the stories of King Arthur and his knights, which were widely read throughout Europe, including Spain. The leitmotif of the enchanted sword, fixed in a rock or pillar and immovable save by a knight chosen by God, was doubtless familiar to all readers.[76] The round of eliminations in the tournament at Binche parallels Malory's tale of the Sangreal, where the champions of Arthur vie to achieve the Quest of the Holy Grail. Like the Grail Quest, the Adventure of the Enchanted Sword featured a hierarchical procession of challengers, each knight greater than the last. In the climax of the narrative, only a young knight of matchless virtue is able to complete the adventure.[77] The name of the Castle of Shadows is even older, appearing as Tenebroc in the twelfth-century Arthurian romance *Erec and Enide* by Chrétien de Troyes.[78] The idea of the hidden fortress guarded from mortal sight by powerful magic also occurs in the Arthurian tales, where the way to the Grail Castle, or Munsalvaeche, cannot be discovered except by those knights who are spiritually worthy.

Philip's pseudonym Beltenebros, however, was lifted straight from *Amadís of Gaul*, the Spanish tale of chivalry the prince had loved as a boy.[79] The idea of the fair unknown, a young knight who arrives incognito to undertake a difficult quest, is found in both the Arthurian cycles and the Amadís stories. The Arthurian motif of the sword in the stone is copied in the Spanish tale of Esplandián, the sequel to *Amadís of Gaul*. Like Philip in the Adventure of the Enchanted Sword, Esplandián storms a dark castle guarded by an evil sorcerer.[80] The structure of Calvete's narrative, however, is closer in many respects to the old Spanish *cantares de gestas* (songs of deeds). These tales were filled with lengthy descriptions of dress and equipment peppered with the boasting of the paladins.[81]

---

[76]For an analysis of some of the probable literary sources for the Adventure of the Enchanted Sword at Binche, see Devoto, "Château Ténébreux," 311–28.

[77]Malory, *Works*, ed. Vinaver, 512–608.

[78]Chrétien de Troyes, *Arthurian Romances*, trans. Owen, 28 lines 2109–36.

[79]Spence, *Myths and Legends*, esp. 94, 116. Parker affirms that *Amadís of Gaul* was one of Philip's favorite books; Parker, *Philip II*, 15.

[80]Spence, *Myths and Legends*, 142–43.

[81]Spence, *Myths and Legends*, 92.

The figures of the two Moorish knights at Binche are also interesting and have several parallels in the legends of Charlemagne as told by Boiardo and Ariosto. In these convoluted tales, Saracen knights perform numerous deeds of valor, yet as Muslims they remain the sworn enemies of Christendom. In the Adventure of the Enchanted Sword at Binche, the Moorish knight Don Guilán, though valiant, is by implication rendered imperfect by his faith and thus barred from completing the quest.

As Roy Strong and others have pointed out, the Adventure of the Enchanted Sword at Binche was essentially a kind of initiation ceremony, one of the deepest and most fundamental of folkloric motifs.[82] Strong also notes that the spectacles at Binche took place in the private world of the western Habsburg court, away from the constraints of civic pageantry with its inevitable references to local liberties and privileges. The planners of the Binche festivals were thus able to state their political point more forcefully, presenting the prince as a divinely ordained deliverer.[83] The Adventure of the Enchanted Sword at Binche was also a significant turning point in the transformation of the tournament from military training into martial spectacle. Whether or not Philip really possessed the prowess to overcome the obstacles in the tournament was irrelevant; what mattered was the presentation of the emperor's son as the epitome of chivalric virtue who reestablishes justice and the rule of law. By illustrating these ideas in the guise of a chivalric romance, the Habsburg agenda was presented in the symbolic language most readily understood by the court nobility of northern Europe.

In spite of the importance of the festivals at Binche, surprisingly few visual records of them were ever made. A series of prints ostensibly illustrating the Adventure of the Enchanted Sword was produced later for an anonymous German tournament book published sometime in the second half of the sixteenth century.[84] These illustrations in fact were reused from an earlier series of prints made for the *Theuerdank* of Maximilian I, first published in 1517. *Theuerdank*, probably written by Maximilian himself, is a semiautobiographical account of the adventures of a knight named Noble Thought and itself relies heavily on the Arthurian legends. The *Theuerdank* was illustrated by Hans Burgkmair the Elder, but since the illustrations for the Adventure of the Enchanted Sword at Binche were reused from the earlier book, they are of little use in reconstructing the tournaments there.

The Adventure of the Enchanted Sword marked the crescendo of the festivities at Binche, though the entertainments continued until the end of the month. The next round of spectacles began indoors, in the

---

[82]For a synopsis of the spectacles at Binche, see Strong, *Splendor*, 109. Strong, however, has reversed the order of several key events.

[83]Strong, *Splendor*, 109.

[84]Heartz, "Un divertissement de palais pour Charles V à Binche," woodcut illustrations.

royal salon of the palace. The masques on this occasion were staged by Mary's court musician, Roger Pathie.[85] On the evening of 28 August, while the ladies were dancing after a magnificent feast, four knights wearing bearded masks entered the chamber, with long gowns over their armor. Each led a lady by the hand, who also wore masks and strange high headdresses in an antique style. They entered all in order and danced a pretty German dance together. Then another squad of knights entered the chamber with visors lowered, led by two knights wearing masks like old men, and they fought with the first four knights.

Suddenly, a band of savages burst into the chamber. They wore garments of green and gold like scales over their armor and panaches of colored feathers on their helmets. Seeing the knights occupied in fighting each other, the savages seized the ladies and tried to carry them off. The knights wheeled about to defend the ladies and danced a fiery *moresca* with the savages, their swords clashing in time with the music (fig. 4.17).[86] But the savages prevailed in the end and retired unopposed, handing the ladies over to their squires, who led them to a fine car waiting at the gates of the palace. The car was fashioned like an antique chariot, covered all in green taffeta, and pulled by four white horses. Though it was after midnight, the ladies were driven through the dark woods to the savages' castle about a league from Binche. The knights threw themselves on their knees before the queen and her guests and tearfully begged permission to pursue the savages and destroy their stronghold from whence they terrorized the countryside, committing robberies and other insults. The emperor nodded his assent and announced he would go himself to witness the combats.[87]

The Siege of the Castle of Savages was to take place at the queen's second palace at Mariemont, less than a day's ride from Binche. The roads were clogged with spectators, not only from Binche but from the nearby towns and villages as well, all eager to see the punishment of the savages. Arriving at Mariemont, Calvete rhapsodizes about the beauties of the site: its fresh gardens and clear waters, grand tree-lined avenues, and grassy expanses strewn with wild flowers, where rabbits, deer, and other game wandered. The palace was richly adorned with tapestries and equipped with a spacious wooden gallery on the end overlooking the palace grounds. The gallery was painted and gilt with an arcade of Ionic columns with gilt bases and capitals. The gallery opened onto a beautiful vista and was probably built specifically to provide a sheltered area for guests to view the queen's fêtes in the park.

---

[85]For a discussion of the music, dances, and costumes on this occasion, see Heartz, "Charles V à Binche," 329-30.

[86]Heartz, "Charles V à Binche," 333.

[87]Calvete de Estrella, *Felicíssimo viaje*, 2:50-52.

Figure 4.17 Flemish, *Dance of the Savages*, ca. 1549. Colored drawing, private collection. Image courtesy of Trustees of the Cadland Estate.

The Castle of the Savages was erected in a small valley across from the gallery. The castle on this occasion was designed like a typical fortress of the mid-sixteenth century, complete with twin bastions and a terraplein adequate for the placement of heavy artillery. The sham walls were built of boards dressed and painted to resemble brick, though the walls and outworks facing the attackers were constructed of actual brick and mortar. A second trench was dug behind the terraplein, filled with soldiers who manned the guns, and before the fortress was a fosse filled with running water. The fortress was defended by a handful of knights and eighty soldiers, stiffened by thirty arquebusiers and some pieces of heavy artillery. On a hillock to the right of the palace were the tents of the besiegers with a squadron of men-at-arms drawn up nearby. Here were stationed the principal knights of Flanders, Brabant, and Hainault, along with several Spanish and Italian knights. Five bands of infantry were placed before them, pikemen and arquebusiers, all in order and glittering in their armor. Facing the fortress on the right was a cordon of panniers, with sixteen pieces of heavy artillery and a pair of culverins to the left of the gallery commanding the fosse.

By midday, the troops were ready and the siege of the fortress commenced. First a band of Spanish knights reconnoitered the defenses, but were driven off by a sally of cavaliers from the fortress. Then the cannon of the attackers thundered until it seemed the heavens echoed with their sound. At this, the queen and her guests sat down to dinner in the gallery. Four youths of the royal household, dressed like Apollo in long gowns with laurel in their hair, entered the gallery playing gentle music on harps. The courses of the feast were served by a procession of gentlemen disguised as fauns and satyrs, led by Bacchus, Silenus, and Pan, who came playing rustic tunes on little flutes. They were attended by beautiful young girls dressed like nymphs, guarded by the virgin goddesses Pomona, Pales, and Diana.

Meanwhile, the siege of the fortress continued. By sunset the defenders of the fortress had been defeated and fled via a secret postern at the rear of the fortress. The besiegers stormed the stronghold of the savages and freed the captives, who had been kept safe from the artillery blasts in a vaulted chamber deep below the fortress. Mounting with their ladies in the same car that had taken them from Binche, the victors passed before the gallery where they doffed their masks and revealed their identities to the queen and her guests. At this the emperor, the queen, and Philip rode back to Binche and finished the evening with another round of feasting and dancing.[88]

The motif of the savage predates the Renaissance and is a common feature of late Gothic art. The shaggy wild man or *homme sauvage* was

[88]Heartz, "Charles V à Binche," 53–61.

another stock character at fancy-dress tournaments of the sixteenth century, especially in northern Europe. Like the giants and centaurs, savages in medieval art represented the forces of anarchy and anticivilization. Their intrusion into the fancy-dress ball at Binche and subsequent battle with the knights could be interpreted as another reference to the emperor's struggle to bring order out of chaos. Daniel Heartz interpreted the Dance of the Savages at Binche as representing the threat to security posed by the Ottoman Turks.[89] The costumes of the knights who faced the savages, in fact, look remarkably like the dress worn by Venetian cavaliers in costume books of the later sixteenth century. The Venetian empire, along with Poland and Hungary, was regarded by sixteenth-century Europeans as one of the eastern bulwarks of Christianity against the Turk and thus was a natural ally to Habsburg interests. The savages at Binche, however, also suggest Renaissance images of Native Americans. Peru had only recently been conquered in the name of the Habsburg emperor and real Peruvian captives in Indian costume were supposedly part of the pageantry at Binche. Mummers dressed as American Indians, in fact, are still part of the annual pageants at modern-day Binche, where tourists are told they represent the Inca warriors presented to Charles V in 1549.

The last of the tournaments at Binche took place at the end of August in the little town square. So far the entertainments had all gone according to plan, though on the morning scheduled for the tournament, the town awoke to find the sky heavy with rain. In spite of the weather the square was packed with spectators, determined to witness the first royal tournament ever held in the public square of Binche.

In the midst of the square was a stockade topped by a row of small pillars of painted wood surmounted by imperial eagles and antique trophies. The stockade was closed on both ends by two stretches of high walls made of boards painted to resemble triumphal arches. Each of the arches had two tall gates and was covered with portraits of ancient worthies. Between the gates on the first arch were figures of two colossal river gods holding antique urns from which two mighty waters flowed, one towards the east and one towards the north; these represented the Danube and the Rhine. The river gods seemed

[89]Heartz, "Charles V à Binche," 338. The savages at Binche, however, could also represent the "savages" enountered by Europeans in the New World. A figure of three savages representing Africa, the Turk, and the New World was shown being trampled by a colossal equestrian figure of the emperor at his entry into Milan in 1541; Albicante, *Trattato del'intrar in Milano di Carlo V*, 47. Prints of these same figures, however, show the figure representing "King Atabalipa" (Atahualpa) with feather headdress and a heroic nude physique. This type of image is closer to later engravings of American tribes by Theodore de Bry, and bears little resemblance to illustrations of the savages at Binche. Peruvian captives were allegedly presented to the emperor at Binche, however, and their colorful costumes are echoed in a type of folk dance still practiced in the town; Michelin, *Belgium ... Luxemburg*, 73.

like giants to the common people, who called that arch the Gate of the
Giants. On the opposite arch was a figure of Victory in a triumphal car,
crushing Envy beneath her wheels. To the left as one entered the
Giant's Gate, a grand gallery had been built for the queen and the
emperor, with two lower boxes alongside. The gallery was raised on six
silvered and gilt Attic pilasters, with another row of pilasters above sup-
porting architraves and cornices in the same style, decorated with eagles
and trophies in raised relief. The grand gallery, which was reached by a
flight of broad steps, was hung with fine tapestries and brocades, with
the seats inside arranged lengthwise along the rear wall like the levels in
a theater.

It was already two in the afternoon when the queen and her
guests took their seats in the gallery. Then a mighty blast of trumpets
was heard, and the Prince of Spain and his squadron entered the lists.
They were preceded by their musicians and four *maréchaux du champ*. The
prince and his companions entered through the Giant's Gate with their
lances in rest, wearing skirts over their armor of ruddy brocade with
roses worked in cloth of silver and fringed with gold. Over this was
another garment, a network of festoons lined with white silk, with
golden pinecones in the hollows and tiny cones repeated in the middle
of the roses on their skirts. Their saddles and horse trappings were of
white velvet, with twists, fringes, and tassels of gold; the panaches on
their helmets and on the chamfrons of their horses were also white with
a touch of ruddy. The prince's second, the Duke of Alba, rode before
him armed only in leg harness.[90] Arriving before the imperial gallery,
they paid their respects to the emperor and the queens and gave a turn
about the stockade, passing through the arches of the Victory Gate and
the Giant's Gate.[91]

The next band of contestants was led by the Prince of Piedmont,
who entered through the Victory Gate. They wore jackets over their
armor of yellow velvet with fringes of gold and silk. After they had
entered, the two princes jousted with their squadrons, five against five
all at once, shattering their lances in the air. The next band entered
through the Giant's Gate, and so on, the tourney continuing through
the afternoon. The perfect order maintained by the competitors was
impressive, especially considering the narrow dimensions of the stockade,
which by the end of the tourney was filled with no less than seventy
men-at-arms and their retainers. According to Calvete, the squadrons of

[90]Calvete de Estrella, *Felicíssimo viaje*, 2:63.

[91]Again, it is difficult to reconstruct the exact arrangement of the monuments from Calvete's
description. The arches might have been simply painted onto the wooden walls at the ends of the
stockade, with two doors side by side, or they might have been built out into the lists, with openings on the flanks of the arches. The description of the prince and his party passing through the
arches as they rode around the stockade suggests that the arches were three-dimensional, and projected into the stockade. Calvete de Estrella, *Felicíssimo viaje*, 62–63.

knights moving in concert in their different liveries were marvelous to see, shifting like the patterns in a kaleidoscope as the combats unfolded.

The tourney was not without its mishaps, however. Blaming the close confines of the square and the unusually heavy lances, Calvete records an unusual number of accidents that day. Don Juan Manrique de Lara received such a blow from his opponent's lance that his horse fell dead in the middle of the lists. Jacques de Herbaix broke his left arm in his encounter, while Francis de Montmorency was more seriously wounded when a fragment of his opponent's lance penetrated his thigh. A number of other competitors were wounded in the hand. To make matters worse, in the middle of the combats the clouds finally broke, drenching the competitors with rain. The spectators ran for cover under the sheds and scaffolds, but the rain stopped as suddenly as it had begun and the combats continued with a *mêlée* of swords. Philip and his companions distinguished themselves in the sword fight as well, but the rain returned in a downpour, forcing an end to the tournament. The emperor and queens left the gallery and returned to the palace, followed by the brave champions, who arrived soaking wet.[92]

At the end of the summer of 1549, the grand entertainments at Binche finally came to a close. The festivals of 1549 were indelibly impressed upon the European imagination and determined the course of western pageantry for the next hundred and fifty years. The fêtes at other European courts, of the later Medici and Tudors, the Valois, and the Stuarts, were inevitably compared to the festivals at Binche and drew heavily on the symbolism of divine monarchy first employed by the Habsburgs.[93] The spectacles for Prince Philip became a byword for fantastic splendor, leading to a saying in old Spanish, "mas brava que las fiestas de Bains" (more sumptuous than the festivals at Binche).[94]

Another splendid triumph and tournaments awaited Philip at Antwerp, however, where the prince had still to be formally accepted as heir to the northern territories of Charles V before proceeding on to Augsburg. The prince entered the city on 12 September via the Caesarean Gate, which had been erected for Charles V's own inauguration in 1515.[95] Philip's entry followed a special triumphal way that had been set up across the center of town, flanked by 2,200 pilasters joined by festoons. Along the way, the prince passed beneath a series of magnificent triumphal arches erected by the guilds of the various foreign merchants residing in Antwerp.[96] The arches were decorated with images alluding

---

[92]Calvete de Estrella, *Felicíssimo viaje*, 61–67.

[93]Strong, *Splendor*, esp. 109.

[94]Devoto, "Château Ténébreux," 311.

[95]Checa, *Philip II*, 84.

[96]According to Strong, the *apparati* at Antwerp were enormously expensive: 280 men are said to have worked on the Arch of the Genoese alone, which took seventeen days to build and cost

to past imperial victories, the new Golden Age, and the ritual of succession, all transposed to an empyrean realm where the Habsburgs mingled with their Olympian counterparts. The Arch of Spain featured an entire avenue of Tuscan Doric columns, culminating in a representation of the Temple of Peace.[97] A freestanding sculpture on the left depicted a figure in classical cuirass holding the keys to the Temple while a pair of sculptures to the right showed another armored figure, the emperor (or perhaps Mercury), guiding Prince Philip into the temple. Another arch bore figures of the emperor and Philip as Atlas and Hercules sharing the weight of the world on their shoulders. Each figure held a drawn sword, symbolizing their right to dispense justice and readiness to defend the Habsburg domains by force.

The Arch of the Genoese was decorated with several thematically related tableaux referring to the divine authority of the emperor and the succession from father to son (fig. 4.18). On the left were shown the Fates who determined human destiny, while on the right an armored warrior (perhaps Aeneas) battled harpies and other monsters. The central panel showed Charles V in the company of the Olympian gods, who are shown presenting divine armor to Prince Philip in the center of the scene. The theme of the gift of divine armor to heroes is ancient and is found in both the *Iliad* and the *Aeneid*. In the Latin epic, Aeneas' armor is made by Vulcan and bestowed on the hero by his mother, Venus.[98] The magical shield was covered with pictures illustrating the future greatness of Rome. Aeneas was one of several ancient heroes linked to Charles V in the mythical genealogy of the Habsburgs and thus the story of the bestowal of heavenly armor on the prince took on a special resonance as Philip prepared to receive the imperial inheritance from his father.[99] In the right of the central scene was a figure of the emperor wearing heroic armor, seated alongside Jove, who offers his thunderbolt (the symbol of heavenly authority) to the prince. Surmounting the arch was a third scene showing Atlas handing over the weight of the world to Hercules, while the ceilings and vault were reportedly decorated with other scenes from the twelve labors of the hero.[100] Hercules was frequently associated with the image of the emperor in Habsburg art, though here the story of the hero accepting

some 9,000 florins. Many of the decorations, however, were left unfinished at the time of Philip's visit; Strong, *Splendor*, 103–4.

[97]Strong, *Splendor*, 104.

[98]Virgil, *The Aeneid*, trans. Knight, 219–23.

[99]Tanner, *Aeneas*, 137.

[100]It is difficult to make out the scenes on the ceilings and vault of the arch in the print, though Checa maintains the scenes on the third arch at Antwerp (the Genoese Arch?) represented the Labors of Hercules; Checa, *Felipe II*, 84. Additional figures in the niches represent Jove (?) and Neptune. The print also shows auxiliary scenes on the plinths below the niche pilasters, which appear to illustrate episodes from the story of Ulysses.

Figure 4.18 Pieter Coecke van Aelst, arch of the Genoese at Antwerp, 1549, from Cornelius Scribonius Grapheus, *Triomphe d'Anvers* (Antwerp, 1550). Paris, Bibliothèque nationale de France. Used by permission.

the weight of the world was borrowed to suggest the devolution of imperial authority from father to son.

Further along the way, another *apparatus* showed a scene of the emperor and Philip driving the Turks from Europe. Father and son are both shown in armor sharing the imperial regalia, holding drawn swords held point upwards. Christian prisoners wait hopefully below, raising their hands in supplication to the emperor and his heir. Following his entry, Philip was ceremonially accepted as head of the Low Countries and the heralds threw gold and silver coins to the crowd assembled in the square. The prince dined in the palace afterwards, while the commoners made merry in the streets outside to the light of fireworks and *luminarias*. Following another round of the obligatory tournaments and other pageantry, at the end of the month Philip and the emperor left for Augsburg.[101]

The emperor and Philip's journey south was a leisurely one, with frequent stops in the German towns along the Rhine, including a pleasure cruise near some particularly scenic spots. On 8 June they stopped at Aachen, where Philip admired the coronation relics of Charlemagne.[102] On 8 July 1550, they entered Augsburg. A full month was spent just waiting for the remaining delegates to arrive, who were coming from all over the empire.[103] On 26 July, the discussions concerning the imperial succession finally began.[104]

The first order of business was the problem of the Turks, who were threatening another invasion up the Danube. The German princes, however, seemed more interested in their own religious controversies. In return for financial support for the emperor's wars, the Protestants demanded the release of the deposed elector of Saxony and Philip, Landgrave of Hesse, two of their leaders who had been captured at the Battle of Mühlberg. The emperor's most formidable obstacle in the discussions proved to be the eastern branch of his own family. While Charles pursued his imperial ambitions in the West, his brother Ferdinand had been left to consolidate his authority over the hereditary Habsburg territories in Austria and Bohemia. Ferdinand wished the imperial crown to pass directly to his own son, the young Archduke Maximilian of Austria, and was strongly supported by the German princes and clergy. The issue was not so much that Philip was Spanish and a Catholic—Ferdinand and Maximilian were both Catholics and had spent many years in Spain. Maximilian spoke fluent Spanish and had even married a Spanish wife.[105] The real reason for the gridlock was the

---

[101]Checa, *Felipe II*, 400–409. Calvete's account of Philip's tournaments essentially ends here, though at least three additional tournaments were held at Augsburg.

[102]Kamen, *Philip of Spain*, 44.

[103]Kamen, *Philip of Spain*, 45.

[104]Foronda y Aguilera, *Estancias y viajes*, 623.

[105]Kamen, *Philip of Spain*, 45–46.

growing might of Charles V. A strong emperor threatened the liberty of the German princes, who were determined to prevent a consolidation of imperial power over their territories.

The negotiations dragged on for six months, with little headway made on either side, leading one exasperated ambassador to report that the German princes seemed to prefer the Turk to Philip. Ferdinand also insisted that his son be present for the discussions concerning his inheritance (Maximilian was still in Spain, having been left in charge as regent during Philip's absence). Maximilian arrived in December and immediately pressed for his full rights. On two separate occasions, Charles had to summon his sister from Brussels to lend her support in person for Philip. The emperor and Ferdinand began to argue violently in public as well as in private.[106] Eventually, Charles was able to impose an agreement on his bickering relatives, though the agreement was not entirely to his advantage. The so-called Family Compact was signed by all parties on 9 March 1551. The imperial crown was to pass first to Ferdinand and only after his death to Philip of Spain. After Philip's death, it would pass to Maximilian. The archduke was understandably unhappy with the settlement and friction continued between him and the emperor, in this and many other matters. Ferdinand, as future events would show, never had any intention of honoring the agreement.[107]

Meanwhile Philip was forced to spend almost an entire year in Augsburg rubbing shoulders with the Germans, whose manners were different from those of Spain. The prince did his best to appear amiable in public, joining with the young nobles in their hunting, jousting, and drinking bouts. Prior to their arrival in the city, the emperor had increased Philip's allowance to 200,000 ducats a year for the maintenance of his household.[108] The prince's expenses during his stay include payments for arms and armor, fine arquebuses ordered from the emperor's gunsmith, prizes for tournaments, gold medallions, and a pair of fancy sleighs made to his specifications when the snows began in November.[109] Philip also paid Titian for more paintings when the artist visited him again in Augsburg.[110] These were presumably copies of the standing portrait of the prince in armor painted at Milan in 1549, which were sent to Cardinal Granvelle and Mary of Hungary.[111] On workdays Philip attended sessions of the Diet, though the prince remained silent in the debates, deferring to his father in all important matters.[112]

---

[106]Kamen, *Philip of Spain*. Philip, in fact, had already written to his cousin urging him to come to Germany.

[107]Kamen, *Philip of Spain*; and Grierson, *Two Worlds*, 32.

[108]AGS, *Secretaría de Estado*, libro 71, 57r–57v.

[109]AGS, *Secretaría de Estado*, libro 71, 63v–113r.

[110]AGS, *Secretaría de Estado*, libro 71, fols. 91r, 104r, 110v, 111v.

[111]Campbell, *Renaissance Portraits*, 241n.

[112]Kamen, *Philip of Spain*, 45.

At least three tournaments were held in Augsburg during the discussions, though regrettably few details are known about them. On 16 October 1550, the emperor and the duchesses of Lorraine and Arschot attended a joust in Augsburg in which Prince Philip participated. As His Majesty watched from a window, six jousted against six, breaking three lances each. On 19 October, another joust was held by the Lord of Hubermont and Ruy Gómez de Silva, judged by the Knights of the Golden Fleece. The prince won first prize, with second place going to the Lord of Hubermont. On 1 February 1551, a particularly grand series of jousts were held in the palace before the imperial court. These jousts took place entirely indoors under artificial illumination, a novelty said to have been introduced by the emperor.[113] On this occasion, the prizes were won by Don Pedro Sarmiento, Don Alvaro of Portugal, and a Greek gentleman.[114]

Three fine armors were completed for Philip around the time of the meetings at Augsburg. In 1550 and 1551, Wolf of Landshut was paid for a pair of armors he was making for Philip while the prince was in Augsburg. The first of these is probably an armor of plain polished steel from this period in the Royal Armory, with pieces of exchange for war and the joust. In July of 1550, Wolf was already working on another armor, a fancy equestrian armor for war known as the "Burgundy-cross" armor (discussed in chapter 3).[115]

The most splendid armor owned by Philip II, however—and arguably one of the finest ever made—is a pageant armor now in Madrid, embossed by Desiderius Colman of Augsburg (fig. 4.19). Separate pieces of this armor are signed and dated 1549, 1550, and 1552. The armor is in fact a small garniture for light cavalry use with pieces of exchange to be worn over a coat of mail and mail leggings. The cuirass is of laminated construction, allowing for more flexibility in the torso. This type of armor, a combination of western and Turkish types, was worn by light

[113]Foronda y Aguilera, *Estancias y viajes*, 620–23. The claim that Charles V invented the indoor joust is difficult to verify, though Gravett notes that the first recorded indoor joust was held at Lille in 1513; Gravett, *Tournament*, 50.

[114]Foronda y Aguilera, *Estancias y viajes*, 623.

[115]AGS, *Secretaría de Estado*, libro 71, fols. 64v, 96r, 103r–103v; payments to "maestre bulff armero, vezino de lançuete." Siegmund Wolf of Landshut can probably be identified as Wolfgang Grosschedel (active 1545–54), another celebrated armorer of Landshut. Recent studies treat Wolf of Landshut and Wolfgang Grosschedel as the same person, though the Conde de Valencia believed them to be different individuals. According to the conde, Wolf of Landshut died in 1544, leaving his four minor sons under the care and tutelage of Wolfgang Grosschedel; Crooke y Navarrot, *Catálogo historico-descriptivo de la Real Armería*, 87–88n1. Whatever his identity, documents state that Franz Grosschedel and Wolf of Landshut were paid 2,350 escudos in 1555 for portions of an armor for Philip of Spain—the year after Wolf's death as given by the conde (Madrid, Royal Armory, A-243). Wolf's mark was a W formed of two crossed Vs. Works ascribed to Wolf of Landshut are found in the Real Armería in Madrid (A231-38, A243-62, A263-73, A274-76, armor of Don Carlos). See AGS, *Secretaría de Estado*, libro 71, fols. 64v, 96r, 103r; Crooke y Navarrot, *Catálogo historico-descriptivo de la Real Armería*, 76, 83, 84 pl. 14, 86, 87 pl. 15, 87–88n1, 89; Lacaci, *Armería del Palacio Real de Madrid*, 14–15, 22, 41 (fig.); and Pfaffenbichler, *Medieval Craftsmen*, 20, fig. 19.

Figure 4.19a and b Desiderius Colman, armor and shield of Philip of Spain, 1549–51. Madrid, Real Armería, A239, A241. Cheekplates on helmet are restored. Used by permission.

cavalry armed in the style of the famous Hungarian and Polish hussars. In addition to the growing tactical importance of light cavalry, as the guardians of the eastern approaches to Europe, the hussars were regarded as the epitome of romantic bravery in the West and are shown this way in contemporary prints depicting life on the eastern frontier. The choice of a hussar-style armor is especially interesting in view of Charles's plans for Philip to eventually inherit the eastern half of the Habsburg empire, which directly faced the Ottoman threat. Philip's fine armor in this case was obviously not intended for real warfare and thus its form may be regarded as essentially symbolic. The decoration on the armor includes embossed representations of the Golden Fleece and lion masks of Hercules on the poleyns or knee-cops, with a pair of female busts on pedestals like classical herms on the couters or elbow-cops. In ancient times, herms marked the boundaries of a place, and the hermlike figures on the couters also resemble ancient personifications of imperial provinces. Both are crowned and wear tiny collars of the Order of the Golden Fleece. The helmet is decorated with battle scenes and the double-headed imperial eagle, whose heads looked both East and West. The shield for this armor (which was not finished in time for the imperial diet) is embossed with four radially arranged medallions showing the triumphs of Wisdom, Peace, War, and Strength. These allegorical figures illustrating royal virtues are based (though somewhat loosely) on Petrarch's famous *Trionfi* and are enclosed by laurel wreaths indicating victory.[116] Around the rim of the shield are scenes of the hunt, including a little vignette showing a Spanish bull goring a warrior with a shield inscribed Negrol, a humorous commentary on the prince's preference for his German armorers over the Negroli of Milan.

Philip seems to have paid for this armor in several installments. At least five payments were made to Desiderius Colman during Philip's stays in Brussels and Augsburg (including a tip of twenty escudos for Colman's apprentices) for a staggering total of 3,690 gold escudos.[117] One of these payments specifically mentions embossed, or "black" armor (fig. 4.20):

> Domingo de orbea mi Thesorero yo vos mando que de qualesquier dineros de vuestro cargo deys y pageys a Desiderio colman armero vezino desta ciudad de Augusta, quatrocientos escudos de oro…los quales son para en quenta y parte de pago de lo que ha de hauer del precio de vnas armas negras que haze para mi seruicio.[118]

> [Domingo de Orbea, my treasurer, I order you to pay, from those moneys that are in your charge, Desiderius Colman, armorer of Augsburg, four hundred escudos of gold…on account and in partial payment of what he is asking for some embossed armor, which he is making for my service.]

---

[116]Godoy, "Royal Armory," 155. Petrarch's triumphs included Love, Chastity, Death, Fame, Time, and Eternity. Pageant cars bearing allegorical figures extrapolated from Petrarch were a regular part of triumphal processions, and prints showing them were sometimes included in festival books. Philip owned a copy of the writings of Petrarch and it is possible the scenes were adapted by the prince himself.

[117]AGS, *Secretaría de Estado*, libro 71, fols. 44v, 74r–74v, 93r, 108v, 110v. A total of five payments are mentioned in the documents, though the Conde de Valencia only mentions two of these; Crooke y Navarrot, *Catálogo historico-descriptivo de la Real Armería*, 78n1. The documents suggest all five payments refer to the same armor and specifically describe *armas negras* (embossed armor). It is possible that, like the bills for Wolf, the payments to Desiderius refer to more than one armor, though this seems unlikely (the bills for the flower garniture, however, have yet to be discovered). Philip's accounts from this period also mention payments to other armorers, Petre Caecen of Ulm and Master Peter of Munich, for pieces of mail armor, probably to be worn with Desiderius's armor; AGS, *Secretaría de Estado*, libro 71, fols. 79v, 100r. No information is available on these armorers (active ca. 1551); they are referred to in the documents simply as mail makers from Ulm. Payments were recorded to other armorers during Philip's stay in Augsburg, to a Master Hans (probably Hans Seusenhofer) and a certain Master John described as one of the emperor's armorers, though no surviving armors have been linked to these payments with any certainty. AGS, *Secretaría de Estado*, libro 71, fols. 79v, 100r.

[118]AGS, *Secretaría de Estado*, libro 71, fol. 93r.

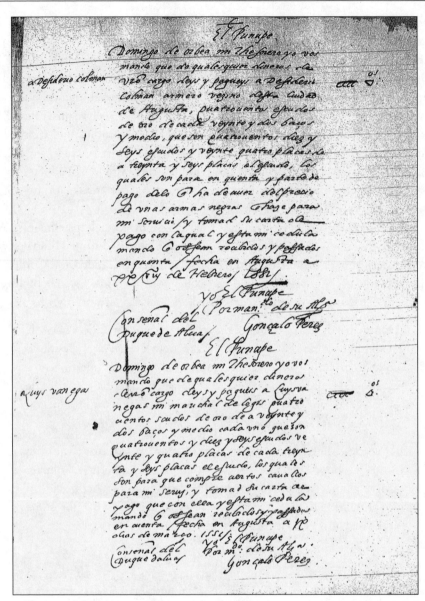

Figure 4.20 *Cédula* to Desiderius Colman, dated Augsburg, 1551. Ministerio de Cultura de España. Archivo General de Simancas (EST-LIB.71.93 y EST-LEG.36.1–15). Used by permission.

These documents are also interesting in another respect. Although the payments are specified in detail, the complex iconography of the armor is not mentioned. Contracts for religious paintings from the Renaissance sometimes indicated that certain images be included in an artist's work. Actual contracts for decorated armor rarely (if ever) survive, though the notes for payment sometimes mention the type of decoration that was used. The documents for this particular armor suggest that, in this case at least, Desiderius was free to select the content of the decoration he produced.

A fine sword was made for Philip around this time by Clement Horn of Solingen, most likely to accompany Desiderius' fine armor. The sword is also preserved in the Real Armería, though the hilt and blade were separated from each other in the nineteenth century. The hilt made for Philip's sword is covered with a decorative pattern of shields, satyrs, and other grotesques, and was once attributed to the famous sculptor and goldsmith Benvenuto Cellini.[119]

Desiderius' embossed armor for Philip of Spain with its imperial message was a magnificent expression of Renaissance statecraft. The dates stamped on different pieces of the armor confirm that Philip could certainly have worn the full suit (minus the shield) in the tournaments at Augsburg in 1551 and portions of it possibly earlier. In addition to the tournaments at Augsburg, it is interesting to note that armor was also traditionally worn at meetings of the Imperial Diet. One can imagine the prince wearing Desiderius' armor, resplendent with the emblems of sacred empire, as he attended the meetings and festivities at Augsburg as the hopeful imperial heir.[120] Many years later, King Philip II was shown wearing Desiderius' armor in a portrait by Sánchez-Coello, painted sometime between 1570 and 1580 (fig. 4.21). Philip's hair has begun to turn gray, though his expression is still lively, and he holds a commander's baton firmly in his right hand, the pillar of Fortitude rising behind him. The pendant of the Golden Fleece hangs from his neck on a small gold chain wound about with a soft silk band. The presumed date of this painting is especially interesting in light of contemporary events. In 1580, Philip II claimed the throne of Portugal after the death of King Sebastian I on a disastrous crusade to Morocco. Sebastian had died childless and Philip stood next in line to the throne through his mother, who had been a Portuguese princess. Despite initial difficulties, Philip pressed his claim successfully and Portugal, with its vast colonial territories in Africa, the Far East, and Brazil, was added briefly to the Spanish crown. Desiderius' armor and its imperial imagery took on a new resonance when Philip's claim to world dominion was renewed, and Sánchez-Coello's portrait may be better understood in this light.

[119]Crooke y Navarrot, *Catálogo historico-descriptivo de la Real Armería*, 221-23. The Conde de Valencia attributed the hilt of this sword to Cellini. For some reason, the conde switched the hilt of this sword with the blade of another sword in the Royal Armory; Bondioli, "Espadas toledanas de la Real Armería," 12–16.

[120]Godoy also notes that Prince Philip probably wore Desiderius' armor for the festivities surrounding the meetings of the imperial diet in 1550-51: Godoy, "Royal Armory," 156.

Figure 4.21 Sánchez-Coello, *Portrait of Philip II*, ca. 1570–80. Oil on panel, Glasgow Museums, formerly Stirling Maxwell Collection. Used by permission.

Chapter 5

EPILOGUE
The Long Journey Home

THE DIET OF AUGSBURG came to a close on 14 February 1551, though Philip remained in Augsburg with his father for the rest of the winter. From a political standpoint, the grand tour of Philip of Spain was a colossal and expensive failure. The Venetian ambassador Soriano shrewdly summed up the problem in his assessment of the impression the prince made on his travels. Philip of Spain, he observed, was "not very agreeable to the Italians, not very acceptable to the Flemings, and odious to the Germans."[1] On the threshold of the modern age, the medieval dream of a Christian empire united under a single monarchy was finally laid to rest.

In the spring of 1551, Philip prepared for the long journey back to Spain, leaving Augsburg on 25 May. The prince stopped briefly in the cities that had fêted him so splendidly on the first part of his journey: Innsbruck, Trent, Mantua, Milan, and Genoa.[2] The streets had fallen silent on his return, however, and Philip was greeted hastily and in private by the local rulers. The prince's galleys made port in Barcelona on 12 July. Philip unexpectedly decided to stay in Barcelona for the rest of the season, as the guest of Luis de Requeséns. The Consell de Cent responded by canceling the celebrations usually held in the city during the summer months. Philip,

---

[1]Grierson, *Two Worlds*, 31.
[2]Kamen, *Philip of Spain*, 47–48.

anxious to maintain a festive mood, had to order the council to hire musicians to play in the streets. Disappointed and depressed, the prince arrived in Valladolid on the first of September 1551.[3]

As soon as he arrived back home, Philip went to pay the obligatory visit to his grandmother, Queen Juana of Castile, at Tordesillas.[4] The prince then headed for Madrid to begin work, stopping on the way to visit his younger sister María in Toro. During his stay, a tournament was held in late September in the nearby town of Torrelobatón, to which all the local knights were invited. Two teams of sixty knights each jousted against each other. Philip's homecoming tournament in Castile was a lavish affair, with the entertainments continuing for two weeks afterwards.[5]

The years following Philip's grand tour were disastrous for Charles V. In 1551 the Turks seized Tripoli from the Spanish garrison, intending to use the city as a base for further action in the western Mediterranean. That same year, the Protestant princes formed a secret alliance with Henri II of France, attacking the emperor simultaneously on two fronts in Franconia and Lorraine. Betrayed by his former ally Maurice of Saxony, the emperor was trapped without an army at Innsbruck. Ferdinand refused to help his brother and Charles was forced to flee with a tiny entourage through the Alps in a blinding snowstorm. The emperor escaped and in October 1552, he laid siege to the city of Metz, though by January he was forced to withdraw due to lack of money and men. Charles retreated to Brussels, where his health rapidly began to deteriorate. Once again, Philip was summoned from Spain. It was around this time that Charles seriously began to consider abdicating as a solution to his dilemma. Forced by circumstances to withdraw from public life, the last of the medieval warrior-kings spent the remainder of his days in a monastery at Yuste in northwestern Spain, tormented by gout and tinkering with his collection of German clocks.[6] Charles brought with him a few carefully chosen artworks and his favorite book, the *Chevalier Délibéré*, a moral tale about an older knight who faces the allegorical adversaries of Weakness, Accident, and Old Age.

The dynastic ambitions of Charles V are summed up in Leone Leoni's bronze statue of Prince Philip of Spain, begun around the time of the meetings at Augsburg though not completed until 1553, two years after Philip's visit to the city (fig. 5.1). Philip is shown standing in the pose of a classical hero, his head and torso turned slightly to the left, the imperial *paludamentum* thrown casually over his shoulder, and a

---

[3]Kamen, *Philip of Spain*, 49–51.
[4]The queen was allegedly insane and had been incarcerated at Tordesillas before Philip was born.
[5]Kamen, *Philip of Spain*, 50.
[6]Kamen, *Philip of Spain*, 53–54.

military commander's baton resting on his knee. The prince wears buskins decorated with Herculean lion masks called *cothurni*, a type of footgear worn by the Olympian gods in classical art. The laminated cuirass worn by the prince in this portrait resembles the real armor made for him by Desiderius Colman in time for the imperial diet, though the decoration on the armor in Leoni's portrait is more complex. On the left shoulder, Philip's armor is decorated with a relief medallion illustrating the Three Graces: Beauty, Love, and Pleasure, a standard trope referring to the qualities of an ideal man and woman (for women, Pleasure was replaced by Chastity).[7] The statue was completed in time for the Tudor marriage and bears a hastily added inscription on the base hailing Philip as King of England.[8] The tabs at the bottom of his breastplate are decorated with figures alluding to his princely virtues and his divine descent, led by Hercules choosing Virtue over Vice. At Philip's side is an eagle-hilted sword of imperial Roman type, based on Roman sculptures like the statue of the Tetrarchs in Venice, which in the Renaissance was believed to represent Aeneas and the heroes of Troy.[9] Philip is shown in heroic armor as the prophesied heir to the Roman Empire, the sword of his divine predecessors by his side. In Leoni's sculp-

Figure 5.1 Leone Leoni, *Philip of Spain*, 1551–53. Madrid, Museo National del Prado (E/272). Used by permission.

ture, Philip's journeys to Augsburg and England were elevated to the status of myth. Following the Augsburg conclave, hope lingered for some

---

[7]This motif appears to have been copied directly from the reverse die of a medal of Prince Philip by Leoni, struck around 1549–50 and probably associated with the festivals at Brussels and Ghent.

[8]The base of the statue is inscribed PHILLIPVS. ANGLIÆ. REX. CAROLI. V. F.

[9]Vecellio, *De gli Habiti antiche et moderni di Diverse Parti del Mondo*, iii.

that Philip might still inherit the imperial crown, provided he survived his Habsburg relatives in the East. When Philip's second marriage was arranged with Mary Tudor, it was a simple matter to add the inscription hailing him as King of England.

Ernest Kantorowicz has called the portraits of Renaissance monarchs in armor "gods in uniform," recalling that western rulers had been depicted as demigods wearing decorated cuirasses since Hellenistic times. Kantorowicz also notes that after the second century AD, statues of Roman emperors were transformed into icons of everlasting or unconquered virtue (*Virtus Perpetuus* or *Virtus Invictus*).[10] A more succinct statement of divine kingship than Leoni's statue of Philip II is difficult to imagine, and had not been seen in the West since the images of the pharaohs.

Charles's own imperial visions are eloquently expressed in another statue by Leoni, *Charles V Trampling Fury* (fig. 5.2). The statue is well documented, revealing a lengthy saga of confusion and delays, though much of it was completed by 1553, five years before the emperor's death.[11] Like Philip, Charles stands in the hip-shot pose of a Greek athlete, his hand resting on the haft of a long spear. The powerful figure of Fury twists beneath his feet, representing the enemies of Charles V subdued by the divine majesty of the emperor. The lion-skin masks of Hercules decorate Charles's shoulders and the visor of his helmet on the ground beside him. The cuirass can actually be removed from the statue, revealing a nude portrait of Charles underneath his armor. In the classical tradition, nudity was always the proper dress for a hero. A story is told that the emperor, embarrassed by the figure's nakedness, belatedly ordered the armor from Leoni to cover the statue.

Painting at the Spanish Habsburg court at the end of the sixteenth century repeated the visual language of universal empire established by artists working for Charles V and Philip II, though by the reign of Philip III they were fast becoming empty clichés. An allegorical portrait of the education of Philip III from about 1585 shows the prince wearing different parts of a pair of real armors for combat at the barriers made for him as a boy (figs. 5.3–5.5). The armors, gifts to the prince from the Dukes of Savoy and Terranova, have been attributed to the famed Milanese armorer Lucio Piccinino and are decorated with a complex network of cartouches containing scenes from ancient history and figures representing military virtues. The breastplate shown in the painting is decorated with a figure of Pallas Athena (Wisdom, who guided Hercules), and the helmet is embossed with the lion mask of Hercules, in a hopeful attempt to transform the prince into a semblance of the

[10]Kantorowicz, *Selected Studies*, 93.
[11]Campbell, *Renaissance Portraits*, 126, 162.
[12]Crooke y Navarret, *Catálogo historico-descriptivo de la Real Armería*, 121–23. Hercules was aided

Figure 5.2 Leone Leoni, *Charles V Trampling Fury*, ca. 1556–58. Madrid, Museo National del Prado (E/273). Used by permission.

Figure 5.3a, b, and c
Italian, boy's armors of
Philip III, ca. 1585. Madrid,
Real Armería, B1, B2, and
B3. Used by permission.

Figure 5.4a and b Italian, boy's armors of Philip III, ca. 1585. Madrid, Real Armería, B4, B5. Used by permission.

Figure 5.5 Justus Tiel, *Allegory of the Education of Philip III*, ca. 1585–95. Oil on canvas, Madrid, Museo National del Prado (1846). Used by permission.

Theban hero.[12] Time is shown pushing Love aside, while Justice steps forward and hands Philip her massive sword. The painting may have been completed to commemorate the prince's elevation to the status of *principe heredero* (crown prince and heir apparent) by his father in 1582, since the iconography refers to the prince's eventual assumption of authority and responsibility. Despite its carefully crafted message, the overall effect of the painting is unconvincing. The descendant of divine Hercules is a pallid and slender little boy who seems unsure about the royal power being conferred upon him.

Habsburg armor and artworks depicting it were integral parts of a collective imagery that announced the emperor as the prophesied heir of a long line of ancient and medieval heroes whose legendary exploits were part of the fabric of Christian Europe. The Habsburg imperial myth was clearly expressed in the chivalric milieu of the tournament, where these ideas could be put across most effectively to those on whom the emperor's authority ultimately depended. The tournaments and pageantry held at the courts of Charles V and Philip II were the climax of a long tradition and served as a model for the martial spectacles at later Renaissance and baroque courts. The tournament remained the proving ground for knighthood and provided an attractive escape for a noble class whose way of life was rapidly fading away. Tournaments at the Spanish Habsburg court presented their audiences with an imaginary world where honor, love, and beauty reigned supreme, and worthiness was shown in the exercise of arms in the sight of God and all the prince's people. Yet they were also a colorful and fascinating part of early modern statecraft, and contained more than meets the eye.

---

by Pallas Athena in his labors and was also believed to have founded a number of cities in Spain.

Appendix I

A Chronology of Tournaments at the Spanish Habsburg Court, 1504–1604

This chronology is based on the principal modern and original printed sources. In some cases, the original sources have been reprinted.

1504 (?)
Cane games in Moorish costume are held before the Catholic Monarchs. Philip the Handsome participates.
—Crooke y Navarrot, *Catálogo historico-descriptivo de la Real Armería*, 143–44.

DECEMBER 1517, 17–23 JANUARY AND 11–16 FEBRUARY 1518, VALLADOLID
Jousts are held for the acceptance of Charles I as King of Spain. Masked jousts, *mêlée*, jousts, and *juegos de cañas*. The king enters the lists in disguise. A colossal effigy of a Turk is burned.
—Foronda y Aguilera, *Estancias y viajes de Carlos V*, 117–18.

18 JULY 1518, ZARAGOZA
Jousts (the king may or may not have participated).
—Foronda y Aguilera, *Estancias y viajes de Carlos V*, 126.

24 JUNE 1519, BARCELONA
The king attends a *juego de cañas* and games involving a "castle."
—Foronda y Aguilera, *Estancias y viajes de Carlos V*, 146.

4 JUNE 1522, GREENWICH
A royal joust is held to celebrate the emperor's arrival in England.
—Jacquot, *Fêtes de la Renaissance*, 2:171.

5 JUNE 1522, GREENWICH
A tourney.
—Jacquot, *Fêtes de la Renaissance*, 2:171.

19 APRIL–1 MAY 1526, SEVILLE
Jousts and *juegos de cañas* to celebrate the emperor's marriage to Isabella of Portugal.
—Foronda y Aguilera, *Estancias y viajes de Carlos V*, 271.

MAY–JUNE 1527, VALLADOLID
The emperor celebrates the birth of his son, Prince Philip of Spain, with bullfights and tournaments. The emperor kills a bull in the arena.
—Grierson, *King of Two Worlds*, 19.

5–6 DECEMBER 1529, BOLOGNA
The emperor and the pope attend a tournament to celebrate the birth of the emperor's nephew.
—Tosi, *Torneo di Belvedere*, 33.

1 JANUARY TO 24 FEBRUARY 1530, BOLOGNA
More festivities, including tournaments, are held to celebrate the New Year and the surrender of Florence to imperial troops. Masses are sung in the presence of the Knights of the Golden Fleece and Santiago. The emperor is crowned by the pope on 24 February 1530.
—Jacquot, *Fêtes de la Renaissance*, 2:422–23.

END OF MARCH 1530, MANTUA
Tournaments are held in the city following the emperor's entry.
—Belluzi, "Carlo V a Mantova e Milano," 47 and notes; and Vasari, *Lives of the Artists*, on Giulio Romano (Vasari does not distinguish between the emperor's first and the second visit to Mantua, in November 1532).

1534, BARCELONA
Hunts and tournaments are held during the preparations of the imperial fleet.
—von Habsburg, *Carlos V*, 179.

25 NOVEMBER 1535 TO 27 MARCH 1536, NAPLES
Jousts, *juegos de cañas*, bullfights on horseback, and a carrousel are held to celebrate the emperor's return from Tunis.
—Sala, *entrata di Carlo V*, 31–35, cc. Alr–C4v.

MARCH 1539
Juegos de cañas are part of the festivities arranged in honor of Isabella of Portugal. The emperor and possibly Prince Philip attend.
—Horn, *Jan Vermeyen*, 25–26.

CHRISTMAS 1539, FONTAINEBLEAU
Tournaments and other "warlike games" follow the emperor's reception by Francis I.
—Jacquot, *Fêtes de la Renaissance*, 2:436-37.

22-29 AUGUST 1541, MILAN
Tournaments are held following the emperor's entry. The emperor reviews the troops of the Marquis del Vasto.
—Bugati, *Historia Universale*, 899-900.

8 DECEMBER 1542, VALENCIA
Fiestas are held following the Day of the Immaculate Conception to celebrate the arrival of Prince Philip to join the emperor (Philip arrived on 4 December). *Carreras de cintas*; Prince Philip wins the prize.
—Foronda y Aguilera, *Estancias y viajes de Carlos V*, 532

11 DECEMBER 1542, VALENCIA
The emperor and Philip attend jousts and a *juego de alcancía*.
—Foronda y Aguilera, *Estancias y viajes de Carlos V*, 532.

12 DECEMBER 1542, VALENCIA
The emperor assists in a barriers in the house of the Duchess of Calabria.
—Foronda y Aguilera, *Estancias y viajes de Carlos V*, 533.

13 DECEMBER 1542, VALENCIA
The emperor and Philip attend a *juego de cañas*.
—Foronda y Aguilera, *Estancias y viajes de Carlos V*, 533.

10-11 DECEMBER 1543, BRUSSELS
The emperor attends a barriers.
—Foronda y Aguilera, *Estancias y viajes de Carlos V*, 556.

23 DECEMBER 1543, SPEYER?
A barriers is held to celebrate the convocation of the Imperial Diet.
—Foronda y Aguilera, *Estancias y viajes de Carlos V*, 556.

1543, SALAMANCA
Prince Philip attends a mock battle upon his arrival at the gates of the city.
—Jacquot, *Fêtes de la Renaissance*, 2:397.

1543, MEDINA DEL CAMPO
Prince Philip attends a tournament held in honor of the entry of Princess María of Portugal. This event features mock battles of "Gypsies," "Christians," and "Moors."
—Jacquot, *Fêtes de la Renaissance*, 2:397, 399.

1543–1544, VALLADOLID
Various tournaments held by Prince Philip in and around the city, including a mishap on an island in the Rio Pisuerga in which the prince and several companions are nearly drowned.
–Parker, *Philip II*, 15.

1544, VALLADOLID
A tournament is held to celebrate the marriage of Prince Philip and María of Portugal.
–Jacquot, *Fêtes de la Renaissance*, 2:393–94.

22–31 OCTOBER 1544, BRUSSELS
The emperor and the queen of France attend a barriers in which the young archdukes of Austria participate.
–Foronda y Aguilera, *Estancias y viajes de Carlos V*, 566.

1–7 NOVEMBER 1544, BRUSSELS
The emperor and the queen of France watch a *juego de cañas* and a tourney of lance and sword, hosted by the Conde de Féria in the city hall. The emperor celebrates the Feast of St. Andrew with the Knights of the Golden Fleece.
–Foronda y Aguilera, *Estancias y viajes de Carlos V*, 566.

1 FEBRUARY 1545, BRUSSELS
The emperor, forced to remain in the city due to an attack of gout, hosts another round of jousts.
–Foronda y Aguilera, *Estancias y viajes de Carlos V*, 569.

9 JULY 1546, GUADALAJARA
Prince Philip holds a tournament on an island in a lake near the city.
–Parker, *Philip II*, 15.

20 DECEMBER 1548 TO 7 JANUARY 1549, MILAN
Jousts, a barriers of Spanish soldiers, a royal barriers of pikes and combat on foot with swords, and a *juego de cañas* to celebrate the entry of Prince Philip and the marriage of Hippolita Gonzaga and Fabrizio Colonna (Prince Philip participates in the royal barriers and combat with swords).
–Albicante, *Intrada de Milano di don Philippo*; Bugati, *Historia Universale*, 961; Calvete de Estrella, *Felicíssimo viaje de don Phelippe*, 1:71–88; Jacquot, *Fêtes de la Renaissance*, 3:443; and Nobili, *La triumphale intrata del serenissimo prence de Spagna*. Albicante's account is substantially different, describing a series of nocturnal festivities including an attack by "centaurs" and a predawn tournament.

23 JANUARY 1549, BRUSSELS
The emperor attends a tournament of nobles.
–Foronda y Aguilera, *Estancias y viajes de Carlos V*, 607.

24–29 JANUARY 1549, TRENT
Prince Philip jousts. The siege of a mock castle is staged, featuring
"giants" and "centaurs," followed by a barriers.
—Calvete de Estrella, *Felicíssimo viaje de don Phelippe*, 1:134–44; and Mariani, *Trento
con il Sacro Concilio et altri notabili*, 358–66.

2? APRIL 1549, THE "SANDY FIELD" (BRUSSELS)
Following his reception by the queen of Hungary at the castle of Wura,
Prince Philip witnesses a mock battle from galleries built especially for
the occasion just outside the city.
—Calvete de Estrella, *Felicíssimo viaje de don Phelippe*, 1:167.

5 MAY 1549, BRUSSELS
Several weeks after the entry of Prince Philip, jousts are held before the
emperor and the queens of France and Hungary in the town square.
Prince Philip participates.
—Calvete de Estrella, *Felicíssimo viaje de don Phelippe*, 1:194–200.

MAY 1549, BRUSSELS
Another joust is held in a park adjoining the palace, followed by an
armed procession on Ascension Day. The papal envoy delivers a sword
and bonnet to Prince Philip.
—Calvete de Estrella, *Felicíssimo viaje de don Phelippe*, 1:202–16.

18 JULY 1549, GHENT
A tournament is held following the emperor's entry into his hometown.
Prince Philip arrives to join his father; a *juego de cañas* is held.
—Calvete de Estrella, *Felicíssimo viaje de don Phelippe*, 1:306–11; and Foronda y
Aguilera, *Estancias y viajes de Carlos V*, 610.

AUGUST 1549, BINCHE, MARIEMONT
The emperor attends a barriers in which the prince participates and
other celebrations on St. Bartholomew's Day. A mock assault on an
improvised fortress is staged, in which Philip participates incognito. On
30 August, the emperor and Philip attend another tournament, hosted
by the queen in honor of the prince.
—Calvete de Estrella, *Felicíssimo viaje de don Phelippe*, 2:1–69; and Foronda y Aguilera, *Estancias y viajes de Carlos V*, 611.

13–15 SEPTEMBER 1549, ANTWERP
The emperor attends a barriers in the great marketplace. The prince
attends a joust in the great marketplace to celebrate his own entry into
the city and the marriage of Madame Policena de Brederode and Thomas
Perrenot. On the Day of the Feast of the Exaltation of the Cross, the
emperor, the prince, and their courtiers watch a barriers. The next day

the emperor attends a royal joust, in which Prince Philip participates.
—Calvete de Estrella, *Felicíssimo viaje de don Phelippe*, 2:208–16; and Foronda y Aguilera, *Estancias y viajes de Carlos V*, 612. Calvete de Estrella's account differs slightly from Foronda y Aguilera's brief note on these events.

MAY 1550, BRUSSELS
The emperor watches a series of jousts beginning on Carnival Day. The prince participates. Another joust follows these, with the prince again participating.
—Calvete de Estrella, *Felicíssimo viaje de don Phelippe*, 2:389–99.

11 MAY 1550, BRUSSELS
The emperor and the prince observe an *escaramuça de caballo* in the park at the palace.
—Calvete de Estrella, *Felicíssimo viaje de don Phelippe*, 2:404–8.

16 OCTOBER 1550, AUGSBURG
The emperor watches a joust in which Prince Philip participates.
—Foronda y Aguilera, *Estancias y viajes de Carlos V*, 620.

19 OCTOBER 1550, AUGSBURG
Another joust is held; Philip wins the prize.
—Foronda y Aguilera, *Estancias y viajes de Carlos V*, 620.

1 FEBRUARY 1551, AUGSBURG
Jousts are held in the presence of the imperial court.
—Foronda y Aguilera, *Estancias y viajes de Carlos V*, 623.

MID-OCTOBER 1554, WHITEHALL
Juego de cañas with Philip and some Spanish lords.
—Loades, *Mary Tudor*, 232.

4 DECEMBER 1554, GREENWICH?
Philip and other English nobles participate in a barriers against English knights. Philip receives second prize in a contest for the "fairest and most gallant entry" and first in the combat with rapiers.
—Young, *Tudor and Jacobean Tournaments*, 31, 200.

18 DECEMBER 1554, GREENWICH?
A "grett tryhumph" is held, followed by a tourney on foot with spears and swords.
—Young, *Tudor and Jacobean Tournaments*, 31, 200.

24 JANUARY 1555, WHITEHALL
Another tournament on foot is held; Prince Philip probably attended.
—Young, *Tudor and Jacobean Tournaments*, 31, 201.

12 FEBRUARY 1555, ENGLAND, LOCATION UNKNOWN
A joust and tourney on horseback with swords is held to celebrate the marriage of Lord Strange and Lady Cumberland, followed by a *juego de cañas* (Prince Philip probably attended).
—Young, *Tudor and Jacobean Tournaments*, 31, 201.

19 MARCH 1555, ENGLAND, LOCATION UNKNOWN
Jousts are held; Prince Philip probably attended.
—Young, *Tudor and Jacobean Tournaments*, 201n.

25 MARCH 1555, WHITEHALL
Prince Philip participates in jousts between Spanish and English knights on Lady Day.
—Young, *Tudor and Jacobean Tournaments*, 31–32, 201.

1560, TOLEDO
Philip II attends a mock battle held to celebrate the arrival of Princess Isabel de Valois.
—Jacquot, *Fêtes de la Renaissance*, 2:397.

1565, BAYONNE
Isabel de Valois, queen of Spain attends a series of tournaments held to celebrate her meeting with her mother, Catherine, the queen of France.
—Yates, *Valois Tapestries*, xxiv.

1570, SEVILLE
A mock-up of a war galley suspended from a pulley is burned for Philip's entry.
—Pizarro-Gómez, *Arte y espectáculo en los viajes de Felipe II*, 21.

1585, TORTOSA
A *naumachia* is presented to King Philip II by the fishermen of the city.
—Jacquot, *Fêtes de la Renaissance*, 2:395.

1586, VALENCIA
A mock assault and *naumachia* representing the Siege of Malta is presented to Philip II.
—Jacquot, *Fêtes de la Renaissance*, 2:398.

1591?, PISUERGA
A *naumachia* is presented to Philip II on his diplomatic visit to Aragon.
—Pizarro-Gómez, *Arte y espectáculo en los viajes de Felipe II*, 16.

18 APRIL 1599, VALENCIA

Marriage of Philip III and Margarita of Styria. Eight days of festivities including bullfights, tournaments, *juegos de cañas*, royal jousts, *alcancías*, and processions. Philip may have participated.
—Bustamante, *Felipe III*, 69.

DECEMBER 1605

Celebrations for the birth of Prince Philip IV. The king holds bullfights, *juegos de cañas*, tournaments, troop reviews, and entries in triumphal cars.
—Bustamante, *Felipe III*, 80–81.

Appendix 2

Tournaments and Competitors on the Grand Tour of Philip of Spain, 1548–1551

Following is a roster of the combats and competitors in the tournaments attended by Philip of Spain on his tour of Italy and the Low Countries, from 1548 to 1551, as listed by Calvete de Estrella. Included are all livery colors, devices, crests, and mottoes described. Where possible, the judges and prizewinners for the competitions are also listed.

Milan

1. TOURNAMENT ON HORSEBACK, THIRD DAY OF CHRISTMAS, 1548
Jousts and combat with swords of seven on seven, tourney with lances of two squadrons, and *mêlée* with swords.

The first squadron
>   Don Francés de Beamont and six knights (red, yellow, and white)
>   The Conde de Gayazo and six knights (white and black)
>   Don Hernando de Lanoy and an unknown number of knights (blue)
>   Don Alvaro de Luna and six knights (murrey and white)
>   Don Ramón de Cardona and an unknown number of knights (green)
>   Alessandro Gonzaga and six knights (murrey)

The second squadron
>   Muzio Sforza (yellow and white)
>   Filippo Tornielo (yellow)
>   Francesco della Somaya and six knights (red)
>   Cesare Gonzaga and an unknown number of knights (white)
>   Niccolò Prosterna and an unknown number of knights (yellow and brown)
>   The signore della Trinità and six knights (red)

2. SKIRMISH OF SPANISH INFANTRY, ST. SILVESTER'S DAY, END OF DECEMBER 1548

Two squadrons engage in a mock artillery duel with field guns, then a skirmish of seven on seven with arquebuses, pikes, and swords.

Alvaro de Sande, maestre de campo, with Andrea Gonzaga and three hundred veteran Spanish soldiers.

3. ROYAL TOURNAMENT ON FOOT, 4 JANUARY 1548

Combat at the barriers of two squadrons, three on three then eight on eight, with pikes and swords, followed by a *mêlée* with pikes and swords.

Crown Prince Philip of Spain and twenty-three knights (white)
The prince's knights
   The admiral of Castile
   Don Antonio de Rojas
   Don Alvaro Osorio
   The Marquis of Pescara
   Don Diego de Córdoba
   The Marquis of Las Navas
   The Prince of Asculi
   The Marquis of Falces
   Don Juan de Benavides
   Ruy Gómez de Silva
   Don Alonso de Tovar
   The Count of Luna
   The Duke of Alba
   The Count of Castañeda
   Don Alvaro de Sande
   Don Francés de Beamont
   Don Alvaro de Luna
   Don Hernando de Aragón
   The grand master of the Order of Alcántara
   Don Bernardino Manrique de Lara
   Don Juan de Silva
   Don Diego de Acuña
   Don Juan de Granada

The prince's seconds
   Don Antonio de Toledo
   Don Gómez de Figueroa
   Gutierre López de Padilla
   Don Alonso de Silva

The Duke of Sessa and twenty-three knights (red and white)
The duke's knights
   The Count of Cifuentes

Don Rodrigo Manuel
Don Fadrique Enríquez
Don Gabriel de La Cueva
Don Pedro de Avila
Don Pedro Manuel
Don Bernardino Manrique
Garcilaso Puertocarrero
Don Luis Zapata
Don Hernando Carillo
Don Diego de Haro
Don Alonso de La Cueva
Don Alvaro de Mendoza
Don Jorge Manrique
Don Luis Méndez de Haro
Don Juan de Saavedra
Don Juan de Castilla
Don Juan Tavera
Don Rodrigo de Benavides
Don Pedro Quintana
Don Diego de Leyva
Garcilaso de La Vega
Don Juan Niño de Rojas

The duke's seconds
Don Juan de Luna, castellan of Milan
Don Sancho de Córdoba
Don Juan de Mendoza
Don Bernardino de Ayala

4. JUEGO DE CAÑAS, KING'S DAY, EARLY JANUARY 1549
Game of six squadrons, three squadrons against three, with staves and shields.

The first squadron, led by the admiral of Castile (white and brown)
The Count of Castañeda
The Marquis of Las Navas
The Count of Olivares
Don Antonio de Rojas
Don Hernando de Aragón
Don Juan de Benavides
Don Juan de Granada

The second squadron, led by the Duke of Sessa (blue)
The Count of Cifuentes
Don Antonio de Toledo
Don Gómez de Figueroa

Don Rodrigo Manuel
Don Sancho de Córdoba
Don Luis de Córdoba
Don Diego de Córdoba

The third squadron, led by the Marquis of Pescara (yellow and red)
The Count of Gelves
The Marquis of Falces
Don Pedro de Avila
Don Diego de Acuña
Don Bernardino Manrique de Salamanca
Don Luis Méndez de Haro
Gutierre Quijada

The fourth squadron, led by the Prince of Asculi (yellow and black)
Don Gabriel de La Cueva
Don Alonso de La Cueva
Don Hernando Carillo de Mendoza
Don Juan Mausino
Don Pedro de Castilla
Don Pedro Quintana
Don Rodrigo de Benavides

The fifth squadron, led by the Count of Luna (yellow and red)
The grand master of the Order of Alcántara
Ruy Gómez de Silva
Don Fadrique Enríquez
Don Pedro Manuel
Don Bernardino Manrique de Lara
Don Juan Manrique de Valencia
Don Iñigo de Baraona

The sixth squadron, led by Don Francés de Beamont (red, all on white horses)
Don Alvaro de Luna
Don Manuel de Luna
Don Diego de Haro
Don Juan de Saavedra
Don Francisco de Ibarra
Don Jorge Manrique
Don Juan del Río, captain of the guard of Ferrante Gonzaga

Trent

1. SKIRMISH OF FOOT SOLDIERS, 24 JANUARY 1549

2. FANCY-DRESS COMBATS AND SIEGE OF A MOCK CASTLE, 24–26 JANUARY 1549

3. TOURNAMENT ON FOOT, 27 JANUARY 1549

Combat at the barriers, two on two, with pikes and swords, and a *mêlée* of two squadrons with pikes and swords, followed by fancy-dress combats.

Four defenders, led by Colonel Niccolò Madruccio, in liveries with the crest of a Phoenix on their helmets, and the motto VT VIVAM (the device of the cardinal of Trent).

Twelve adventurers, in diverse liveries.

Brussels

1. BATTLE AND TOURNAMENT IN THE "SANDY FIELD," 1 APRIL 1549

Skirmish of two armies of infantry, men-at-arms, hussars, and mounted pistoleers, with lances, swords, handguns, and field artillery.

The Army of the East, in white, the hussars bearing shields with a gold eagle on a blue ground surrounded by a gold orle, and pennoncels with a red St. Andrew's cross on a white ground

Joachim de Rie, captain general and imperial sumiller de corps, leading four hundred men, including the following princes, lords, and knights:
    Adolph, Duke of Holstein
    Albrecht, Marquis of Brandenburg
    Nicholas of Lorraine
    Count Waldemont
    Charles de Croy, the Prince of Simay
    Jean, Marquis de Berghes
    Amoral, Prince of Gaure and Count of Egmont
    Hugo de Meleung, Prince of Spinoy
    Peter Ernst, Count of Mansfelt
    Philippe de Montmorency, Count of Horne
    Jean de Lignes, Count of Aremberghe
    Charles de Brymeu, Count of Meghen
    Jacques de Lignes, Count of Faulquenberghe
    Hermann, Count of Nieuwenare and Moerss
    Philippe de St. Aldigonde, Lord of Noircarmes
    Jean de Poupet, Lord of Lachaulx
    Guillaume de Croy, Lord of Chièvres
    Jacques de Herbaix
    Thomas Perrenot
    Don Hernando de Lanoy
    Baudoin de Blois
    François de Noyelles
    Simon de Vernoy
    Charles de Berniemicourt
    Antoine de Breda

Jean de Tyan
Jean de Pouligny
Philippe de Blois
Filibert de Charnot
Jacques de Quarrè
Karl Darmstorff
Antoine de Canòt
Guillaume de Canòt
Jean de Bransion
and the following Spanish gentlemen:
Don Luis de Requeséns, *commendador mayor* of Castile
Don Hernando de la Cerda
Don Juan Manrique de Lara
Don Antonio de Zúñiga
Don Fadrique Enríquez de Ribera
Don Alonso de Aguilar
Don Pedro de Guzmán
Don Pedro de Toledo
Hernando de Vega
Juan Zapata de Cárdenas
Onofre Zaposa
Rafael Caldés

The Army of the West, in green, the hussars bearing shields with either a gryphon or eagle's wing of unspecified colors with a red orle on a green ground, and pennoncels with a St. Andrew's cross of unspecified color on a green ground.

The Prince of Piedmont and his lieutenant Giovanni Battista Castaldo, leading the following lords and knights:
Antoine de Lalaing, Count of Lalaing
Philippe de Lalaing, Count of Hoogstraten
Maximilian of Burgundy, Lord of Beures and admiral of Flanders
Louis, Count of Mall
Pont de Lalaing
Humbert de Peleaux
Filibert, Baron of Salmeurs
Jérôme Perrenot
Claude Bouton
Charles de Trasegnies
Martin de Cilly
André de Sucre
Corneille Wandereecke
Jean de Lanoy de Mingoval
André de Busanton

Frederick of Sombref
Adrien de Wailleux
Antoine de Rubemprey
Philippe de Chassey
Maximilian de Marzille
Jean de Dumey
and the following Italian gentlemen:
The Count of Fossas
Francesco Delfino
Sir Lamberto
Girolamo Pinatelo
Antonio dello Campo
Ascanio Cafarello
and the following Spanish gentlemen:
Don Alonso de Aragón y Mendoza
Don Juan Pimentel
Don Alonso Pimentel
Don Juan de Ayala
Don Alonso de Silva
Don Juan de Acuña
Don Suero de Quiñones
Don Bernardino de Velasco
Alonso de Ulloa
Don Hernando de Acuña
Don Bernardino de Granada
Don Francisco de Mendoza
Don García de Ayala
Don César de Silva
Don Juan Aguilón
Don Felipe Carillo
Don Diego de Carvajal
Gaspar de Robles

2. JOUST IN THE SQUARE, 5 MAY 1549 (QUASIMODO SUNDAY)
Single jousts over the barrier and jousts in quadrille, with barred shields, and a *mêlée*.

The defenders (white and yellow)
Peter Ernst, Count of Mansfelt
Philippe de Montmorency, Count of Horne
Jean de Lignes, Count of Aremberghe
Floris de Montmorency, Lord of Hubermont
and the "Duke Adolph"

The first band of adventurers (brown, letter M in gold)
   Charles de Brymeu, Count of Meghen
   Pierre de Vaudrey, Baron of Corlaou
   Thomas Perrenot
   Humbert de Peleaux
   Hieronymus Perrenot
   Francis de Lambert

Don Hernando de Lanoy (black)

André de Sucre (black)

The second band of adventurers (white, blue, and yellow)
   Jean Marquis de Bergues
   Philippe de Lalaing, Count of Hoogstraten
   Jacques de Herbaix
   Baudoin of Blois
   and the Marquis Albrecht of Brandenburg

The third band of adventurers (blue-gold and white)
   Maximilian de Melun, Lord of Chaumont
   Georges de Beaufort
   Jacques de Claron
   Charles de Berniemicourt

Maximilian of Schenck, Lord of Tautenburg (gold)

André de Busanton (red-gold)

The first band of Spanish adventurers (brown and yellow)
   Don Claudio de Quiñones, Count of Luna
   Ruy Gómez de Silva
   Don Antonio de Aguilar

The second band of Spanish adventurers, jousting in quadrille (black and white)
   Don Luis Zapata
   Don García de Ayala
   Don Bernardino de Granada
   Don Bernardino de Mendoza
   Don Juan de Acuña
   Don Luis Méndez de Haro
   Don Cristóbal Fenollet
   Don Felipe de Cervellón
   Gaspar de Robles

The third band of Spanish adventurers (orange, white, and black)
   Don Luis de Requeséns, *commendador mayor* of Castile
   Don Hernando de La Cerda

Don Alonso Pimentel
Don Luis de Beamont

Philip, Prince of Spain and his followers (scarlet, murrey, and yellow)
Emmanuel Philibert, Prince of Piedmont
Amoral, Prince of Gaure and Count of Egmont
Don Juan Manrique de Lara, imperial grand chamberlain
and their seconds, in the same livery
Don Luis Enríquez, admiral of Castile
Don Gonzalo Hernández de Córdoba, Duke of Sessa
Jean de Henin, Lord of Bossù and imperial marshall
Don Antonio de Toledo, grand marshall of the prince
Don Antonio de Rojas
Don Juan de Benavides
Filibert de La Bauvie, Baron of Montfalconet and imperial grand
    chamberlain
The Count of Fossas

The judges
The Duke of Alba
Sir Francesco de' Este
Renault, Lord of Brederode

The prizewinners
The Prince of Spain
The Prince of Piedmont
Count of Egmont
Francis de Lambert

3. JOUST IN THE PALACE PARK, SUNDAY, 13 MAY 1549
Single jousts over the barrier.

The defenders (orange, white, and black)
Don Alonso Pimentel
Don Gaspar de Quiñones

The adventurers
The Prince of Spain and five followers (white)
The Prince of Piedmont
The Count of Egmont
The Count of Meghen
Don Antonio de Toledo
Ruy Gómez de Silva
and the prince's second, Don Antonio de Rojas, His Highness's *sum-
    iller de corps.*

The other adventurers
André de Sucre
Gaspar de Robles
Don Pedro Sarmiento
Don Hernando de Lanoy
The Count of Mansfelt
Don Rodrigo de Bazán
Jacques de Herbaix
The Count of Aremberghe

The prizewinners
Don Hernando de Lanoy
The Prince of Spain
Don Gaspar de Quiñones
Don Pedro Sarmiento
The Count of Mansfelt
Don Rodrigo de Bazán
Jacques de Herbaix
Don Alonso Pimentel

Ghent

1. JUEGO DE CAÑAS, 18 JULY 1549
Game of two teams, three squadrons each, with staves and shields.

Don Juan Pimentel's team (yellow pennoncels)
The first squadron, led by Don Juan Pimentel (black, white, and yellow)
Don Luis Manrique, Count of Castañeda
Don Rodrigo Manuel
Don Diego de Córdoba
Don Sancho de Córdoba
Don Diego de Guzmán
Don Bernardino Manrique de Salamanca
Don Gómez Suarez de Figueroa
Don Juan de Acuña Vela
Don Diego de Acuña
Luis Quijada
Juan Quijada

The second squadron, led by Don Diego de Acevedo (black and white)
Don Gabriel de la Cueva
Don Francisco de Mendoza
Don Pedro Manuel
Don Alonso de Silva
Don Bernardino Manrique de Lara
Don Pedro de Velasco
Don Diego de Leyva

Don Juan Mausino
Don Diego de Haro

The third squadron, led by Don Luis de Avila y Zúñiga, grand master of the Order of Alcántara (black, yellow, and white, with green crosses of the Order of Alcántara on their shields)
Don Pedro de Avila
Don Hernando Carillo de Mendoza
Don Juan de Saavedra
Don Luis Zapata
Don Alonso de Córdoba
Don Pedro de Toledo
Don Juan de Acuña
Don Juan de Ayala
Don García de Ayala
Don Juan de Mendoza
Don Luis Méndez de Haro

Prince Philip's team (white banners)
The first squadron, led by Don Antonio de Zúñiga (scarlet and white)
Don Alvaro de Portugal, Count of Gelves
Don Luis de Córdoba
Don Alonso de la Cueva
Don Pedro de las Roelas
Don Iñigo de Mendoza
Don García Sarmiento
Juan Zapata de Cárdenas
Don Iñigo de Baraona
Gutierre Quijada
Don Rodrigo de Benavides
Don Rodrigo de Avila

The second squadron, led by the Prince of Spain (dark red with red pennoncels)
Don Antonio de Toledo, His Highness's grand marshall
The Prince of Piedmont
The Duke of Alba
The Marquis of Pescara
Don Antonio de Rojas
The Count of Cifuentes
Ruy Gómez de Silva
The Count of Egmont
Don Hernando de la Cerda
Don Diego López de Zúñiga y Velasco, Count of Nieva
Don Juan de Benavides

The third squadron, led by Hernando de Vega (red, murrey, and white, with pennoncels of the same colors)

 Don Fadrique Enríquez de Ribera
 Don Alonso de Aguilar
 Don Hernando de Toledo
 Don Juan de Acuña Padilla
 Don Alonso Puertocarrero
 Don Pedro Manrique
 Don Hernando de Cárcamo
 Antonio de Guzmán
 Garcilaso Puertocarrero
 Don Enrique Manrique
 Garcilaso de la Vega

Binche

1. TOURNAMENT ON FOOT IN THE COURTYARD OF THE PALACE, 23 OR 24 AUGUST 1549 (ST. BARTHOLOMEW'S DAY)

Single combats without barrier, with pikes, swords, spears, and ferrules, javelins, two-hand swords, and battle-axes, and a *mêlée* at the barrier with pikes and swords.

The defenders (red and white)
 The Marquis of Berghes
 Baudoin de Blois
 François de Berniemicourt
 Charles de Trasegnies
 Robert de Trasegnies
 Jean de Trasegnies
 and twelve gentlemen seconds.

The adventurers
The Prince of Piedmont and his squadron (black)
 The Count of Mansfelt
 The Count of Meghen
 Philippe de St. Aldigunde
 Humbert de Peleaux
 Floris de Montmorency
 Pierre de Vaudrey
 Don Juan de Acuña
 Juan Quijada
 Gaspar de Robles
 and seventeen seconds.

The second band of adventurers (white, blue, and red)
 Antoine de Ronsgin
 Louis de Sonmain

Renault Argenteau
and six seconds.

The *"Pilgrims"* (brown)
Jacques de Claron
Daniel de la Marcke
Joseph de Melissan
Mos de St. Martin

The fourth band of adventurers, led by Don Luis de Avila y Zúñiga, Grand
Master of the Order of Alcántara, with five knights (red)
The Count of Cifuentes
The Count of Castañeda
Don Gómez de Figueroa, captain of the Spanish guard
Ruy Gómez de Silva
Don Luis Zapata
and many gentlemen seconds.

The fifth band of adventurers (silver and black)
Duke Adolph of Holstein
The Count of Mansfelt (second match)
Philip, Count of Eberstein
and five seconds.

Don Alvaro of Portugal, Count of Gelves, with five knights (blue and white)
Don Juan de Saavedra
Don García de Ayala
Don Pedro de las Roelas
Don Martín Cortés
Don Carlos de Arellano
and six seconds.

The *"hunters"* (no colors mentioned)
Jean de Lanoy de Mingoval
Georges de Beaufort

The Prince of Asculi with five knights (black and silver)
The Count of Egmont
Don Alonso Pimentel
Don Francisco de Mendoza
Don Alvaro de Mendoza
Don Diego de Leyva
and six seconds.

The *"savages"* (no colors mentioned)
André de Busanton
Don Diego de Croy
and one second.

The *Prince of Spain* and his squadron (crimson-murrey and yellow)
  The Prince of Piedmont
  The Count of Meghen
  Don Juan Manrique de Lara
  Don Juan de Benavides
  Don Rodrigo Manuel
  and twelve seconds.

The judges
  The Duke of Alba
  The Count of Lalaing
  The Count of Hoogstraten
  Reginald of Brederode
  Claude Bouton, Count of Hoogstraten [*sic*]

The prizewinners
  Juan Quijada, for combat with the sword
  Daniel de la Marcke, for combat with the pike
  Gaspar de Robles, for casting the spear
  André de Busanton, for combat with the two-hand sword
  Mingoval, for combat with the ferrule of the spear
  The Count of Egmont, for combat with the battle-axe
  The Prince of Spain, for the *mêlée*

2. FANCY-DRESS JOUSTS AND COMBATS ON FOOT IN THE GARDENS
OUTSIDE THE PALACE, 25–26 AUGUST 1549
Single jousts and combat on horseback and foot with swords.

The defenders
  The Knight of the Red Gryphon (Jean de Lignes, Count of Arem-
    berghe; Floris de Montmorency, Lord of Hubermont; and Philippe
    de Montmorency, Count of Horne)
  The Knight of the Black Eagle (Philippe de Lalaing, Count of
    Hoogstraten; Baudoin de Blois, Lord of Trelon; and Adolf of Bur-
    gundy, Lord of La Chapelle)
  The Knight of the Golden Lion (Count Amoral de Egmont, scarlet
    and yellow; and Louis de Traulliere)
  and the enchanter Norabroch (Claude Bouton).

The adventurers (first day)
  The Black Knight (Maximilian de Melun)
  The Knight of the Sun (Don Juan de Acuña)
  The Knight of the White Mule (Peter Ernst, Count of Mansfelt)

The adventurers (second day)
  The Knight of the Green Shield (Humbert de Peleaux, blue and red
    with a green shield)

The Knight of the Three Stars (Baron Pierre de Vaudrey, blue-gold)

The Untried Knight (Don Rodrigo de Bazán, white)

The Sorrowful Knight (the Count of Mansfelt, no colors listed)

The Forlorn Knight (Don Juan de Acuña, no colors listed)

The Knight of the Blue Shield (Antoine de Montigny, Lord of Noyeles, no colors listed, but with a blue shield)

The second Untried Knight (Don Diego de Leyva, black)

The "Hungarians" (scarlet and yellow)

Don Luis de Avila y Zúñiga, grand master of the Order of Alcántara

The Prince of Asculi

and their ladies, with their minstrel Luisillo.

The "Moors" (murrey gold)

Don Guilán the Watchful (Don Juan Quijada)

Angriote de Estranaus (Don Diego de Acuña)

and two little Moors.

Further adventurers

The second Knight of the White Mule (the Prince of Espinoy, black)

The Knight of Death (Guillaume de Croy, Lord of Chièvres, black with three skulls on his shield)

The Knight of Fortune (Don Hernando de la Cerda, red and white)

The Sad Knight (Don Juan de Saavedra, black)

The Unprovided Knight (Maximilian de Melun, red)

Florestan (Lambert de Verlucey, blue)

Gabarte de Valtemeroso (Don Luis Zapata, yellow)

Sir Bruno of the Mount (Filippo di Hama, no colors listed)

The second Knight of the Sun (Charles de Brymeu, Count of Meghen, device of the sun in a garland, with white heron plumes)

The Knight of the Stars (Hieronymus Perrenot, crest of stars)

The Knight of the Moon (Gaspar de Robles, no colors listed)

The Knight of Esboye (Floris de Gravenbroude, green)

The second Knight of Death (Don García de Ayala, black with a device of skulls)

The Knight of the Basilisk (Mingoval; orange, blue, and white)

The Knight of the White Rose (Antoine de Werchin, white)

The Adventurous Knight (Louis de Stradiot, white)

Guidon Sauvage (André de Sucre, device of blue rock on a silver field)

The last band of adventurers (red and white)

The Knight with No Name, or the third Untried Knight (Don Francisco de Avalos, Marquis of Pescara) and his second, Don Juan de Benavides

The second Knight of the White Rose (Philippe de St. Aldegonde) and his second, Jean de Poupet

The Blue Knight (the Marquis Jean de Berghes) and his second, Jean de Lyminges

The Chevalier Ebré (the Prince of Piedmont) and his second, the Count of Frossasco

Beltenebros (Prince Philip of Spain)

The judges
The Fortunate Pass
The Baron de Montfalconet
Don Juan Manrique de Lara
Gutierre López de Padilla
each with his king of arms.

The Perilous Tower and the Blessed Isle
The Marquis of Astorga
The Lord of Bossù, grand marshall of the emperor
Joachim de Rie, imperial *sumiller de corps*
each with his king of arms,
and Don Francisco de Mendoza, maréchal du champ.

3. FANCY-DRESS COMBATS IN THE PALACE AT BINCHE, WITH A SIEGE OF A MOCK FORTRESS IN THE GARDENS OUTSIDE THE NEARBY PALACE OF MARIEMONT THE FOLLOWING DAY, 28–29 AUGUST 1549
Staged sword fight, skirmishes, and assault on a mock fortress with light and heavy artillery.

The defenders of the fortress, led by Philippe de Lalaing, Count of Hoogstraten, with some knights, around eighty soldiers, and thirty arquebusiers.

The besiegers of the fortress, led by Duke Adolf, with some Spanish and Italian knights, and five squadrons of infantry, pikemen, and arquebusiers, with the Prince of Piedmont, captain general, and Giovanni Battista Castaldo, *maestro del campo*.

The first assault, led by Don Juan de Acuña and two other knights.

The relief force, led by Duke Philippe of Arschot
Charles de Boniere
Floris de Tserclaes
Corneille Wandereecke
Louis de Stradiot
Ferri Laurens
Antonio de Landas
Roberto de Landas
Jean de Lafontaine
and approximately fifty other knights.

4. Tournament on horseback in the town square, 30 August 1549

Single jousts, jousts of five on five, and *mêlée* with swords.

The Prince of Spain and his squadron, entering through the Giants' Gate (white and red)
    The Count of Cifuentes
    Don Antonio de Toledo
    Joachim de Rie
    Ruy Gómez de Silva
and the prince's second, the Duke of Alba, with four *maestres de campo*
    The Baron of Montfalconet
    Gutierre López de Padilla
    Pont de Lalaing
    Giovanni Battista Castaldo.

The Prince of Piedmont and his squadron, entering through the Victory Gate (yellow)
    The Count of Froslas, His Highness's grand marshall
    Vespasiano de' Gonzaga
    Hieronymus Perrenot
    Don Juan de Acuña

The third band, entering through the Giants' Gate (orange)
    Amoral, Count of Egmont
    Jacques de Herbaix
    Antoine de Montegnies
    Richard de Merodes
    Don Diego de Leyva

The fourth band, entering through the Victory Gate (brown)
    Philippe de Lalaing, Count of Hoogstraten
    Juan de Lanoy
    Philippe de Hamalles
    Charles de Trasegnies
    André de Bailleul

The fifth band, entering through the Giants' Gate (light blue)
    The Marquis of Berghes
    Thomas Perrenot
    Jean de Failly, grand marshall of the queen of Hungary
    Baudoin de Blois
    Jean de Lyminges

The sixth band, entering through the Victory Gate (turquoise blue)
    Jean de Lignes, Count Aremberghe
    Duke Adolf of Holstein

Hermann, Count of Nieuwenare and Moerss
Floris de Gravenbroude
Adrien of Burgundy
Jacques de Quoaresme

The seventh band, entering through the Giants' Gate (tawny and yellow)
Charles de Wignacourt, second to Peter Ernst, Count of Mansfelt
(wounded at previous event)
Jean de Locguingen
Francis de Stranchaux
Jean de St. Omer
Lambert de Verlucey

The eighth band, entering through the Victory Gate (light brown)
Hugo de Melun, Prince of Espinoy and Baron of Antoine
Guillaume de Croy
Antoine de Werchin
Pierre de Quaderebbe
Robert de Trasegnies

The ninth band, entering through the Giants' Gate (white)
Charles de Brymeu, Count of Meghen
André de Bailleul
Pierre de Vaudrey
Francis de Lambert
Don Luis Zapata

The tenth band, entering through the Victory Gate (murrey)
Philippe de Montmorency, Count of Horne
Philippe de St. Aldegunde
Humbert de Peleaux
Juan de Lanoy y Mingoval
Gaspar de Robles

The eleventh band, entering through the Giants' Gate (black and silver)
Jean de Henin, Lord of Bossù and grand marshall of the emperor
Don Juan Manrique de Lara
Don Hernando de La Cerda
Jean de Poupet
Luis Quijada

The twelfth band, entering through the Victory Gate (red)
Jacques de Lignes, Count of Faulquenberghe
Antoine de Montegnies
Francis de Montmorency
Georges de Beaufort
Maximilian de Melun

Antwerp

1. TOURNAMENT ON HORSEBACK, 13 SEPTEMBER 1549

Tourney of two teams without barrier, tourney of three on three, a *mêlée*, and a skirmish of knights and Spanish arquebusiers. The names of the individual participants are not listed.

2. TOURNAMENT ON FOOT, 14 SEPTEMBER 1549

Single combats with pikes, spears, javelins, and swords.

The defenders (gold and silver)
  The Marquis of Berghes
  The Count of Hoogstraten
  The Count of Horne
  The Count of Meghen
  and their seconds.

The adventurers
The first band
  William of Nassau, Prince of Orange
  Hieronymus Perrenot
  Peter de Waldrey
  Humbert de Peleaux
  Jean de Lanoy de Mingoval
  and the Prince of Orange's second, the Master Pedro de Felices,
    ambassador of the Order of St. John at the imperial court.

The other adventurers (gold and silver, and "many-colored silks")
  The Count of Egmont
  Philippe de St. Aldegonde
  Floris de Montmorency
  François de Berniemicourt
  The Count of Gelves
  Don Pedro de Velasco
  Don Alonso Pimentel
  Felipe de Castro
  Don Diego de Córdoba
  Don García de Ayala
  Don Diego de Leyva
  Don Diego de Acuña
  Don García Sarmiento
  Don Pedro de las Roelas
  Don Juan Mausino
  Don Gabriel Zapata
  Gaspar de Robles
  and other knights.

3. ROYAL JOUST, 15 SEPTEMBER 1549
Single jousts over the barrier, and a *mêlée*.

The team of Captain Jean de Lignes, Count of Aremberghe. Having been wounded in the tournament at Binche, the team is led by his second, Floris de Montmorency, Lord of Hubermont (white and red, with crests on their helmets conforming to the arms on their shields)
  The Marquis of Berghes
  The Count of Horne
  The Count of Meghen
  Philippe de Hamalles
  Thomas Perrenot
  Don Hernando de la Cerda
  Don Luis de Carvajal
  Don Francisco de Mendoza
  Don Diego de Acevedo Pimentel
  Don Juan de Acuña
  Don Diego de Acuña
  Don García de Ayala
  Each with two seconds.

The team of Jacques de Herbaix, gentleman of the imperial chamber and Margrave of Anvers. De Herbaix having been wounded at Binche, the team is led by his second, the Prince of Piedmont (yellow, red, and murrey, with crests on their helmets conforming to those on their shields)
  The Prince of Spain
  The Count of Egmont
  The Count of Mansfelt
  The Count of Hoogstraten
  Guillaume de Croy
  Antoine de Montegnies
  Charles de Trasegnies
  Pierre de Vaudrey
  Humbert de Peleaux
  Francis de Lambert
  Don Luis Zapata
  Don Luis Méndez de Haro
  Each with two seconds.

The judges
  The Duke of Alba
  The Marquis of Astorga
  Jean de Henin, Lord of Bossù and grand marshall of the emperor
  Joachim de Rie, first imperial *sumiller de corps*

Brussels

1. JOUSTS IN THE PARK OF THE PALACE, SHROVE TUESDAY, 1550
Single jousts over the barrier, with barred shields.

The defender, Don Alonso Pimentel, and fourteen seconds (black)
  The Count of Cifuentes
  The Count of Castañeda
  Don Alonso de Aragón
  Don Rodrigo Manuel
  Don Felipe Manrique
  Don Juan de la Nuza
  Don Gaspar de Quiñones
  Don Enrique Manrique
  Don Diego Ferrer
  Alonso de Ulloa
  Don Hernando de Acuña
  Don Francisco Manrique
  Don Juan de Silva
  Don Luis de Beamont

The first band of adventurers (white and murrey)
  The Prince of Spain
  The Prince of Piedmont
  The Count of Egmont
  Don Diego de Acuña
  and the prince's second, Don Antonio de Toledo, His Highness's
    grand marshall.

The other adventurers (colors not listed)
  Don Hernando de Toledo
  Don Luis de Carvajal
  Don Diego de Acevedo Pimentel
  Carlos de Sango

The judges
  Don Pedro de Avila, Marquis of Las Navas
  Jean de Henin, grand marshall of the Emperor
  Gutierre López de Padilla, the prince's chamberlain
  Filibert de Baume, Baron of Monfalconet, imperial chamberlain

The prizewinner
  The Count of Egmont, best man-at-arms

2. JOUSTS IN THE PARK OF THE PALACE, FIRST SUNDAY OF LENT, 1550
Single jousts over the barrier, fully armed with barred shields, and a
mêlée.

The defender, Ruy Gómez de Silva, and his seconds, Don Diego de Córdoba and Don Diego de Haro (white and murrey).

The first adventurers, then joining the defender (white)
The Prince of Spain
Don Antonio de Toledo, His Highness's grand marshall
and their seconds, the Duke of Alba and Don Alonso de Silva.

The second band of adventurers, led by the Prince of Piedmont (white and red)
The Count of Egmont
The Count of Mansfelt
The Count of Meghen
Floris de Montmorency
Jacques de Herbaix
Hieronymus Perrenot
Guillaume de Croy
Humbert de Peleaux

The other adventurers (colors not listed)
Don Alonso Pimentel
Don Rodrigo de Bazán
Count Annibale Visconti
Don Luis Zapata
Pompeo Colonna
Juan Quijada

The fourth band of adventurers (no colors listed)
The Marquis of Pescara
Don Diego de Acuña
Lambert de Verlucey
Gaspar de Robles

Don Luis de Carvajal and eight seconds (blue and yellow; jousting alone)

The fifth band of adventurers (white, yellow, and murrey)
The Count of Gelves
Don Diego de Leyva
and six seconds.

The judges
The Marquis of Astorga
Don Juan Manrique de Lara
Claude Bouton (in place of Adrien de Croy)

The prizewinners
Don Antonio de Toledo, best man-at-arms
The Prince of Piedmont, for the Lance of the Ladies

Don Luis de Carvajal, for the most gallant entry
Jacques de Herbaix, for the *mêlée*

3. SKIRMISH ON HORSEBACK IN THE PARK OF THE PALACE, SUNDAY, 11 MAY 1550

Skirmish and battle without barrier, forty on forty.

The first team, led by Captain Garcilaso Puertocarrero, the Duke of Alba; Don Manrique de Lara, keeper of the Order of Calatrava; and Don Antonio de Rojas, His Highness's first *sumiller de corps* (yellow and brown), and thirty seven other knights, with three *maestres del campo* and four additional captains with their squads

The Marquis of Pescara
The Count of Cifuentes
The Count of Castañeda
The Marquis of Berghes

Garcilaso's squadron (left sleeves brown and white)
The Prince of Spain
Don Antonio de Toledo, His Highness'a grand marshall
Ruy Gómez de Silva
Don Hernando de Toledo
Don Juan de Silva

The Marquis of Pescara's squadron (left sleeves black and white)
Don Pedro de Avila
Don Juan de Benavides
Don Rodrigo Manuel
Don Diego de Acuña
Don García de Ayala
Don Juan de la Nuza
Don Juan de Ayala

The Count of Cifuentes' squadron (left sleeves red and black)
Don Diego de Acevedo Pimentel
Don Pedro Manuel
Don Diego Hurtado
Don Francisco de Mendoza
Don Diego de Haro
Don Alonso de Córdoba
Iñigo López de Zúñiga

The Count of Castañeda's squadron (left sleeves brownish yellow and white)
Don Alvaro de Mendoza
The Marquis of Val Siciliana
Don Diego de Córdoba
Don Rodrigo de Moscoso

Don Juan Manrique
Don Pedro Manrique
Don Juan de Castilla

The Marquis of Berghes' squadron (left sleeves brown, yellow, and red)
Don Gonzalo Chacón
Don Lope Zapata
Don Jerónimo Pinatelo
Scipión Vilono
with three other Flemish knights and Polidoro, the emperor's standard
    bearer, with a standard of the team's colors and the letter Y (intial
    of Garcilaso's lady).

The second team, led by Captain Don Alvaro of Portugal, Count of
Gelves, Gutierre López de Padilla, Joachim de Rie, first imperial *sumiller
de corps,* and Giovanni Battista Castaldo (murrey and white), and four
additional captains with their squads
The Prince of Piedmont
The Count of Egmont
The Prince of Asculi
Don Luis de Carvajal

The Count of Gelves' squadron (left sleeves white and murrey)
Don Hernando de la Cerda
Don Pedro de Velasco
Don Luis Méndez de Haro
Don Pedro de las Roelas
Pompeo Colonna
Marcial Colonna

The Prince of Piedmont's squadron (left sleeves white and black), and seven
Burgundian and Flemish knights.

The Count of Egmont's squadron (left sleeves blue, white, and red), and an
unknown number of Flemish and Burgundian knights.

The Prince of Asculi's squadron (left sleeves orange, white, and black)
Don Gabriel de la Cueva
Don Hernando Carillo de Mendoza
Don Diego de Leyva
Don Rodrigo de Benavides
Don Rodrigo de Bazán

Don Luis de Carvajal's squadron (left sleeves blue, white, and yellow)
Don Antonio de Velasco
Don Juan Tavera
Don Gómez Manrique
Don Pedro Quintana

Don Gabriel Zapata
Carlos de Sango
and their standard bearer, with a standard of the team's colors and
   the letter V (initial of the Count of Gelves' lady).

Glossary

adargas   heart-shaped shields of hide used by Spanish light cavalry. *Adargas* were used in the *juego de cañas* or cane game.

adventus   ceremonial entry of a ruler into a subject city or town (also called an *entrata* or *intrata*).

alcancías   Spanish game in which contestants threw earthen balls filled with flowers or perfume at each other.

all'antica (*alla romana*)   armor or costume in ancient Roman style.

allemande   a slow and stately dance for couples.

amantecas   Indian featherworkers whose skills were prized by the Aztecs.

apparati   temporary architecture and mechanical devices made for Renaissance festivals.

armas negras   lit. "black armor"; Spanish term referring to embossed armor with raised designs left black from the hammer.

assegai   Moorish javelin.

attaint   a hit on an opponent's shield or armor.

bard   armor for a horse.

barriers   a combat on foot with pikestaffs or swords over a central wooden barrier.

bezants   gold coins or coinlike decorations (usually a heraldic motif).

bordonasse   a jousting lance with a fluted hollow shaft.

brigandine   light body armor composed of many small steel plates riveted to a facing of leather or cloth.

bucrania   skulls of oxen, used in ancient and Renaissance art as symbols of time and immortality.

buff   in the sixteenth century, a reinforcement for the lower half of the helmet protecting the neck and face.

burgonet   light open-faced helmet for infantry or light cavalry use.

cane game   see *juego de cañas*.

carreras de cintas   Spanish game of indeterminate type.

213

carrousel   game in fancy costume between teams of horsemen armed with staves or swords. In the carrousel, emphasis was placed on horsemanship rather than skill at arms.

cartellino   in chivalric parlance, a letter declaring the rules and prizes for a tournament.

chamfron   face-plate for a bard or horse armor.

champ clos   enclosure for armored combat on foot with sword or pollaxe, without a central barrier.

chimalli   feather-decorated shield used by the Aztecs.

close helmet   form-fitting helmet completely enclosing the head, usually opened from the side.

cloth of gold   fancy cloth interwoven with real gold thread.

cloth of silver   fancy cloth interwoven with real silver thread.

coronel   lance tip split into three points for greater safety.

couters   armor for the elbows.

crupper   plates for the hindquarters of a horse.

culverins   light artillery pieces.

en armes   wearing armor.

entrata   ceremonial entry of a ruler or pope into a subject city or town (also called an *adventus*).

escaramuça   skirmish of soldiers. A skirmish on horseback was called an *escaramuça de caballo*.

ferrule   tournament exercise of indeterminate type, in which opponents apparently cast spears at each other.

festival book   printed book describing the entry, tournaments, and feasts of a visiting ruler or prince.

Freiturnier   in the later sixteenth century, a *mélée* on horseback without a tilt barrier, wearing regular armor for war with reinforcing pieces.

Fusskampf   in the later sixteenth century, a tournament on foot with sword or pollaxe without a central barrier, wearing a tonlet armor.

garniture   a suit of armor including all its reinforcements and pieces of exchange.

Gestech   joust, in German.

gorget   armor for the throat.

grandguard   in the later sixteenth century, a reinforcing piece of armor shaped to conform to the jouster's left side and shoulder, worn in place of a shield in the Italian-style joust or tilt.

graper   metal ring with teeth near the butt of a jousting lance, designed to fit into corresponding slots on the lance rest.

great helm   massive helmet for jousting worn in the Middle Ages.

gupfe   reinforcing piece of armor for the top of a knight's helmet, worn in the *Freiturnier* or *mêlée*.

halberd   staff weapon with an axelike head with a spike on the opposite side.

half-armor   armor worn only down to the thighs for combat on foot, usually with full arm-harness and pieces of exchange for the shoulders.

harness   plate armor.

heaume (*helm*)   oversized helmet, in the Renaissance worn only in the joust and bolted directly to the breastplate.

herms   busts on pedestals (originally representing the god Hermes) used to mark boundaries in Greek and Roman art.

hussars   eastern European light cavalry, armed in a combination of Western and Turkish styles.

impresa   personal emblem or device.

joust   tournament combat in which a pair of horsemen wearing special armor charged each other with leveled lances. The joust was called a *Gestech* in Germany.

jousting at the ring   jousting exercise in fancy-dress or civilian costume in which an unarmored horseman attempts to spear rings of various sizes hanging from a crosspiece on a pole.

jousting check   scoring sheet for a joust.

juego de cañas   "cane game"; game on horseback in which opposing teams attacked each other with blunt cane spears, then wheeled to retreat. In Spanish Italy, this game was called a *gioco de canne*.

justa real   "royal joust"; term for the joust with blunt lances in Spain.

karr wa farr   Muslim tactic in which lightly armored horsemen repeatedly attacked and retreated in an effort to tire more heavily armored opponents. This tactic was probably the ancestor of the Spanish cane game.

Kufic   script in Arabic letters.

Landsknechts   imperial mercenaries armed with pikes, swords, and guns.

Lapiths   family in Greek mythology who fought the centaurs at a wedding feast.

livery   uniform for a servant in the colors of his master's coat of arms, usually with a badge on the left breast.

locking gauntlet   special gauntlet for the right hand made to lock to the underside of the wrist, preventing a tourneyer from losing his weapon. The locking gauntlet was prohibited in some tournaments.

manifer   large gauntlet for the left hand worn in the joust, tilt, and *Freiturnier*.

manteau   small curved shield tied to the left shoulder on a jousting armor. In the later sixteenth century, the *manteau* was bolted directly to the breastplate. A *manteau* with a trellised surface (designed to catch and break an opponent's lance) was called a *manteau des armes*.

masque   courtly dance in fancy-dress costume and masks.

mêlée   tournament combat in which teams of armored horsemen attacked each other all at once. The *mêlée* was also referred to as the *tournois* or tourney, or the *Freiturnier* in Germany.

morrion   light open-faced helmet.

naumachia   mock sea battle.

occularium   vision-slot on a helmet.

paludamentum   the imperial mantle of ancient Rome.

panoply   in the sixteenth and seventeenth centuries, a set of matching helmet and shield *all'antica*.

pas d'armes   collectively, all the contests in a tournament: the joust, combat on foot, and *mêlée*.

pasguard   large reinforcing plate for the left arm, worn in the joust, tilt, and *Freiturnier*.

pauldrons   armor for the shoulders.

peytral   armor for the chest and forequarters of a horse.

piece of exchange   piece of armor designed to reinforce or replace another piece for different types of combat, decorated en suite with the rest of the armor.

Plankengestech   joust over a tilt barrier. Contestants in the *Plankengestech* aimed at their opponent's shield with the object of breaking a lance or knocking the opponent out of his saddle.

plus ultra   "more beyond," the imperial motto of Charles V, referring to a passage in Strabo's geography asserting the world ended at the Pillars of Hercules (Gibraltar).

poleyns   armor for the knees.

pollaxe   staff weapon with a long haft and a head with an axelike blade on one side and a war hammer on the other, designed to be used with two hands for combat on foot.

principe heredero   crown prince of Spain.

prospettive   scenes illustrated in perspective.

putti   in ancient and Renaissance art, figures of winged children representing love and matrimony. *Putti* are also sometimes referred to as *amorini*.

queue   brace behind a jouster's right arm that ensures the lance was pointed at the proper angle.

quintain joust   jousting exercise in which a horseman charged at a spinning target fitted with a hanging sack designed to strike jousters who failed to duck in time. The quintain was sometimes shaped like a dragon or a Turk.

ravelin   secondary platform in front of the main wall of a fortress designed to resist an artillery assault.

rebated blunted and dulled weapons for safety in tournament combats.

Reichsadler in European art, the double-headed imperial eagle.

renovator imperii restorer of the Roman Empire.

royal joust (justa real) the joust with blunt lances in Spain.

sallet light helmet, usually worn with a separate face guard called a bevor.

Scharfrennen joust with sharp lances.

Stechsack padded sack protecting the neck of a jouster's horse, designed to prevent collisions with the tilt barrier.

Stradiots mercenary light cavalry from the Balkans.

tassets armor plates protecting the upper thighs.

terraplein raised embankment for the placement of heavy artillery.

tilt a long barrier designed to separate jousters and prevent collisions. Also, a joust specifically over a tilt barrier.

tiltyard a temporary or permanent space set aside for jousting over a barrier.

toison the emblem or jeweled collar of the Order of the Golden Fleece, an order of chivalry dedicated to the recapture of Jerusalem (also *Toison d'Or*).

tonlet a metal skirt worn as a reinforcement over armor for combat on foot with sword or pollaxe in the *champ clos (Fusskampf)*.

tournament public event featuring sporting combat on horseback and foot, originally intended as knightly training for war.

tournois à theme tournament with a prearranged program or theme, held in fancy-dress costume.

traite des armes a book describing the forms and rules of a tournament.

trionfi poems describing a procession of virtues in decorated cars.

triumphal arch arch intended to commemorate a victorious Roman general. In the Renaissance and baroque periods, temporary triumphal arches in Roman style were erected for the ceremonial entry of a visiting prince.

triumphator person to whom a triumphal procession is dedicated.

vamplate flaring sheet of metal on a jousting lance to protect the hand.

Victory in ancient and Renaissance art, a winged female figure representing military conquest.

Bibliography

Archives

AGS   Archivo General de Simancas

Published Sources

Administrazione Provinciale di Viterbo, Regione Lazio. *Spettacoli conviviali dall'antichità classica alle corte Italiane del' 400.* Viterbo: Centro di studi sul teatro medioevale e rinascimentale, 1982.

Albicante, Giovanni Alberto. *Al gran Maximiliano d'Austria granduca, intrada de Milano di don Filipo d'Austria re di Spagna, capriccio d'historia de l'Albicante.* Venice: le Case di Marcolini, [ca. 1549–56].

———. *Trattato del'intrar in Milano di Carlo V.* Milan: Andrea Calvi, 1541.

Anonymous. *Amadís de Gaula, Tomos I–IV.* Edited by Edwin B. Place. Madrid: Instituto Miguel de Cervantes, 1962.

Apollonius of Rhodes. *The Voyage of Argo.* Translated by E. V. Rieu. London: Penguin Books, 1959.

Ariosto, Ludovico. *Orlando Furioso.* Edited by Piero Nardi. Verona: Editore Arnoldo Mondadori, 1964.

Armas, Frederick A. de. *The Return of Astraea: An Astral-Imperial Myth in Calderón.* Lexington: University Press of Kentucky, 1986.

Aroldi, Aldo. *Armi e armature italiane fino al XVIII secolo.* Milan: Bramante, 1961.

Ashdown, Charles Henry. *British and Continental Arms and Armor.* London: T. C. & E. C. Jack, 1909.

Baines, Barbara Burman. *Fashion Revivals, from the Elizabethan Age to the Present Day.* London: B. T. Batsford, 1981.

Barber, Richard, and Juliet Barker. *Tournaments: Jousts, Chivalry, and Pageants in the Middle Ages.* Woodbridge: Boydell Press, 1989.

Beer, Rudolf. "Acten, Regesten und Inventare aus dem Archivo General zu Simancas." *Jahrbuch der Kunsthistorischen Sammlungen des Allerhöchsten Kaiserhauses* 12 (1890): 91–204.

Belluzi, Amadeo. "Carlo V a Mantova e Milano." In *La città effimera e l'universo artificiale del giardino: La Firenze dei Medici e l'Italia del '500*, edited by Marcello Fagiolo, 47–62. Rome: Officina Edizioni, 1980.

Bober, Phyllis Pray, and Ruth Rubinstein. *Renaissance Artists and Antique Sculpture.* London: Harvey Miller Publishers, 1986.

Boccia, Lionello Giorgio. *Armi antiche delle raccolte civiche reggione.* Reggio Emilia: Comune, 1984.

——— and E. T. Coelho, *L'arte dell'armatura in Italia.* Milan: Bramante, 1967.

Böheim, Wendelin. "Augsburger Waffenschmiede, ihre Werke und ihre Bezeichnungen zum kaiserlichen und zu anderen Höfen." *Jahrbuch der Kunsthistorischen Sammlungen des Allerhöchsten Kaiserhauses* 12 (1891): 165–227.

Bondioli, Miriam. *Armature milanesi.* Milan: A. Vallardi, 1965.

————. "Espadas toledanas de la Real Armería: Siglos XVI y XVII." *Reales Sitios* 11 (1974): 12–16.

Braudel, Ferdinand. *The Mediterranean World in the Age of Philip II.* New York: Harper-Collins, 1992.

Brown, Jonathan. *The Golden Age of Painting in Spain.* New Haven, CT: Yale University Press, 1991.

Bugati, M. Gaspare. *Historia universale di M. Gaspare Bugati Milanese, nella quale con ogni candidezza de verita si racconta brevemente, e con bel ordine tutto quel ch'a successo dal principio del mondo fino all'anno M.D.L.XIX.* Venice: Gabriel Giolito di Ferrarii, 1570.

Bustamante, C. Pérez. *Felipe III: Semblanza de una monarca y perfiles de una privanza.* Madrid: Estados Evaristo, San Miguel, 1950.

Cadenas y Vicent, Vicente de. *El Milanesado: De Vicariato del Imperio al problema de España.* Madrid: Asociación Universal de Entusiastas de la obra de Emperador Carlo V, 1989.

Calvete de Estrella, Juan Cristóbal. *El felicíssimo viaje del muy alto y muy poderoso Príncipe Don Phelippe, hijo del Emperador Don Carlos Quinto Maximo, desde España a sus tierras de la baxa Alemaña: Con la descripción de todos los estados de Brabante y Flandes.* Antwerp: Martin Nucio, 1552. Facsimile reprint, n.p.: Miguel Artigas, 1950.

Campbell, Lorne. *Renaissance Portraits: European Portrait-Painting in the 14th, 15th, and 16th Centuries.* New Haven, CT: Yale University Press, 1990.

Campbell, Thomas P. *Tapestry in the Renaissance: Art and Magnificence.* New Haven, CT: Yale Universtiy Press, 2002.

Cano, Marina. "Leone y Pompeo Leoni, medallistas de la casa de Austria." In Museo del Prado, *Los Leoni (1509–1608), escultores del Renacimiento italiano al servico de la corte de España,* 180–81. Madrid: Museo del Prado, 1994.

Carlos, Alfonso de. "Espadas del siglo XVI en la Real Armería." *Reales Sitios* 28 (1991): 17–27.

Carretero, Concha Herrero. "Renaissance Tapestries from the Patrimonio Nacional." In Antonio Domínguez Ortiz, Concha Herrero Carretero, and José A. Godoy, *Resplendence of the Spanish Monarchy: Renaissance Tapestries and Armor from the Patrimonio Nacional,* 29–64. New York: Metropolitan Museum of Art, 1991.

Castaldo, Antonio. *Dell'istoria di notar Antonio Castaldo, libri quattri.* In *Raccolta di tutti i più rinomati scrittori dell'istoria generale del regno de Napoli principiando dal tempo che queste provincie hanno preso forma de regno,* vols. 6 and 8. Naples: Giovanni Gravier, 1769–70.

Centro di Studi Storici (Narni). *La civiltà del torneo (sec. XII–XVIII): Giostre e tornei tra medioevo ed età moderna.* Narni: Centro di Studi Storici, 1991.

Checa, Fernando. *Felipe II, Mecenas de las artes.* Madrid: Nerea, 1992.

————. *Tiziano y la Monarquía Hispánica: Usos y funciones de la pintura veneciana en España (siglos XVI y XVII).* Madrid: Editorial Nerea, S.A., 1994.

Clamorinus, Bartholomaeus. *Thurnierbüchlei–Darinnen Sechs und dreiszig Thurnier, von Keyser Heinrich dem I angesangen, bis auff Keyser Maximilianum den ersten so ganz Ritterlich sind gehalten worden.* N.p., 1591.

Clephan, R. Coltman. *The Tournament: Its Periods and Phases.* London: Methuen, 1919.

Colum, Padraic. *The Golden Fleece and the Heroes Who Lived before Achilles.* New York: Macmillan, 1921.

Comparetti, Domenico. *Virgil in the Middle Ages.* Translated by E. F. M. Benecke. London: Swan Sonnenschein, 1895.

Crooke y Navarrot, Juan. *Catálogo historico-descriptivo de la Real Armería de Madrid.* Madrid: Fototipias de Hauser y Menet, 1898.

Davenport, Millia. *The Book of Costume.* New York: Crown Publishers, 1948.

De' Nobili, Alberto. *La triumphale intrata del serenissimo prence de Spagna nell'inclitta città di Melano el di. XIX de decembre M.D. XLVIII.* N.p.: ca. 1548–49.

Devoto, Daniel. "Folklore et Politique au Château Ténébreux." In *Les fêtes de la renaissance.* Vol. 2, *Fêtes et cérémonies au temps de Charles Quint,* edited by Jean Jacquot, 311–28. Paris: Centre National de la Recherche Scientifique, 1975.

Dumont, Catherine. *Francesco Salviati au Palais Sacchetti de Rome et la décoration murae italienne (1520–1560)*. Rome: Institut Suisse, 1973.

Edge, David, and John Miles Paddock. *Arms and Armor of the Medieval Knight: An Illustrated History of Weaponry in the Middle Ages*. Greenwich, CT: Brompton Books, 1988.

Eisler, William. "Celestial Harmonies and Hapsburg Rule: Levels of Meaning in a Triumphal Arch for Philip II in Antwerp, 1549." In *All the World's a Stage: Art and Pageantry in the Renaissance and Baroque*, edited by Barbara Wisch and Susan Scott Munshower, 332–56. University Park: Pennsylvania State University, 1990.

———. "The Impact of the Emperor Charles V upon the Visual Arts." PhD diss., Pennsylvania State University, 1983.

Elliott, J. H. *Imperial Spain, 1469–1716*. London: Edward Arnold, 1963.

Fagiolo, Marcello, ed. *La città effimera e l'universo artificiale del giardino: La Firenze dei Medici e l'Italia del '500*. Rome: Officina Edizioni, 1980.

Felipe II, Rey de España. *Testamento de Felipe II*. Edited by Manuel Fernández Alvarez. Madrid: Editorial Nacional, 1982.

Ferguson, George. *Signs and Symbols in Christian Art*. New York: Oxford University Press, 1954.

Ffoulkes, Charles. *The Armourer and His Craft, from the XIth to the XVIth Century*. London: Methuen, 1912.

Fletcher, Jennifer. "Titian as a Painter of Portraits." In *Titian: Essays*, edited by Charles Hope and David Jaffé, 29–42. Exhibition catalogue. London: National Gallery Company Limited, 2003.

Foligno. *La società in costume: Giostre e tornei nell'italia di antico regime*. Città di Foligno: Palazzo Alleori Ubaldi, 1986.

Forcella, Vincenzo. *Tornei e giostre, ingressi trionfali e feste carnevaleschi in Roma sotto Paolo III*. Bologna: Forni Editore, 1885.

Foronda y Aguilera, Don Manuel. *Estancias y viajes de Carlos V, desde el día de su nacimiento hasta él de su muerte*. Madrid: La Sociedad Geográfica de Madrid, 1895.

Freedberg, Sydney Joseph. *Parmigianino: His Works in Painting*. Westport, CT: Greenwood Press, 1950.

Gaya, Louis de. *Gaya's Traité des armes, 1678*. Edited by Charles Ffoulkes. London: Henry Frowde, 1678. Facsimile reprint, London: Clarendon Press, 1911.

Gnecchi, Francesco and Ercole. *Le monete di Milano, da Carlo Magno a Vittorio Emanuele II*. Milan: Fratelli Dumolard, 1884.

Godoy, José A. "La Real Armería de Madrid." *Reales Sitios* 25 and 26 (1989): 189–200.

———. "The Royal Armory." In Antonio Domínguez Ortiz, Concha Herrero Carretero, and José A. Godoy, *Resplendence of the Spanish Monarchy: Renaissance Tapestries and Armor from the Patrimonio Nacional*. New York: Metropolitan Museum of Art, 1991.

———, and Silvio Leydi. *Parures triomphales: La maniérisme dans l'art de l'armure italienne*. Geneva: Musées d'art et d'histoire, 2003.

Gorse, George. "Between Empire and Republic: Triumphal Entries into Genoa During the Sixteenth Century." In *All the World's a Stage: Art and Pageantry in the Renaissance and Baroque*. Part 1, *Triumphal Celebrations and the Rituals of Statecraft*, edited by Barbara Wisch and Susan Scott Munshower, 188–256. Papers in Art History from the Pennsylvania State University 6. University Park: Pennsylvania State University, 1990.

Grant, Michael. *The Army of the Caesars*. New York: Charles Scribner's Sons, 1974.

Gravett, Christopher. *Knights at Tournament*. London: Osprey Publishing, 1988.

Gravier, Giovanni, ed. *Raccolta di tutti i più rinomati scrittori dell'istoria generale del regno de Napoli principiando dal tempo che queste provincie hanno preso forma de regno*, vols. 6 and 8. Naples: Giovanni Gravier, 1769–70.

Greenhalgh, Michael. *Donatello and His Sources*. New York: Holmes & Meier, 1982.

Grierson, Edward. *King of Two Worlds: Philip II of Spain*. London: Collins Press, 1974.

Hale, J. R. *Artists and Warfare in the Renaissance*. New Haven, CT: Yale University Press, 1990.

Hall, James. *Dictionary of Subjects and Symbols in Art*. New York: Harper & Row, 1974.

Hart, Harold. *Weapons and Armor: A Pictorial Archive of Woodcuts and Engravings*. New York: Dover, 1978.

Hartley, C. Gasquoine. "The Madrid Royal Armoury." *Connoisseur* 4, no. 16 (1902): 239-47.

Hartt, Frederick. *Giulio Romano*. 2 vols. New York: Hacker Art Books, 1981.

―――. *History of Italian Renaissance Art: Painting, Sculpture, Architecture*. 2nd ed. New York: Harry N. Abrams, 1979.

Haskell, Francis. *History and Its Images: Art and the Interpretation of the Past*. London: Yale University Press, 1993.

Hayward, John F. "The Revival of Roman Armour in the Renaissance." In *Art, Arms, and Armour: An International Anthology*, edited by Robert Held, 144-63. Chiasso: Acquafresca Editrice, 1979.

Heartz, Daniel. "Un divertissement de palais pour Charles V à Binche." In *Les fêtes de la renaissance*. Vol. 2, *Fêtes et cérémonies au temps de Charles Quint*, 329-42. Paris: Centre National de la Recherche Scientifique, 1975.

Heintze, Helga. *Roman Art*. New York: Universe Books, 1972.

Hibbard, Howard. *Michelangelo*. 2nd ed. New York: Harper & Row, 1974.

Hibbert, Christopher. *The House of Medici: Its Rise and Fall*. New York: William Morrow, 1975.

Hill, G. F., and G. Pollard. *Renaissance Medals from the Samuel H. Kress Collection at the National Gallery of Art*. London: Phaidon Press, 1967.

Holme, Bryan. *Medieval Pageants*. London: Thames & Hudson, 1987.

Hope-Moncrieff, A. R. *Romance & Legend of Chivalry*. New York: William Wise, 1934.

Horn, Hendrik J. *Jan Cornelisz Vermeyen, Painter of Charles V and His Conquest of Tunis: Paintings, Etchings, Drawings, Cartoons, & Tapestries*. 2 vols. Meppel: Davaco, 1989.

Hughes, Quentin. *Military Architecture*. London: Hugh Evelyn, 1974.

Huizinga, Johan. *The Waning of the Middle Ages: A Study of the Forms of Life, Thought and Art in France and the Netherlands in the Dawn of the Renaissance*. 3rd ed. Garden City, NY: Doubleday, 1954.

Jacquot, Jean. "La fête chevaleresque." In *Les fêtes de la renaissance*. Vol. 2, *Fêtes et cérémonies au temps de Charles Quint*. Edited by Jean Jacquot. Paris: Centre National de la Recherche Scientifique, 1975.

Janzen, Reinhild. *Albrecht Altdorfer: Four Centuries of Criticism*. Ann Arbor: UMI Research Press, 1980.

Junquera, Paulina. "Aeneas tapestries." *Reales Sitios* 11(1974): 17-29.

―――. "Los trabjos de Hércules: una serie inedita del Patrimonio Nacional." *Reales Sitios* 11 (1974): 18-24.

―――. "Tapices de una serie de Escipión en el Real Armería de Madrid." *Reales Sitios* 10 (1973): 20-36.

Kamen, Henry. *Philip of Spain*. New Haven, CT: Yale University Press, 1997.

Kantorowicz, E. H. *Selected Studies*. Locust Valley, NY: J. J. Augustin, 1965.

Karcheski, Walter J. Jr. *Arms and Armor in The Art Institute of Chicago*. Chicago: The Art Institute of Chicago, 1995.

Katzenellenbogen, Adolf. *Allegories of the Virtues and Vices in Medieval Art*. Toronto: University of Toronto Press, 1989.

Kavaler, Ethan M. "Being the Count of Nassau: Refiguring Identity in Space, Time and Stone." *Nederlands Kunsthistorisch Jaarboek* 46 (1995): 13-51.

Keen, Maurice. *Chivalry*. New Haven, CT: Yale University Press, 1984.

Konstam, Angus. *Pavia, 1525: The Climax of the Italian Wars*. Reed International Books, 1996.

Krenn, Peter, and Karcheski, Walter J., Jr. *Imperial Austria: Treasures of Art, Arms & Armor from the State of Styria*. Munich: Prestel-Verlag, 1992.

Lacaci, Guillermo Quintana. *Armería del Palacio Real de Madrid*. Madrid: Editorial Patrimonio Nacional, 1987.

Lageirse, Marcel. "L'entrée du prince Philippe à Gand." In *Les fêtes de la renaissance*. Vol. 2, *Fêtes et cérémonies au temps de Charles Quint*. Edited by Jean Jacquot. Paris: Centre National de la Recherche Scientifique, 1975.

Leguina, Enrique de. *Glosario de voces de Armería*. Madrid: Librería de Felipe Rodríguez, 1912.

Lensi, Alfredo. *Museo Stibbert: Catalogo delle sale delle arme europee*. Florence: n.d.

Loades, David. *Mary Tudor: A Life*. Oxford: Blackwell, 1989.

Malatesta, Enzio. *Armi ed armaioli*. Milan: B. C. Tosi, 1939.

Malory, Thomas. *Works*. Edited by Eugène Vinaver. 2nd ed. London: Oxford University Press, 1971.

Mariani, Michel'Angelo. *Trento con il Sacro Concilio et altri notabili [...] descrittion' historica*. Book 3. Trent, 1672.

Marsden, C. A. "Entrées et fêtes espagnoles au XVI siècle." In *Les fêtes de la renaissance*. Vol. 2, *Fêtes et cérémonies au temps de Charles Quint*, 389–411. Edited by Jean Jacquot. Paris: Centre National de la Recherche Scientifique, 1975.

Martín, Fernando A. "Tres espadas de la época de Felipe II conservados en la Armería del Palacio Real de Madrid." *Reales Sitios* 27 (1985): 11–16.

Martindale, Andrew. *The Triumphs of Caesar by Andrea Mantegna in the Collection of Her Majesty the Queen at Hampton Court*. London: Harry Miller Publishers, 1979.

Martínez del Romero. *Catálogo de la Real Armería*. Madrid: Impresor de Camara de S.M. y su Real Casa, 1854.

Michelin Guides. *Belgium, Grand Duchy of Luxemburg*. N.p.: Michelin Tyre, 1997.

Miller, Douglas. *The Landsknechts*. London: Osprey Publishing, 1976.

Mitchell, Bonner. *Italian Civic Pageantry in the High Renaissance: A Descriptive Bibliography of Triumphal Entries and Selected Other Festivals for State Occasions*. Florence: Leo S. Olschki, 1979.

———. *The Majesty of the State: Triumphal Progresses of Foreign Sovereigns in Renaissance Italy (1494–1600)*. Florence: Leo S. Olschki, 1986.

Mode, Heinze. *Fabulous Beasts and Demons*. London: Phaidon Press, 1975.

Moreno Garbajo, Justa. "Real Armería." *Reales Sitios* 6 (1969): 185–88.

Morterero-Simón, Conrado. *Archivo General del Palacio Real de Madrid: Inventario-guía del fondo documental*. Madrid: Patrimonio Nacional, 1977.

Murrin, Michael. *History and Warfare in Renaissance Epic*. Chicago: University of Chicago Press, 1994.

Museo del Prado. *Los Leoni (1509–1608): Escultores del Renacimiento italiano al servicio de la corte de España*. Madrid: Museo del Prado, 1994.

Necipoglu, Gülru. "Suleyman the Magnificent and the Representation of Power in the Context of Ottoman-Hapsburg-Papal Rivalry." *Art Bulletin* 71, no. 3 (1989): 401–27.

Newton, Stella Mary. *Renaissance Theatre and Costume and the Sense of the Historic Past*. London: Rapp and Whiting, 1975.

Niccoli, Ottavia. *Prophecy and People in Renaissance Italy*. Translated by Lydia Cochrane. Princeton, NJ: Princeton University Press, 1990.

Nickel, Helmut. *Arms and Armor from the Permanent Collection*. New York: Metropolitan Museum of Art, 1991.

———, Stuart W. Pyhrr, and Leonid Tarrasuk. *The Art of Chivalry: European Arms and Armor from the Metropolitan Musuem of Art*. New York: Metropolitan Museum of Art, 1982.

Nicolle, David. *The Age of Charlemagne*. Reprint, London: Reed International Books, 1984.

Oakeshott, R. Ewart. *The Archaeology of Weapons: Arms and Armour from Prehistory to the Age of Chivalry*. London: Lutterworth Press, 1960.

———. *European Arms and Armour from the Renaissance to the Industrial Revolution*. London: Lutterworth Press, 1980.

———. *A Knight and His Armour*. London: Lutterworth Press, 1961.

O'Connor, John J. *Amadís de Gaule and Its Influence on Elizabethan Literature*. New Brunswick, NJ: Rutgers University Press, 1970.

Ovid. *The Metamorphoses.* Translated by Mary M. Innes. Reprint, Harmondsworth: Penguin Books Ltd., 1955.

Panofsky, Erwin. *Problems in Titian, Mostly Iconographic: The Wrightsman Lectures.* New York: New York University Press, 1969.

Parker, Geoffrey. *Philip II.* Chicago: Open Court, 1995.

Pastor, Ludovico. *Storia dei papi dalla fine del medioevo.* Vol. 5, *Paolo III (1534–1549).* Rome: Desclée Editori, 1914.

Perlingieri, Ilya Sandra. *Sofonisba Anguissola: The First Great Woman Artist of the Renaissance.* New York: Rizzoli International, 1992.

Pfaffenbichler, Matthias. *Medieval Craftsmen: The Armourers.* Toronto: University of Toronto Press, 1992.

Pinson, Yona. "Imperial Ideology in the Triumphal Entry into Lille of Charles V and the Crown Prince (1549)." *Assaph* 6 (2001): 205–32. Available online at http://www.tau.ac.il/arts/projects/PUB/assaph-art/assaph6/articles_assaph6/Pinson.pdf.

Pizarro Gómez, Francisco Javier. *Arte y espectáculo en los viajes de Felipe II (1542–1592).* Madrid: Ediciones Encuentro, 1999.

Place, Edwin, ed. *Amadís de Gaula.* Madrid: Consejo Superior de Investigaciones Científicas, 1971.

Plaza Bores, Angel de la. *Archivo General de Simancas: Guía del investigador.* Madrid: Ministerio de Cultura, 1992.

Plon, Eugène. *Les maîtres Italiens au service de la maison d'Autriche: Leone Leoni, sculpteur de Charles V et Pompeo Leoni, sculpteur de Philippe II.* Paris: E. Plon, Nourrit et Cie, Imprimeurs-Éditeurs, 1887.

Pollard, J. Graham. *Medaglie italiane del rinascimento nel Museo Nazionale del Bargello.* Vols. 1–3. Firenze: Studio per Edizione Scelte, 1985.

Popham, A. E. "The Authorship of the Drawings of Binche." *Journal of the Warburg and Courtauld Institutes* 3, no. 1/2 (Oct. 1939–Jan. 1940): 55–57.

Pyhrr, Stuart W., and José A. Godoy. *Heroic Armor of the Italian Renaissance: Filippo Negroli and His Contemporaries.* New York: Metropolitan Museum of Art, 1998.

Rangström, Lena. *Riddarlek och tornerspel.* Stockholm: Livruskammaren och författarna, 1992.

Robertson, William, and William H. Prescott. *The History of the Reign of the Emperor Charles the Fifth.* Vols. 1–3. Philadelphia: J. B. Lippincott, 1869.

Rodríguez, Ledesma. "Armaduras." *Reales Sitios* 111 (1992): 49–55.

Romero García, Eladi Teresa. *El imperialismo hispánico en la Toscana durante el siglo XVI.* Lérida: Dilagro, 1986.

Ronchetti, G. *Dizionario illustrato dei simboli: Simboli, emblemi, attribuiti.* Milan: Ulrico Hoepli, 1922.

Rosso, Gregorio. "Istoria di Napoli." In *Raccolta di tutti i più rinomati scrittori dell'istoria generale del regno de Napoli principiando dal tempo che queste provincie hanno preso forma de regno.* Vols. 6 and 8. Edited by Giovanni Gravier. Naples: Giovanni Gravier, 1769–70.

Roubaud, Silvia. "Les fêtes dans les romans de chevalerie hispaniques." In *Les fêtes de la renaissance.* Vol. 3. Edited by Jean Jacquot. Paris: Centre National de la Recherche Scientifique, 1975.

Ruíz Alarcón, María Teresa. "Armaduras de caballos en la Real Armería de Madrid." *Reales Sitios* 9 (1972): 65–75.

———. "Sillas de montar de Diego de Arroyo, Real Armería." *Reales Sitios* 10 (1973): 49–54.

Sala, Andrea. *La triomphale Entrata de Carlo V Imperadore Augusto i la inclitta citta di Napoli, i di Missina, con il significato delli Archi triomphale, i de le figure Antiche in prosa i versi latin: Le sontuose feste, giostre,* etc. ca. 1535.

Scalini, Mario. *Armature all'eroica dei Negroli.* Florence: Museo Nazionale del Bargello, 1987.

Schalkhausser, Erwin. "Peter Peck, the Emperor's Gunsmith." In Robert Held, ed., *Art, Arms, and Armour: An International Anthology.* Vol. 1 (1979–80). Chiasso: Acquafresca Editrice, 1979.

Sepúlveda, Juan Ginés de. *De rebus gestis Caroli V.* Vol. 1. Granada: Servicio de Publicaciones de la Universidad, 1994.

Sheard, Wendy Stedman. *Antiquity in the Renaissance: Catalog of the Exhibition Held April 6–June 6, 1978.* Northampton, MA: Smith College Museum of Art, 1979.

Shearman, John. *Mannerism.* Reprint, London: Penguin Books, 1967.

Silver, Larry. "Paper Pageants: The Triumphs of Emperor Maximilian I." In *All the World's a Stage: Art and Pageantry in the Renaissance and Baroque.* Part 1, *Triumphal Celebrations and the Rituals of Statecraft,* edited by Barbara Wisch and Susan Scott Munshower, 292–331. Papers in Art History from the Pennsylvania State University 6. University Park: Pennsylvania State University, 1990.

Simon, Kate. *A Renaissance Tapestry: The Gonzaga of Mantua.* New York: Harper & Row, 1988.

Smith, Bradley. *Spain: A History in Art.* New York: Doubleday, 1966.

Smith, Jeffrey Chipps. "Venit nobis pacificus Dominus: Philip the Good's Triumphal Entry into Ghent in 1458." In *All the World's a Stage: Art and Pageantry in the Renaissance and Baroque.* Part 1, *Triumphal Celebrations and the Rituals of Statecraft,* edited by Barbara Wisch and Susan Scott Munshower, 258. Papers in Art History from the Pennsylvania State University 6. University Park: Pennsylvania State University, 1990.

Sociedad de Bibliófilos Españoles. *Relaciones de los Reinados de Carlos V y Felipe II.* 2 vols. Madrid: Imprenta Aldus, 1941.

Spence, Lewis. *Spain: Myths and Legends.* London: Bracken Books, 1985.

Strong, Roy. *Art and Power: Renaissance Festivals 1450–1650.* London: Boydell Press, 1973.

———. *Splendor at Court: Renaissance Spectacle and the Theater of Power.* Boston: Houghton-Mifflin, 1973.

Tanner, Marie. *The Last Descendant of Aeneas: The Hapsburgs and the Mythic Image of the Emperor.* New Haven, CT: Yale University Press, 1993.

Tasso, Torquato. *La Gerusalemme Liberata.* Vols. 1–2. Brussels: Luigi Hauman, 1836.

"Tesoros Mexicanos en colecciones Espanoles." *Artes de Mexico* 22 (1993–94).

Thomas, Bruno, and Ortwin Gamber, *Kunsthistorisches Museum, Wien: Waffensammlung: Katalog der Leibrüstkammer.* Vol. 1, *Der Zeitraum von 500 bis 1530.* Vienna: Anton Schroll, 1976.

———. "L'arte Milanese dell'armatura." In *Enciclopedia della storia de Milano,* 697–841. [Milan], 1958.

———, and Hans Schedelmann. *Arms and Armor: Masterpieces by European Craftsmen from the Thirteenth to the Nineteenth Century.* Translated by Ilse Bloom and William Reid. Munich: Keyserche Verlagsbuchhandlung, 1963.

Thurnier Buch von Anfang, Ursachen, Ursprung und Herkommen der Thurnier im heiligen Römischen Reich Teutscher Nation. Frankfurt am Main: Sigmund Feyerabend, 1566.

Tosi, Mario. *Il torneo di Belvedere in Vaticano e i tornei in Italia nel Cinquecento.* Rome: Edizioni di storia e letteratura, 1945.

Tracy, James D. *Emperor Charles V: Impresario of War.* Cambridge: Cambridge University Press, 2002.

Trevor-Roper, Hugh. *Princes and Artists: Patronage and Ideology at Four Habsburg Courts, 1517–1633.* London: Thames and Hudson, 1976.

Troyes, Chrétien de. "Erec and Enide." In *Arthurian Legends.* Translated by D. D. R. Owen. London: J. M. Dent, 1987.

Vale, Malcolm. *War and Chivalry: Warfare and Aristocratic Culture in England, France and Burgundy at the end of the Middle Ages.* Athens: University of Georgia Press, 1981.

Valgoma, Dalmito de la. "El toro en la heraldica española." *Reales Sitios* 5 (1908): 78–80.

Van de Put, Albert. "Two Drawings of the Fêtes at Binche for Charles V and Philip (II) 1549." *Journal of the Warburg and Courtauld Institutes* 3, no. 1/2 (Oct. 1939–Jan. 1940): 49–55.

Van Dorme, Maurice. *Les Archives générales de Simancas et l'histoire de la Belgique (IXe–XIXe siècles).* Vols. 1–4. Brussels: Académie Royale de Belgique/Commission Royale d'Histoire, 1964.

Vasari, Giorgio. *Lives of the Most Eminent Painters, Sculptors, and Architects.* Vols. 1–3. Translated by Gaston du C. de Vere. New York: Harry N. Abrams, 1979.

Vecellio, Cesare. *De gli Habiti antiche et moderni di Diverse Parti del Mondo,* 1st ed. Venice: Damian Zenaro, 1589–90.

Ventrone, Paolo, ed. *Le tems revient/l'tempo si rinuova: Feste e spettacoli nella Firenze dei Medici e l'Italia del '500.* Florence: Silvana Editoriale, 1992.

Virgil. *The Aeneid.* Translated by W. F. Jackson Knight. London: Penguin Books, 1956.

Vital, Laurent. *Primer viaje a España de Carlos I con su desembarco en Asturias.* Oviedo: Grupo Editorial Asturiano, 1992.

von Habsburg, Otto. *Carlos V: Un emperador para Europa.* Translated by Pilar Burgos Checa. Madrid: Editorial EDAF, 1992.

Warry, John. *Alexander, 334–323 BC.* London: Reed International Books, 1991.

Wasserman, Jack. *Leonardo da Vinci.* New York: Harry N. Abrams, 1984.

Wethey, Harold E. *The Complete Paintings of Titian.* Vol. 2, *The Portraits.* London: Phaidon Press, 1971.

Wheatcroft, Andrew. *The Habsburgs: Embodying Empire.* London: Viking, 1995.

Wheeler, Mortimer. *Roman Art and Architecture.* New York: Thames & Hudson, 1964.

Wilenski, R. H. *Flemish Painters, 1430–1830.* Vol. 1. New York: Viking Press, 1960.

Wind, Edgar. *Pagan Mysteries in the Renaissance.* New York: W. W. Norton, 1958.

Wittkower, Rudolf. *Art and Architecture in Italy, 1600–1750.* New Haven, CT: Yale University Press, 1958.

Yates, Frances A. *Astraea: The Imperial Theme in the Sixteenth Century.* London: Routledge & Kegan Paul, 1975.

———. "Charles Quint et l'idée d'empire." In *Les fêtes de la renaissance.* Vol. 2, *Fêtes et cérémonies au temps de Charles Quint,* edited by Jean Jacquot, 57–97. Paris: Centre National de la Recherche Scientifique, 1975.

———. *The Valois Tapestries.* 2nd ed. London: Routledge & Kegan Paul, 1975.

Young, Alan. *Tudor and Jacobean Tournaments.* Dobbs Ferry, NY: Sheridan House, 1987.

About the Author

Braden Frieder is assistant professor of art history at Morehead State University. His research interests range from Renaissance and baroque art to Latin America and the decorative arts. He has published articles in books and journals, and critical reviews on art, music, and cultural history. He received his doctorate in art history from the University of Wisconsin-Madison.

Index